THE HISTORY OF
AMERICAN LEAGUE
BASEBALL

Also by Glenn Dickey:

The History of National League Baseball
Champs and Chumps
The Great No-Hitters
The Jock Empire

THE HISTORY OF AMERICAN LEAGUE BASEBALL

SINCE 1901

Glenn Dickey

STEIN AND DAY / *Publishers* / New York

First Published in 1980
Copyright © 1980 by Glenn Dickey

All rights reserved
Designed by Louis Ditizio
Printed in the United States of America
Stein and Day/*Publishers*/Scarborough House
Briarcliff Manor, N. Y. 10510

Library of Congress Cataloging in Publication Data

Dickey, Glenn.
      The history of American League baseball.

      Bibliography: p. 311
      Includes index.
      1.   American League of Professional Baseball
Clubs—History.   I.   Title.
GV875.A15D52   796.357′64′0973   79-3693
ISBN 0-8128-2700-7

To Nancy and Scott, for their love and support

ACKNOWLEDGMENTS

The American League office and American League clubs were of great help on this project, offering me information and access to their picture files.

The Baseball Encyclopedia, The Official Encyclopedia of Baseball, and *The Sports Encyclopedia: Baseball,* provided me with information that could otherwise have been gained only with great difficulty. A complete bibliography is located in the back of the book.

My editor, Benton Arnovitz, conceived this project.

Finally, a word of thanks to my parents, whose love has always meant a great deal to me. It was my father who first sparked an interest in baseball which has remained with me.

Contents

Introduction

by REGGIE JACKSON

The American League has been my home ever since I signed a bonus with the Kansas City A's in 1965, and I haven't regretted that for a moment. I've enjoyed playing in the league, and I think the league has improved a great deal since I first came up at the end of the 1967 season.

Just look at the division my team, the New York Yankees, plays in now. With Baltimore, Boston, Milwaukee, and us, I think you'd have to say that's the strongest division in baseball. In the other division, Kansas City, California, and Texas have really improved in recent years, and we've got great competitive balance in the league.

I'm proud to have been a member of two great champions, the Oakland A's and the Yankees. I especially enjoyed playing on the A's because we were a close-knit group. We used to get a lot of publicity for fights in the clubhouse, but that happens with any team, because of the pressure. The truth was, we were all friends on that team. Part of that was because most of the guys lived in Oakland or the area around there, so we saw each other in the off-season, too.

We had a common bond on the A's: Everybody hated Charlie Finley. I don't feel sorry for Finley now. I do think that if he really intended to use the money to buy players, he should have been allowed to sell Rollie Fingers, Joe Rudi, and Vida Blue. But he hasn't done anything since then that indicates he really wanted to build his club back up.

Finley did a lot for baseball, though. He had some good ideas. He made speed very important, using pinch runners so much. And he had pitchers working on being relievers in the minor leagues, instead of switching starters over when they came to the majors.

That was a great team, the A's, and I think we would have gone on to win a few more pennants if we hadn't split up. Even now, most of us still have some good years left.

We had a great defense, which is more important than a lot of people realize; all the great teams have that.

We had three guys—myself, Rudi, and Sal Bando—who could drive in the run from third when it was needed. And we had guys like Campy Campaneris and Billy North who could get in position to be knocked in. That's what you need.

We had great pitching, both starting and relieving. Who ever had better than Catfish Hunter, Ken Holtzman, and Vida Blue? And nobody could touch Rollie Fingers when he came in for the bottom of the ninth. We had such great relief pitching that a guy like Jim Todd was only the number 3 reliever; he'd have been number 1 on some staffs.

That club knew how to win. We had a manager, Dick Williams, who would get on us if we made mental errors, so we didn't beat ourselves. Our statistics weren't impressive to a lot of people because we didn't care about them. All we cared about was winning.

A lot of people don't understand that. They judge a guy by his numbers. That happens to me in New York. Even if we're winning, people will say, "But Reggie only has ten home runs." In Oakland, we didn't have to worry about that. We only worried about winning.

A lot of guys can have good stats when there's no pressure on. Don't talk to me about a guy who has good numbers and his team is 30 games out of first place. I want to know what he can do when the pressure is on.

The guy who can hold the spotlight doesn't get enough credit. It's like a war: You can always find guys who will say they'll back you up as long as you go over the hill first.

Take relief pitching. It's easy to come in once a week and get a save when the score is 7–3. What you need is a guy who can come in when the score is tied and the winning run is on third base and Jim Rice is hitting with Carl Yastrzemski coming up next.

We've got a guy like that on the Yankees: Rich Gossage. When Gossage was hurt last year, it affected the whole pitching staff. We even had to use Ron Guidry in relief for a while. Gossage just makes a tremendous difference.

The American League has always had stars like that, going back to guys like Ty Cobb and Babe Ruth, and they're all in this book, the most complete I've ever seen about American League baseball. You'll even find my name in there once or twice.

Reggie Jackson was on five World Championship teams and became the focal point of controversy with manager Billy Martin in New York.
(New York Yankees)

Preface

As I did in my companion volume, *The History of National League Baseball,* I have divided this book into what seems to be distinct eras, with a heavy concentration on important players, teams, and events.

Inevitably, some accomplishments get slighted in this kind of treatment, so I have provided a table of historical moments in the back of the book, along with the statistics that are the lifeblood of baseball fans.

Finally, I should say that this was a labor of love for me, because the American League was always my favorite when I was growing up, and the colorful, maddening Boston Red Sox my favorite team. At one point, I was determined to be the next Ted Williams. Alas, only in the field did my play ever approach Ted's.

THE HISTORY OF AMERICAN LEAGUE BASEBALL

THE EARLY YEARS

1. A Stormy Beginning and a Strong Foundation

For the final 25 years of the nineteenth century, major league baseball meant primarily one thing: the National League.

There had been challenges to the dominance of the National League. The American Association had been formed in 1882, the Union Association in 1884, the Players League in 1890. All had foundered because they lacked organization and sufficient financial backing. At the start of the twentieth century, the National League was the sole major professional baseball league.

One year later that situation changed. The American League, a very different operation from its predecessors, was established as a major league and a worthy rival of the Senior Circuit. Well organized and well financed, the staying power of the new league was obvious from the start.

One man was primarily responsible: Byron Bancroft "Ban" Johnson, the American League's founder and president until 1927, and the strongest league executive in baseball history.

Johnson was not an easy man to like. Even Charles Comiskey, who brought Ban into baseball, eventually became his enemy. Johnson was, by the accounts of the day, a vain, arrogant, humorless man, and he was cursed with a never-satisfied thirst for publicity; his critics claimed he would make a speech any time he saw three people gathered together.

He was quick-tempered, hard-drinking, and autocratic. There was always only one way to do things in Ban Johnson's league, and when club owners finally decided his powers had to be curtailed, he resigned.

His sense of morality was hardly unassailable. While he was league president, he had holdings in the Boston and Cleveland clubs. When Comiskey first asked him to investigate the 1919 World Series, he refused, and when

Johnson finally did begin the probe a year later, it was primarily because he thought he could drive Comiskey out of baseball.

None of that concerns us now. What is important is that Johnson's planning and leadership enabled the American League to reach parity with the National League immediately, which strengthened the structure of the game. He was resented by National League owners because he cracked their monopoly, but the changes he brought about benefited all of baseball. We feel his influence even now.

Johnson had a lifelong interest in baseball. He had played it growing up in Ohio, and he continued playing through his college years. He was regarded as a good college catcher, but he made no attempt to play professionally, perhaps because there was very little money in the game then.

Upon graduation in 1887 from Marietta College, he took a job as a sportswriter for the *Cincinnati Commercial-Gazette.* While covering the Reds, he began a friendship with Comiskey, the club's manager, and the two had many long discussions about the future of the game.

Like many sportswriters, Johnson had theories about how a league should be operated. Unlike his colleagues, past and present, he had an opportunity to put his theories into practice.

Autocratic Byron Bancroft "Ban" Johnson founded the American League and got it off to a good start. *(George Brace)*

In 1893 the Western League, which had operated as a minor league since 1879, folded. Comiskey met with some club owners after the season and persuaded them to revive the league, this time with Johnson in charge.

On November 20, 1893, representatives of franchises from Sioux City, Toledo, Indianapolis, Detroit, Kansas City, Milwaukee, Minneapolis, and Grand Rapids met in Detroit and elected Johnson president of the revived league.

For Johnson's second season as league president, he was joined by Comiskey. Fired as Cincinnati manager, Comiskey took over the Sioux City franchise in the Western League and moved it to St. Paul. Johnson also persuaded Connie Mack to purchase the Milwaukee franchise, which Mack eventually moved to Philadelphia.

In common with other minor leagues of that era, there was a lot of franchise movement in the Western League. But under Johnson's leadership, it seems that most of the clubs in the league made money. That was not at all common.

Johnson ran the Western League with dignity, as he would later run the American League. He gave his umpires an authority which was lacking elsewhere in baseball. He encouraged club owners to improve and police their parks, so women would come to games. And he made plans to upgrade the Western League into a major league.

In 1899, the National League cut back from twelve clubs to eight, dropping franchises in Washington, Baltimore, Cleveland, and Louisville. At Johnson's suggestions, the Grand Rapids franchise moved into Cleveland, Comiskey moved his St. Paul franchise to Chicago, and club owners renamed their circuit the American League.

Johnson was still in charge of a minor league, because he agreed to abide by the National Agreement, a pact that made the operating rules for all of professional baseball and which designated the National League as the only major league.

But, after the 1900 season, he announced that the American League was withdrawing from that agreement, and that it would not honor the reserve clause in National League player contracts. He put teams into Boston, Philadelphia, Baltimore, and Washington (to go with Chicago, Cleveland, Detroit, and Milwaukee franchises) which erased the regional character of the league. The league, he said, would operate as a second independent major league.

Unwittingly, by establishing a salary limit of $2,400, the National League owners had made it easy for the new league to get players. The financially sound American League owners offered more money, and they came away with both quality and quantity when they raided National League rosters; 111 of the 182 American League players in 1901 were former National Leaguers.

The best of the players who jumped was probably Nap Lajoie, a second baseman who merely came across town in Philadelphia from the Phillies to the Athletics. Lajoie batted .422, hit 14 home runs, and batted in 125 runs to capture the league's Triple Crown.

There were other quality players: pitchers Cy Young, Eddie Plank, and Joe McGinnity; third basemen John McGraw and Jimmy Collins, both of whom doubled as managers; catchers Wilbert Robinson and Roger Bresnahan. All later were named to the Hall of Fame—along with Johnson, Comiskey, and Mack.

Comiskey's Chicago team, the White Sox, won the first American League pennant by four games over Boston. More significantly, in the three cities where the two leagues both had teams—Chicago, Boston, and Philadelphia—the American League team had the better attendance.

For the 1902 season, the Milwaukee franchise was shifted to St. Louis, and again, the American League franchise outdrew its National League rival. But despite that encouraging news, it took all of Johnson's ingenuity and leadership to keep the league together.

The first problem came when the Pennsylvania Supreme Court ruled that Lajoie, Bill Bernhard, and Chick Fraser had to leave the Athletics and return to the Phillies. Fraser did, but Johnson quickly had Lajoie and Bernhard transferred to the Cleveland club, where they could not be touched by Pennsylvania state law. When Cleveland played in Philadelphia, the two players took a paid vacation outside the state.

The second problem was far more serious and difficult to solve, and it resulted from a series of personality clashes between Johnson and the fiery McGraw. Probably the two could never have gotten along for very long, because McGraw never was willing to recognize any authority other than his own.

Johnson was determined that American League umpires would have complete authority on the playing field. To illustrate his point, he fined managers and players who abused umpires; on one day in 1903, he fined both Boston manager Collins and Washington manager Clark Griffith.

In other leagues, clubs had usually paid player or manager fines. Johnson stopped that practice. He insisted that nobody could even touch an umpire, and that umpires' decisions were final. Given that official standing, umpires even speeded up games by hurrying players on and off the field, which pleased the fans.

Naturally, nobody had more problems with this than Baltimore manager McGraw, whose umpire-baiting was one of the least pleasant aspects of his personality. He felt it should be possible to hit an umpire if verbal coercion failed.

Several times in the 1901 and 1902 seasons, Johnson had fined or suspended McGraw. Finally, in July of 1902, he suspended McGraw indefinitely. McGraw then began negotiations which finally resulted in the Baltimore club being purchased by John T. Brush, owner of the New York Giants franchise in the National League and chairman of that league's executive committee.

Brush then released McGraw, McGinnity, Bresnahan, Dan McGann, Cy Seymour, Joe Kelley, and Jack Cronin to sign with National League clubs. McGraw, of course, became manager of the Giants, a position he held until he resigned early in the 1932 season. Some baseball historians think that McGraw was negotiating for that position even as early as the 1901 season.

With so many players gone, the Orioles could not even field a team for a game against St. Louis on July 17. Johnson revoked the Baltimore franchise, stocked it with players from other clubs in the league, and appointed Robinson the manager. The club finished the season in last place, but Johnson's decisive action had saved the league.

And after the season, he got his revenge, moving the Baltimore franchise to New York to challenge the Giants. That franchise, first known as the Highlanders, became the Yankees, the team that has dominated baseball for much of the time since. To stock that first American League team in New York, Johnson raided the National League rosters one more time.

That convinced the National League club owners that the American League was here to stay. It was obvious that further unbridled competition would be ruinous, so in January 1903 the two leagues began to negotiate a peace.

The strength of the American League, because of Johnson's planning and leadership, was obvious from the results of those negotiations. The National League wanted a complete merger, but Johnson resisted, and the two leagues remained separate. The American League was allowed to keep a team in New York, which the Giants had bitterly opposed. The American League was allowed to keep all the players it had signed from its raids on the National League. The one "concession" the American League had made was to agree not to put a team in Pittsburgh, so the National League Pirates would have a monopoly in that city.

Most important, both leagues agreed to respect contracts and reserve clauses, so there would be no more raiding. Peace once again reigned in baseball.

The peace, and its conditions, made possible that most hallowed of post-season competitions, grandly named the World Series, though it was a small world so described, contained within the Atlantic Ocean on the east and the Mississippi River on the west.

Neither pennant race was close that year, with Pittsburgh in first place in the National League from June 19 on and eventually winning by 6½ games and Boston winning by a lopsided 14½ games in the American League.

So, in August, Pittsburgh owner Barney Dreyfuss and Boston owner Henry Killilea were able to sit down and work out details of the competition. (It was not, incidentally, the first post-season baseball competition, as some think; the National League and American Association champions had met as early as 1884.) The competition would be a best-of-nine series, the first three games in Boston, the middle four in Pittsburgh, and the final two, if needed, in Boston.

Dreyfuss had initiated the discussion because he was confident his Pirates could win. His confidence seemed to be justified as Pittsburgh knocked out the already legendary Cy Young en route to a 7–3 win in the opening game, and then went on to win three of the first four games.

But the Boston Pilgrims, as they were then called, came back to win four straight and take that first Series.

Boston won the American League pennant again in 1904, this time by only 1½ games over New York, but got no chance to repeat its World Series triumph. The New York Giants, easy winners in the National League, refused to play.

Why? Brush, the Giants' owner, said it was because the American League was inferior, a claim rendered ridiculous by Boston's win of the year before.

The real reasons were not hard to find. As usual, they centered around Johnson. McGraw hated the American League president, for reasons already spelled out. Brush had owned the Cincinnati club when Johnson was a sportswriter, and Brush still resented Johnson's criticism at that time. And Brush was also irritated because Johnson had put an American League team in New York.

It was apparently McGraw who first wanted to pass up the Series. Some people then close to McGraw thought that he changed his mind and was willing to play by the last month of the season, but by that time, Brush was determined to keep the Giants out of the Series. His position was heavily criticized in the press, but he did not waver.

But history's little ironies continued. In the off-season, Brush proposed that the World Series be made mandatory for the league champions, and it has been played every year since, even during the two world wars. And when the Series resumed in 1905, it was Brush's Giants who won, 4–1, in a most remarkable competition: Each of the five games ended in a shutout.

The baseball peace also made it possible for Johnson to rule all of baseball, instead of just one league, through the National Commission.

The National Commission was a three-man body which was established by the 1903 truce. Each of the league presidents served on it, and a chairman who was acceptable to both men was to be appointed. That chairman— the only one the commission ever had—was Garry Herrmann, owner of the Cincinnati Reds.

It would seem that, with a National League president and a National League owner on the commission, the American League would be short-changed. In reality, it worked exactly the opposite. Herrmann had been a friend of Johnson's since Ban's days as a sportswriter in Cincinnati, and he usually took Johnson's side if there were a split in voting.

The commission ruled on everything in baseball, from club disputes to player fines. In general, it worked well for most of its existence, bringing the game through some difficult years.

But, from 1915 on, the commission had serious problems as the owners became more and more critical of its decisions. Most of the criticism stemmed from opposition within the American League itself to Johnson, including much from Johnson's former friend, Comiskey. The commission was obviously doomed, and the only real question was what would replace it.

Club owners debated forming another commission, with a chairman from outside baseball. Finally, it was decided instead to bring in one man—Judge Kenesaw Mountain Landis—and give him virtually unrestricted powers.

That move, in January 1921, ended Johnson's reign as baseball strong man; he understood the action and resented it. Even within the American League he no longer was able to rule autocratically as he had for so long. His final years as league president were bitter ones.

In 1911, Johnson had been reelected American League president for a 20-year term. In 1925, that contract had been extended an additional five years, which meant that he could have served through the 1935 season. He didn't last that long, and it was his attempt to buck Judge Landis that ended his career.

In 1926, another potentially damaging scandal had surfaced, with a charge by retired pitcher Dutch Leonard that Ty Cobb and Tris Speaker had been involved in a fixed game in 1919. Leonard produced letters from Smokey Joe Wood and Cobb himself to substantiate his claim, though the letters were hardly conclusive evidence.

Johnson decided that the letters were proof enough. He passed them on to Landis, after having allowed Cobb and Speaker to announce their retirements.

Landis wasn't convinced by the letters, however, and made the whole story public as he announced that Cobb and Speaker would be reinstated. Since their clubs did not want them back, Cobb was traded from Detroit to Philadelphia and Speaker from Cleveland to Washington, each playing two more seasons.

Johnson was enraged. He accused Landis of seeking publicity by making the case public and then dropping the charges against the players. Johnson's claim was not without merit. The principals in the case are all long since dead, and we will never know the complete truth of the affair, but it seems that Landis's decision was based more on what the public wanted than on the facts of the case.

But that did Johnson no good. The American League club owners, except for Phil Ball of St. Louis, supported Landis; they wanted no more scandals, especially one involving two of the league's greatest players. They decided to strip Johnson of his remaining powers and make him merely a figurehead. But Johnson moved more quickly than his adversaries and announced his resignation as of the end of the 1927 season.

Johnson lasted less than four years in retirement, dying of diabetes on March 28, 1931, but his place in baseball history was secure. He was elected to the Hall of Fame in 1937.

2. Starlight and Animal Crackers

In its first decade of play, the American League had many stars. Besides those mentioned earlier, consider a few of these names: Sam Crawford, Ed Delahanty, Chief Bender, Harry Hooper, Frank "Home Run" Baker, Hal Chase, Wee Willie Keeler, Addie Joss, and Eddie Cicotte.

We'll look at the careers of Ty Cobb and Walter Johnson later, but some other players deserve special mention here, either for an extraordinary season or a distinguished career.

There were, for instance, the two great second basemen, Nap Lajoie and Eddie Collins. Each has a special distinction. Lajoie was the first second baseman elected to the Hall of Fame; Collins had the longest career of any twentieth century player—25 years.

Lajoie started his career in the National League with the Phillies and played four full seasons with that club, averaging .349. But the bulk of his 21-year career, and his greatest seasons, were played in the American League. Of all those who jumped from the National League, he was the best of the everyday performers.

It was not difficult to get Lajoie to jump. Connie Mack merely offered him a $6,000 yearly salary, more than double the $2,400 he was allowed under the National League's salary limit.

Nap Lajoie hit .422 to win the first American League batting title and set a record that has never been equalled. *(George Brace)*

In his American League debut, Lajoie hit .422, and American League hitters have been trying in vain to match that ever since. Lajoie went on to hit more than .350 seven more times in his career, finishing with a career mark of .339. His 3,251 hits included 657 doubles, a record at his retirement and still fourth in major league history. And writers of the time claimed that he was as good a fielder as hitter.

Lajoie won four batting titles, but it was one he didn't win which caused the most comment. In 1910, he finished one point behind Ty Cobb, at .384. The unpopular Cobb sat out the final two games of the season to protect his lead, and that strategy nearly backfired. On the last day of the season, Lajoie got eight hits in a double-header against St. Louis. Six of them were bunts, as the St. Louis third baseman, Red Corriden, played nearly back on the outfield grass, conceding bunt hits.

Collins was probably at least Lajoie's equal as a fielder, an equally effective hitter (.333 lifetime), though with less power and a considerably better base runner. He led the American League in stolen bases four times, going as high as 81 in 1910, and his career mark of 743 is second in the American League, third in major league history.

Circumstances and his own ability conspired to make Collins one of the best-paid players of his era. In 1914, Collins was the league's Most Valuable Player as the Philadelphia Athletics won their fourth pennant in five years, but he was sold to the Chicago White Sox after the season in a deal engineered by Ban Johnson.

Johnson had feared that Collins would jump to the Federal League, a newly established rival league, because Connie Mack could not afford to match the new league's salary offer. Thus, he persuaded Chicago owner Charles Comiskey to buy Collins for $50,000, and Collins was then able to command a salary of $15,000, very high for those days—and especially so coming from Comiskey, a man of legendary penuriousness.

Collins was worth it, to his new team and to the league. Had the Federal League been able to lure stars of Collins's reputation and ability away from the established circuits, it might have stayed in business. Without such stars, it folded within two years.

Meanwhile, Collins was a key man on the White Sox team that won pennants in 1917 and 1919, before being ruined by the "Black Sox" scandal. Collins was untouched by the scandal, and he played through the 1926 season in Chicago, acting as playing manager the final two years. He closed out his career where he had started, playing his final four seasons in Philadelphia.

Like Collins, Tris Speaker was a great player whose career started in the first decade of the American League but extended far beyond it.

Speaker was such an outstanding hitter that he might have made the Hall of Fame on that alone. He averaged .344 over a 22-year career, including a league-leading .386 in 1916. Among his 3,515 hits is a major league record 793 doubles.

Or, consider just one season, his best: In 1923, at the age of 35, Speaker averaged .380, with 218 hits, 59 doubles, 11 triples, 17 home runs, 133 runs scored, and 130 RBIs!

And yet, it was Speaker's fielding which was the distinguishing feature of his performances. He invented a daring type of center field play which very few have dared try since.

Speaker played a very shallow center field, so close to the infield that he occasionally took pickoff throws at second from the pitcher! In one ten-day stretch in 1918, he twice caught line drives just behind second and doubled the base runner off. Once he was even the middleman in a double play.

By playing so shallow, Speaker was playing the percentages. Far more games are lost because of balls which drop in front of a center fielder than from those which go over his head. Speaker got countless outs for his pitchers on drives that would have been base hits against any other team.

Tris Speaker is still considered by many the finest defensive center fielder of all time, and he was also a fine hitter. *(George Brace)*

The spitball gave Jack Chesbro the extra pitch he needed as he won a major league record 41 games in 1904. *(George Brace)*

All center fielders know this, but few are willing to play a shallow center field for a very human reason: Fans think nothing of the balls that fall in front of a center fielder, but the one that is hit over his head is remembered for a long time. No center fielder likes to be so embarrassed.

That didn't bother Speaker. His great speed and anticipation allowed him to get back for the balls which were hit deep. He was a marvel.

If anything, that first decade of play was best known for pitching exploits. Certainly, the two greatest seasons in American League history were enjoyed in that period, by Jack Chesbro in 1904 and Ed Walsh in 1908. Chesbro won 41 games and Walsh 40, and nobody has approached those figures since.

Chesbro and Walsh had a lot in common. Neither won 200 games in his career, but both made the Hall of Fame—in each case, primarily because of the one great season. Both discovered the spitball midway through their careers, and that became the key pitch for each of them.

Chesbro actually was a successful pitcher with just a fastball and a curve, with a 14–12 record in 1900 and 21–9 in 1901 for Pittsburgh of the National League. But when he discovered the spitter the next season, he was much better, compiling a 28–6 record, including 12 straight wins in one stretch, with eight shutouts.

The spitter, a pitch which was outlawed in 1920 along with other trick pitches which involved roughing up or defacing the ball, was a pitch which few were ever able to master. It was difficult to control, and not just for the pitchers; infielders sometimes got hold of the damp side and threw wildly to first base.

But for a pitcher who could control it, the spitter was an excellent pitch.

Unlike the knuckleball, which can break in any direction, the pitch was predictable, usually breaking down like a very sharp curve. It was especially effective for a pitcher with a good fastball—like Chesbro—because it came to the plate at the same speed. The batter, looking for a fastball, would find the ball dipping beneath his bat at the last moment.

Chesbro was one of the last players to jump from the National to the American League, going from Pittsburgh to the New York Highlanders before the 1903 season—just before peace was declared between the leagues. Money was the reason, as always.

Chesbro had a good season his first year with the Highlanders, winning 21 and losing 15 as his team finished fourth, 17½ games behind the league champion Boston Pilgrims, but he was only warming up. The next year, he nearly won the pennant by himself.

His statistics in 1904 seem fictional, and not just the 41 wins (against only 12 losses). He completed the first 30 games he pitched that year, and 48 of 51 for the season. He won 14 games in a row. He even pitched in four games in relief, winning three of them, and threw 454 2/3 innings, roughly a third of all the innings pitched by the New York staff that year.

He gave up only 338 hits, and had an earned run average of 1.82. He led the league in games won, percentage (.774), games pitched (55), games started, complete games, and innings pitched.

And yet, for all that, his season ended in disappointment. He could not, finally, do it all himself, though nobody could fault him for trying.

The schedule that year had Boston and New York playing each other for the final week of the season. Chesbro beat the Pilgrims on Friday, October 7, for his 41st win of the season, putting the Highlanders ahead by a half game.

Two double-headers remained, one in Boston on Saturday, the second in New York on Monday. New York player-manager Clark Griffith wanted Chesbro to stay in New York and rest for the Monday games, but Chesbro traveled on his own to Boston and insisted on pitching the first game of the Saturday double-header.

It was a mistake. Boston battered Chesbro, 13–2, in that first game and also won the second to move back into first place by a game and a half. That meant the Highlanders would have to sweep the Monday double-header to win.

They almost did. Chesbro was matched against Bill Dineen, whose 22 wins paled in comparison to Jack's 41, in the first game. Both men pitched well into the ninth inning, with the score tied at 2–2.

In the Boston half of the ninth, Lou Criger reached base on an infield hit, advanced to second on a sacrifice by Dineen, and to third on a groundout by Kip Selbach. Chesbro got two strikes on Fred Parent, but his third pitch to Parent sailed over the head of catcher Jack Kleinow, and Criger scored.

The Highlanders could not score in the bottom of the inning, and, though they won the second game of the double-header, 1–0, the pennant was lost. And Chesbro spent the off-season answering questions about his wild pitch; his 41 wins were forgotten.

There is a footnote to that game: For Dineen, it was the 37th game he had started that year—and the 37th he had completed.

If there were ever a better season than Chesbro's in American League history, it would have to be Walsh's 1908 season. But again, one man could not do it by himself, and the Chicago White Sox finished third, though just a game and a half behind pennant-winning Detroit, despite Walsh's heroics.

Walsh won one less game than Chesbro, but he saved seven games in relief. His statistics, too, seem unreal: 40 wins, 66 games, 49 starts, 40 complete games, 464 innings, only 343 hits allowed. He struck out 269, walked only 56, and had 12 shutouts. He led the league in wins, games, games started, complete games, innings pitched, strikeouts, shutouts, and saves.

Walsh had come to the majors in Chesbro's great year, 1904, but he was no better than an average pitcher until he learned to throw the spitter. He actually learned it in spring training that first year from teammate Elmer Stricklett, but he was reluctant to try it in a game until he felt he had mastered it. Without the spitter, he was only 5–4 and 9–4 in his first two seasons.

In 1906, he felt confident enough to use the spitter, and his record climbed to 19–15. The next season, he won 25 games, and the season after that, he challenged Chesbro's mark.

The White Sox battled Detroit, Cleveland, and St. Louis in one of the great pennant races in 1908, and Walsh almost carried them in on his back. The big right-hander worked seven of the last nine games of the season, winning four games in that stretch. His one loss in that time came when Cleveland's Addie Joss pitched a perfect 1–0 game, but Walsh had nothing to apologize for: He had given up only four hits and struck out 15.

But even with Walsh's great pitching, the weak-hitting Sox (they hit only three home runs, one by Walsh, all season) couldn't make it, as Detroit won the pennant on the final day of the season.

Chesbro had two good seasons after his great one, winning 19 games in

1905 and 24 in 1906. He tailed off quickly after that and was out of the majors by 1910.

Walsh had four good seasons left, winning 15, 16, 26, and 27 in the next four years. But he developed arm trouble in 1913 and, though he hung on through the 1917 season, won only 13 games in the last five years of his career.

A sore arm was something that never bothered the incredible Denton True (Cy) Young in a 22-year career that remains without parallel. He believed that if he kept his legs in shape, he would never have arm trouble, and he was right.

It's difficult to categorize Young because he split his career evenly between the two leagues, his first 11 in the National and his last 11 in the American. Had he pitched his entire career in the National League, he would be considered that league's premier pitcher; had he pitched his entire career in the American League, he would be that league's best. When a separate pitching award was established in 1956, it could have only one name: the Cy Young Award.

Young won 289 games in the National League, and then added 222 in the American; pitchers—including Chesbro and Walsh—have made the Hall of Fame with less than 200 total wins.

He had an excellent fastball (his nickname was short for "Cyclone," a compliment for his fastball), but he seldom tried for strikeouts, preferring to use fewer pitches.

Young was already 33 when he jumped from St. Louis of the National League to Boston of the American League in 1901, but he was still a very effective pitcher and, with Lajoie, unquestionably the biggest name star to jump. He led the new league in wins for the first three seasons, with totals of 33, 32, and 28.

In 1904, he won 27, far behind Chesbro's 41, but led the league with ten shutouts and pitched what Connie Mack called the finest game he had ever seen. Considering how many games Mack saw in a playing and managing career that spanned 65 major league seasons, that is high tribute.

The game, on May 5, 1904, matched Young with Rube Waddell, who was having his best season. Waddell went on to win 25 games that season and set a strikeout record of 349, and just four days earlier, he had pitched a one-hitter against this same Boston club, giving up a leadoff single and then retiring 27 batters in a row.

But even Waddell couldn't match Young on this day, when the great

Rube Waddell set a major league strikeout record that lasted for decades. *(George Brace)*

right-hander was literally perfect. Young set down 27 men in order, striking out eight and allowing only six balls to be hit out of the infield. In a mere 1 hour and 25 minutes, he was a 3–0 winner.

In almost every way, Waddell and Young were opposites, starting with the fact that Rube was a left-hander. Young took his regular turn, year in and year out; Waddell would take off to ride a fire engine or go fishing. Young won 20 games or more for 14 consecutive seasons, Waddell for only three. Waddell was a spectacular strikeout pitcher; Young was not.

In terms of sheer ability, Waddell may have been the best of all time. Connie Mack thought so. When asked by Grantland Rice who had the best combination of speed and curve, Mack immediately answered Waddell. "Waddell had terrific speed," said Mack, "and his curve was even better than his speed. The Rube had the fastest and deepest curve I've ever seen."

There is simply no telling how good Waddell could have been, or what kind of a record he could have achieved, if he had had a better-balanced character. He seemed at times able to do anything he wanted. In exhibition games, he would call his outfielders in and then strike out the side. One time against Chicago, he decided to throw nothing but fastballs and pitched a four-hitter.

But Waddell cared little for fame or success. He spent much of the early part of his career pitching for semipro teams, earning enough for his next drink, always a primary concern. He disliked the constraints that went with pitching for a major league team; if he felt like going fishing, it mattered little how important the game was that he was supposed to pitch. Mack babied, cajoled, and flattered him and got, oh, perhaps 70 percent of Waddell's potential from him. Other managers got considerably less.

Though Waddell was difficult to handle, Mack didn't complain. He wouldn't even have had Rube on the roster otherwise. Waddell had pitched as early as 1897 for Louisville of the National League and was purchased by Pittsburgh in 1900. But as it happened, both clubs were managed by Fred Clarke, a stern disciplinarian, and Waddell simply could not pitch well for Clarke.

By 1902, Waddell's cumulative big league career showed 28 wins and 33 losses. Barney Dreyfuss, the Pittsburgh owner, had had enough, and when Mack came to buy Waddell's contract, Dreyfuss quickly agreed.

Waddell was an immediate success in Philadelphia, winning 25 games his first season and starting a run of six straight seasons in which he led the league in strikeouts. His high mark came in 1904. Originally, he was credited with 343 strikeouts, and his record was broken by Bob Feller's 348 in 1946. Later, historians have generally agreed on a figure of 349, thus negating Feller's "record." It all became academic when Nolan Ryan struck out 383 in 1973.

Even under Mack's gentle handling, Waddell had problems. Sometimes, they were only amusing: He had a habit of eating animal crackers in bed and roommate/catcher Ossie Schreckengost had it written into Waddell's contract that he was forbidden to do that. Other incidents weren't so amusing. In September of 1905, Waddell got into a playful tussle on a train with teammate Andy Coakley and hurt his shoulder. He pitched no more that year and watched from the bench as the Athletics lost the World Series.

By 1908, even Mack had lost his patience, a process no doubt accelerated by the knowledge that Waddell was declining. Mack traded Rube to St. Louis. Waddell had enough left to win 19 games in 1908, but he slipped to 12–3 in his next two seasons and was dropped by St. Louis. In 1914, only 37, he died of tuberculosis.

3. Crazy Cobb?

In baseball, more than any other sport, legend often outstrips fact, but not in the case of Ty Cobb, the first man voted into the Hall of Fame and still considered by many the greatest player in baseball history. Cobb's accomplishments were so great, his personality so strange, that nobody could have embellished on either.

Cobb was a man at war with the world, and that animosity was returned; there has never been a man more hated in sports. He burned with a searing flame that was never extinguished, and he ended his life a rich but embittered old man, estranged from his family and without friends.

He fought with everybody. Early in his career, he had so many verbal (and sometimes physical) battles with his teammates that he was ostracized. Teammates went years without speaking to Cobb, which was fine with him. On the field, he was as individualistic as it is possible to be in a team sport; off it, he went his own way, eating alone and keeping his own counsel.

He lived by his own rules, not the club's. He showed up late for practice, but no manager dared to do anything about it. Once, he jumped the club for a time in spring training because he didn't want to play against the New York Giants. Another time, he moved out of a hotel the team was staying in because it was too noisy.

Convinced that Cobb was bad for the team's morale, Detroit manager Hughey Jennings tried to trade him in 1907—when Cobb was on his way to the first of 12 league batting titles—to Cleveland for 31-year-old infielder Elmer Flick, who was nearing the end of his career. Cobb's reputation was already such that Cleveland would not make the trade.

When Cobb managed Detroit, from 1921 to 1926, he had constant squabbles with team owner Frank Navin, and he later claimed that Navin had cost the Tigers the 1924 pennant by refusing to bring up first baseman Johnny Neun from the minors and had thrown away a chance for several pennants by failing to buy Paul Waner for $45,000 from San Francisco of the Pacific Coast League. Waner, of course, was bought by Pittsburgh and eventually joined Cobb in the Hall of Fame.

Never one to back down from anybody, Cobb also battled American

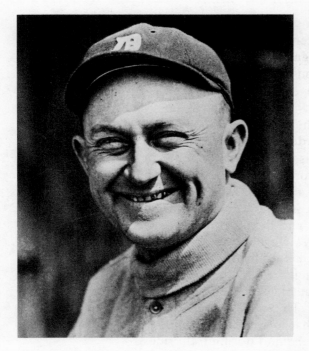

Ty Cobb, who set career
hitting marks which have
never been equalled, didn't
smile on the diamond.
(Detroit Tigers)

League president Ban Johnson for years. The climactic episode (related in
the first chapter) came when Johnson suspended Cobb and Tris Speaker for
allegedly fixing a 1919 game. That decision was reversed by Judge Kenesaw
Landis, the game's commissioner, and forced Johnson's resignation.

He was a big man for his time—6'1" and 208 pounds—and a bully; other
players were terrified of him. He frequently slid into base with spikes high,
although he claimed that was to prevent his spikes from catching in the dirt
and causing an injury rather than an attempt to injure an infielder; the
infielders weren't so certain.

Pitchers seldom dared throw at him. Cobb himself recounted with glee
many years later what happened when one, Hub Leonard, tried it. Cobb
bunted down the first baseline so Leonard had to cover first. Leonard took
the throw and quickly ran from the bag but Cobb ran after him and slid into
him from behind.

But it was more than Cobb's physical actions that inspired fear of him in
other players. The accounts of the day speak of Cobb's consuming desire to
win and a "demonic" look in his eyes when he was at bat. The thought went
unspoken: that Cobb may have been crazy.

It is difficult, more than a half century after the man last played, to assess

Cobb's mental balance. It is possible to say that his competitiveness went far beyond the bounds of his contemporaries, even the most successful, and that his actions exhibited classic signs of paranoia. He was convinced everybody was against him, and his actions made that a self-fulfilling prophecy.

Cobb was certainly a man of high intelligence, as he displayed in his financial dealings as much as on the baseball field, but his personality seemed to tilt back and forth between moments of lucidity and times of towering rages. He was a powder keg with an impossibly short fuse.

Cobb himself recognized this in his lucid moments. In a tape recording he did while working with Al Stump on his autobiography, *My Life in Baseball: The True Record*, Cobb said: "I was like a steel spring with a growing and dangerous flaw in it. If it is wound too tight or has the slightest weak point, the spring will fly apart and then it is done for. . . ."

What made Cobb this way? He blamed it on the hazing he got from teammates when he was a rookie, unheard of even by the rough standards of the time. He twice got into fights in that period, with Charlie Schmidt and Ed Siever. He was locked out of the hotel bathroom that players shared when it was time for a shower. He was shouldered aside in batting practice. The crown was cut out of his hat in a restaurant. A soggy wad of newspaper would be thrown at him from behind during train rides.

But it seems likely in retrospect that this behavior from Cobb's teammates was more effect than cause. They were reacting to a personality they hated from the beginning, a personality that was already warped by an earlier event.

The event that seems to have so greatly affected Cobb's character was the death of his father in August, 1905, when Ty was still playing minor league ball. His father had been a dominant factor in Ty's life.

The death was a tragic one. The senior Cobb had suspected his wife of being unfaithful. He left home one night and announced that he was going to a neighboring village. Doubling back, he crept through the window of his wife's bedroom. But his wife was alone. Thinking the noise that she heard was caused by a burglar, she grabbed the shotgun she kept by the bed and fired at him, killing her husband instantly.

Just before the end of his life, Ty told that story to his biographer, Stump. "I didn't get over that," he said. "I've never gotten over it."

Ty went on to say that he fought so hard through his baseball career because of his father. ". . . I knew he was watching me."

Controversy surrounded Cobb throughout his career, on and off the field.

Once, in a dispute over a bill, he beat up a young butcher's assistant. He spiked Frank "Home Run" Baker of Philadelphia in a celebrated incident in 1909, spawning letters threatening Cobb's life.

He was reported in 1907 to have hit a black groundskeeper in spring training, and then to have hit the man's wife when she joined the dispute; a teammate who chided Cobb almost got hit, too.

The Chicago Defender, a leading Negro newspaper, reported that Cobb had kicked a black chambermaid in the stomach and knocked her down the stairs in the Hotel Pontchartrain in Detroit because she objected to being called "nigger." The maid later sued for $10,000, but the case was settled out of court.

But three specific incidents probably show best what Cobb was like during his baseball years:

—Before the 1917 season, the Tigers and Cobb were playing the New York Giants in a series of exhibition games. The Giants started riding Cobb, with second baseman Buck Herzog leading the attack. Cobb, never one to allow this kind of treatment, plotted his revenge.

When Ty next reached first, he made his move to second on the first pitch, delaying so that Herzog was certain to be at the base. Herzog took the throw while Cobb was still several feet away. Cobb, who outweighed Herzog by 50 to 60 pounds, made no attempt to reach the base but instead slammed into the lighter man, knocking him down. The two sprang up fighting, until separated by other players.

That night in the hotel dining room, Herzog came by Cobb's table and challenged him to continue the fight in a hotel room. They did, and Cobb administered a fierce beating to Herzog.

Cobb then left the Tigers for the rest of that series with the Giants, saying he wanted to have nothing to do with the Giants and their "roughhouse stuff."

—In May 1912, the Tigers were playing a series in New York. A Highlander fan, Claude Lueker, had taunted Cobb at earlier games in New York, and this time he got to Cobb. Ty came over to the stands and swore at Lueker. When Lueker swore back, Cobb climbed into the stands and knocked Lueker down; Leuker insisted later that Cobb had spiked him, too, while he was down.

American League president Ban Johnson, in the stands to witness the incident, immediately suspended Cobb. That set up one of the most bizarre episodes in baseball history. This time, Cobb's teammates supported him and refused to take the field on May 16 against Philadelphia. Detroit manager Hughey Jennings put together a collection of semipro players who lost to the A's, 24–2.

The next day, Cobb persuaded his teammates to call off their strike. After a hearing before Johnson, he was fined $50 and suspended for ten days.

—The final incident went unreported during Cobb's playing days. In June 1912, while on his way to a train, he was set upon by three thugs. Cobb always carried a pistol with him, but the gun would not fire, and he was cut badly by one of the men's knives.

Nevertheless, he fought the men and chased them off. Incredibly, he then chased them, catching one and beating him badly with the pistol.

Nearly 50 years later, he still had a scar from that knife wound, but it wasn't enough to stop him or even slow him down at the time. He got a double and triple in three at-bats in his next game.

It was that kind of drive that made Cobb a great player and, indeed, kept him in the game at the start when another man, less dedicated, might have quit.

It is generally assumed that Cobb was a natural player and a star from the beginning. Nothing could be further from the truth. Playing for Augusta in the Sally League in 1903, he hit only .237 in 37 games and was released. He played semipro ball and got another chance with Augusta, and he was promoted to Detroit for part of the 1905 season. But in 41 games in his rookie season, he hit only .240.

Cobb was not discouraged. He knew he had trouble with low pitches, and he worked and worked at that weakness. In his second year, 1906, in 97 games he hit .320, a remarkable improvement but only the beginning for him. For the rest of a career which stretched through 1928, he never again hit as low as that!

His statistics are mind-boggling. For 23 straight years, he hit more than .300, and in three of those years, he exceeded .400. He won twelve batting titles, nine of them in succession. He had a career average of .367; in the last four decades, only Ted Williams (three times) and Rod Carew (once) have exceeded that mark for a season. In 1926, just before his 40th birthday, he hit .339 and struck out only twice all season. In his last season, nearing his 42nd birthday, bothered by a cataract in his right eye and by legs that had taken a terrific beating over the years, he hit .323!

Some good hitters—Williams among them—never reach 3,000 hits; Cobb is the only one ever to pass 4,000. and his 4,191 hits constitute a record that will probably never be broken.

His base-running exploits were equally remarkable. He stole 96 bases in 1915 and 892 in his career, and both remain American League records. He had 17 seasons when he stole more than 20 bases, and 14 seasons in a row. For 12 straight seasons, he stole more than 30 bases. Nine times, he stole more than 40 bases; eight times, he had more than 50 steals; six times, he stole more than 60. In the 1909–1912 period, he averaged 71 stolen bases a year.

Cobb's value, as with all great players, went beyond his statistics. He put a tremendous psychological pressure on the other team. There seemed to be no way to pitch to him because he had no great weakness. He batted with his hands apart, one down at the end, the other further up the handle. Against the best pitchers, he would slide his bottom hand up and just poke at the ball, content to get a single. Against lesser pitchers, he would slide the top hand down and go for extra bases. Because he hit most of his career against the dead ball, he never exceeded 12 home runs in a season and ended with 118 for his career. But he also hit 297 triples and 724 doubles.

The pressure didn't ease when Cobb got on base, either, because he could steal, take the extra base and—perhaps most important—disrupt the pitcher's concentration.

There seemed very little he couldn't do. Mickey Cochrane started his great catching career with Philadelphia in 1925, and he was cautioned by Athletics' manager Connie Mack not to rile Cobb. Cochrane thought he knew better. He taunted Cobb until Ty stepped out of the batter's box and told Cochrane that he was going to hit the next pitch for a triple. Cochrane called for a pitchout, but Cobb somehow got his bat on it and wound up on third base, as he had promised. Cochrane kept quiet after that.

The lively ball that came into the game late in Cobb's career infuriated Ty, because he felt it took the science out of batting. He took a different stance every time, disguising where he would hit the ball; the sluggers dug in at the same point every time.

Cobb contended that anybody could hit the long ball, and he demonstrated his point in two games in May 1925, when he was nearly 40. He told sportswriters before the first game, on May 5, that he was deliberately going for the long ball the next two games. The first day, he hit three home runs against the Browns. The next day, he hit two more—tying a 41-year-old major league record—and had two more balls which hit the top of the fence but stayed in the park.

After that, he went back to scientific hitting.

For a time, it seemed that Cobb and the Tigers were reaching athletic maturity together, as Cobb won his first three batting titles, from 1907 to '09, and the Tigers became the first American League team to win three straight pennants.

Cobb's best year of the three was 1909, in which he was a Triple Crown winner, leading in average, .377, runs batted in, 115, and even home runs for the first and last time in his career. His home run total was only nine, but this, remember, was the dead ball era. He also led the league in hits (216), runs (116), stolen bases (77), and slugging percentage (.517).

The first two Detroit pennants came at the end of memorable races, the first of which resulted in an outbreak of the fighting that often marred baseball in those days. There was another factor in both those races: the fact that teams did not have to make up rained-out games, and the championship was decided on percentage if teams played an uneven number of games.

The Tigers came into Philadelphia in the closing days of September trailing the A's by only three percentage points at the start of what was supposed to be a three-game series. The Tigers won the first game to take the lead.

The second game was rained out and rescheduled as part of a doubleheader on September 30. The Philadelphia fans jammed into the park, some 25,000 of them overflowing into a roped-off area in center field. Another 5,000 milled around outside the park, angry because they could not get in.

The A's jumped off to a 7–1 lead and were still ahead, 8–6, in the ninth inning, when Cobb hit a two-run homer to tie the game. Philadelphia manager Connie Mack fell off the bench in surprise, sprawling over a pile of bats. Mack's surprise was understandable. Cobb had hit only four home runs that season going into the game, and this one came off Rube Waddell, usually so overpowering a pitcher that Cobb choked the bat and tried only for singles. It was just another case of Cobb doing what he wanted when he wanted.

Both teams scored in the tenth, and it remained that way until the fourteenth inning when the A's Harry Davis sent a long drive toward the crowd in center field. A policeman posted to control the crowd moved in front of Sam Crawford, who was trying to catch the ball. The ball bounced into the crowd.

The Tigers screamed that it was interference, and umpire Tom Connolly agreed. A's players poured off the bench in anger and several fights started.

The police as well as umpires tried to break up the fights, and the police threatened to arrest Detroit pitcher Bill Donovan and first baseman Claude Rossman but were quickly persuaded not to.

Sam Crawford played in the same Detroit outfield with Ty Cobb and set a league career record for triples. *(George Brace)*

The field was finally cleared and the game went three more innings without score before being called by the umpires because of darkness. The Tigers moved on to Washington where they won four straight to take the pennant. The final standings: Detroit, 92–58, .613; Philadelphia, 88–57, .607.

Cobb held out during most of spring training the next season, demanding $5,000, thought to be a tremendous salary for one so young in those days; the long-established Honus Wagner was getting that amount in the National League.

Ty finally compromised on $4,500, but his late arrival unsettled the Tigers, who started slowly for the first two months. From that point, they climbed back into contention, and a tremendously exciting pennant chase with Detroit, Cleveland, and Chicago ensued. The three teams battled down to the wire, and the race was not decided until the final day.

A scheduling quirk had Cleveland playing a double-header with St. Louis on the next-to-last day of the season, while Detroit and Chicago played each other a day later—after the Indians had ended their season. The Indians could have won the pennant by sweeping the Browns, but they got only a split.

At that point, Cleveland had more wins than the other two teams, but it was mathematically eliminated. The Indians had played a full season and finished with a 90–64 record. The Tigers and White Sox had each had a game rained out and had 89–63 records. Whichever team won on the last day would finish a half game ahead of Cleveland.

The odds favored Chicago. Ed Walsh, who had won 40 games already in a marvelous season described in detail in chapter 2, was pitching for the White Sox. Donovan, a 17-game winner, was going for the Tigers—if he were ready. Donovan had developed a rheumatic condition in his arm, and the club trainer stayed up all night with him, putting on mustard plasters and hot towels.

So, Donovan got no sleep that night. His teammates got very little. Chicago fans invaded the Lexington Hotel, where the Tigers were staying, and made so much noise that Cobb claimed he couldn't get to sleep until 4 A.M.

None of that mattered the next day. Donovan pitched a magnificent game, allowing but two hits, striking out ten. Walsh, tired by his superhuman efforts down the stretch, was battered. Cobb got three hits, Crawford four, and the Tigers won, 7–0. The pennant was theirs by the margin of the rained-out game.

Cobb had his best season yet the next year, and so did the Tigers. Crawford hit .314 to back up Cobb. George Mullins won a league-leading 29 games and was supported by 22-game winner Ed Willett and 19-game winner Ed Summers. The Tigers slumped in midseason but came on strong down the stretch to win by 3½ games over Philadelphia.

But one prize was denied Cobb: a World Series championship. The Tigers lost all three Series, going down meekly in five games in the first two. Cobb had only one good Series himself, hitting .368 in 1908, though his team lost to the Chicago Cubs.

The third Series was the most disappointing of all for Cobb. After his great season, the Series was billed as a duel between him, the rising young star, and Honus Wagner, the National League's best. But it was no contest. Wagner hit .333 as his team won in seven games; Cobb hit only .231. Wagner stole six bases, Cobb only two. And both men took a backseat to Pittsburgh pitcher Babe Adams, who won three games, including the deciding one.

Cobb never got another chance at the World Series. The Philadelphia A's, the American League's first real dynasty, came with a rush to win four of the next five pennants, and the Tigers fell far back. Only three times in the remainder of Cobb's Detroit career did the Tigers have a real chance of winning the pennant: In 1915, they finished second with 100 wins, just 2½ games behind the champion Boston Red Sox; in 1916, they finished third, but only four games back; in 1924, with Cobb managing, they finished six games back in third place.

Ironically, if Cobb had played just one season longer, he would have made it back to the Series. He played for Philadelphia in 1927 and 1928, and the A's started a three-season championship run in 1929, the year Cobb retired.

Cobb did not mellow in retirement. He constantly railed at the changes made in the game by the lively ball. He contended that baseball was meant to be played within the confines of the fences, and not decided by a ball hit over one of the fences. He felt that fans wanted to see runs produced by bunts, steals, sacrifices, hit-and-run plays; in other words, as he had played the game. His was a classic case of vanity obscuring the facts.

Nevertheless, the crochety Cobb was sought out by many still connected with the game because he had a very clear vision of how to play the game. Nobody better understood the mechanics and subtleties of the game.

One of Cobb's most attentive pupils was Ted Williams, who ranks with Cobb and Babe Ruth among the top three American League hitters of all time. Williams didn't always take Cobb's advice—he would seldom, for instance, hit to left field, even when it was left nearly vacant by the other team—but he listened avidly to Cobb's theories.

The relationship between the two great hitters ended abruptly the year before Cobb's death, and in typical style. Cobb and Williams were discussing the best players of all time, and Williams insisted that Rogers Hornsby should be the second baseman. Cobb disagreed. Williams pointed out that Hornsby was a great hitter and had, in fact, had a one-season average (.424) that was higher than any Cobb had had. Cobb broke off the discussion and never talked to Williams again!

Cobb could afford his independence, because he was a rich man. He had bought General Motors and Coca-Cola stock in the early years of the century and had also traded very successfully in other stocks. He studied the market as closely as he had studied opposing pitchers. At his death, some estimates of his worth put it at $12 million. But his money didn't give him peace of mind.

In 1960, Cobb asked Al Stump to ghostwrite his autobiography. It was Ty's last chance to get even. No man is a villain in his own mind, and Cobb invariably came out as the wronged man in his recounting of the controversies that had surrounded him.

Stump later wrote a vivid and terrifying article for *Argosy* magazine on

Cobb in his final days. Cobb, wrote Stump, was drinking heavily and hardly eating; taking medicine indiscriminately and ignoring doctor's orders; driving recklessly at night on icy, snow-covered mountain roads in the Lake Tahoe area; and threatening those who crossed him with a Luger.

When they returned to Cobb's palatial 18-room house in Atherton, a wealthy area 30 miles south of San Francisco, Stump learned that the house had no power because Cobb refused to pay a $16 Pacific Gas & Electric bill.

By this time, Cobb was fading fast, cancer eating away at his body. He finally went home to Georgia, his birthplace. On July 17, 1961, he died in an Atlanta hospital.

From all of baseball, only Mickey Cochrane, Ray Schalk, and Hall of Fame director Sid Keener were at his funeral.

4. Nobody Faster

The letters from the traveling salesman in Idaho came pouring in to Washington manager Joe Cantillon that hot and unhappy summer of 1907. One typical letter read:

You better come out here and get this pitcher. He throws a ball so fast nobody can see it and he strikes out everybody. He throws a ball so fast it's like a little white bullet going down to the catcher and his control is so good that the catcher just holds up his glove, shuts his eyes, then picks the ball out of the pocket.

He's a big nineteen-year-old fellow, like I told you before, and if you don't hurry up, someone will sign him and he will be the best pitcher that ever lived.

History does not record the name of the traveling salesman, and there is even some question about the commodity with which he dealt: Some accounts have said liquor, others cigars. But it is certain that he was a good judge of talent. The pitcher he raved about was Walter Johnson, and a credible argument could be made that Johnson was the best pitcher ever.

Certainly, he was the best pitcher among those who have worked exclusively in the American League, a category that excludes Cy Young, of course.

Johnson's totals of 416 wins is by far the best in league history; Eddie Plank is a distant second with 327. He holds the American League record of 58 consecutive scoreless innings, and that string should have been even longer; in a relief appearance, he was unfairly charged with a run that should have been the responsibility of the pitcher he had relieved.

Nobody has approached Johnson's major league mark of 113 shutouts. His career strikeout mark of 3,508 has been approached, but not yet matched or surpassed.

He won 95 fewer games than Young, but Johnson's career extended into the lively ball era, when pitchers could not throw as frequently or easily, which inevitably diminished win totals.

And Johnson usually pitched for weak clubs. Ten times in his 21 seasons, the Senators finished in the second division. Even so, he made those teams

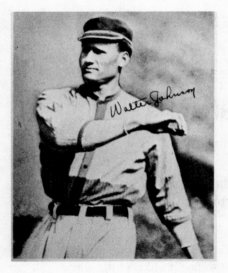

Walter Johnson is the winningest pitcher in American League history and, say many, the fastest pitcher ever. *(Washington Senators)*

look better than they were. Six times, he had more than a third of the Senators' wins in a season. Another six times, he had at least one-fourth of their wins.

Twelve times, Johnson won 20 or more games, twice more than 30. Half of those 20-win seasons came when he was pitching for second division clubs. Three times, he won 25 games with clubs which finished seventh.

Earned run averages were not kept officially until 1912. The next year, Johnson had an ERA of 1.14, which is still the American League record for pitchers with 300 or more innings in a season. The demon statisticians who put out that invaluable reference work, *The Baseball Encyclopedia,* went through old box scores and, using their stats for the years before the ERA was officially tabulated, determined that Johnson allowed less than two earned runs a game in ten of his first twelve seasons.

Johnson had so many great games that it is difficult to single out his best performances, but two stand out, one a single game, the other a series.

On July 1, 1920, he pitched the only no-hitter of his career against Boston, missing a perfect game only because of an error by second baseman Bucky Harris.

In his first full season, 1908, Johnson pitched three consecutive shutouts against the New York Highlanders, improving with each outing. On Friday, September 4, he pitched a six-hitter, on Saturday a four-hitter, and on Monday (there were no games on Sunday at that time) a two-hitter.

Johnson did it all with his fastball and control. He never had more than a fair curve, one that batters were quite happy to see. He never developed a reliable change, nor any trick pitches. Even near the end of his career, when even those with overwhelming speed in their youth develop guile to get batters out—as Lefty Grove and Bob Feller did, for instance—Johnson was still getting batters out with his fast ball.

When the subject is speed, a few names always come up: Feller, Grove, Nolan Ryan, Rube Waddell, Sandy Koufax, Tom Seaver, Dazzy Vance, Dizzy Dean, Sam McDowell. And, usually first, Walter Johnson.

There is no way of knowing who was the fastest. Officially, Ryan is, having been timed at more than 100 mph. But Ryan's edge over Feller's 98 mph timing may be no more than the fact that more sophisticated machinery was used in the measurement. And none of those who pitched before Feller, including Johnson, was ever timed.

Basically, then, it comes down to opinion, and the opinion of those who saw Johnson in his prime has always been that he was faster than anybody. He has always been the measuring stick: A pitcher was "nearly as fast as Johnson," or "the fastest since Johnson."

When he threw his fastball, Johnson was as nearly unhittable as any pitcher ever. Curiously, he didn't always throw it in the logical situations. Fairly often, for instance, when he had two strikes on a batter, he would throw his curve, an idiosyncracy which kept his strikeout total from being even higher than it was. Ty Cobb said he would take two strikes against Johnson in the hopes of then seeing that curve. Even so, Cobb didn't make the Hall of Fame on the basis of what he did against Johnson.

As a person, Johnson was the antithesis of Cobb: gentle, considerate, kind. He went out of his way to be nice to people, on and off the field. Two stories best illustrate Johnson's character:

—Though he was of German-Dutch descent, the story got around early in Johnson's career that his background was Swedish, an error which still crops up in books today, and he was known as "Big Swede." He never bothered to correct that. "They're good people, the Swedes," he said, "and I don't want to offend them."

—In a hotel lobby in St. Louis one time, just before Johnson was to go to a movie with teammate Joe Judge, a stranger came up and struck up a long conversation before finally leaving. The impatient Judge asked why Johnson hadn't cut the conversation short.

"He said he knew my sister," explained Johnson.

"I didn't know you had a sister," said Judge.

"I don't," said Johnson.

Because of his gentle personality, it was often said that Johnson was so afraid that he might hurt a batter if he hit him with a fastball that he wouldn't pitch inside. Cobb bragged that he dug in against Johnson, knowing he wouldn't be brushed back. In fact, though, Johnson hit 206 batters in his career, and nobody in major league history is even close; Don Drysdale, who had a reputation for that, is second with 154. That hardly suggests a reluctance to pitch inside.

Johnson was born in Kansas, and his parents moved first to California and then to Idaho. As early as 14 he was pitching—and having trouble finding somebody who could catch him—but it wasn't until he was 19 that he attracted attention.

The anonymous salesman who discovered Johnson apparently also wrote letters to the Detroit Tigers and New York Highlanders. He was quite florid in his descriptions, as well as prolific. Not only did Johnson have a great fastball, he wrote in one letter, but he knew where it was going. "Otherwise, there would be dead bodies scattered all over Idaho."

But this kind of thing was very common in those days, when there was very little organized scouting. Men would write clubs, hoping to get a bonus or a job if a prospect made it. The Tigers had heard it all before and, on their way to the pennant, didn't need help. Clark Griffith, manager of the Highlanders, paid a little more attention but didn't follow through.

The Senators, though, couldn't afford to pass up any lead. Holding up the rest of the league, they won only 49 games that year, finishing 43½ games behind the Tigers and 11 behind seventh-place Boston. They sent Cliff Blankenship out to scout Johnson.

As it happened, Johnson lost the game Blankenship saw—1–0 in 12 innings on a teammate's error, the kind of game that would become all too familiar to Johnson in his Washington career. Blankenship realized what a find Johnson was and wrote out a contract on a loose piece of paper, adding a $100 bonus as a sweetener.

Johnson was a totally unsophisticated, unpolished young man when he arrived in Washington. His coat sleeves ended just past his elbows, and his pants cuffs were at the high-water mark.

Not realizing there was a team bus, Johnson walked back to the hotel in his uniform after his first major league game. That night, he was standing outside the hotel when a stranger came up to him and pointed out the "Johnson Hotel" across the street, telling him that the hotel was named after him. "Do you know," laughed Johnson years later in retelling the story, "I was so green, I believed him."

He was just as green on the mound. He hadn't learned anything about

Wily Clark Griffith was a pitcher, manager, and club owner in the early years of the league. *(Chase Limited)*

vinced Chicago White Sox owner Charles Comiskey to pay the bonus, arguing that if Johnson played for Chicago in the Federal League, that would cut into the White Sox' gate.

Comiskey paid Johnson, who gave the money to a brother to pay a debt, and everybody in the American League was happy, except for the batters who had to face Johnson.

In 1920, Johnson's stretch of 20-win seasons was broken as he came down with the only sore arm of his career, winning only eight games and pitching only 143 innings. He was 33 after that season ended, at a point in his career where fastball pitchers usually either learn new pitches or fade from the majors.

Johnson did neither. He came back to win 17, 15, and 17 games in his next three seasons, not spectacular but decent years for a club which was cumulatively under .500 during that period. But they were hardly Walter Johnson years. For the first time in his career, he was giving up more hits than innings pitched, and his earned run averages were uncharacteristically high—3.51, 2.99, 3.54.

But in 1924, the Senators won the first pennant in their history, and Johnson was the league's Most Valuable Player, winning 23 games and losing only seven, leading the league with 158 strikeouts and a 2.72 ERA as well.

The Series that year was less a match between Washington and the New York Giants, winners of the National League pennant, than an opportunity for Walter Johnson to finally get a chance for the Series win that had been denied him—the one honor in baseball he had missed.

He pitched 12 strong innings in the opener, but finally went down, 4–3. The next time out, in the fifth game, he was less of a mystery to the Giants. Griffith let him pitch the entire game again, but he was soundly beaten, 6–2. That gave the Giants a 3–2 edge in the Series and made it all but certain that Johnson would not get that Series win.

Washington came back to tie the Series with a 2–1 win in the sixth game. It all came down to the seventh game, in Washington.

The Senators got a run in the fourth, the Giants three in the sixth, the Senators two more in the eighth to tie the game, 3–3. In the ninth, buoyed by the enormous vocal support of the Washington fans, Johnson came on to pitch four innings of strong relief, blanking the Giants and striking out five as the day got darker and darker.

In the bottom of the 12th, the Senators' luck suddenly turned all good. With one out, Muddy Ruel hit a pop-up behind the plate, but New York catcher Hank Gowdy stepped on his mask and failed to make the catch. Given a reprieve, Ruel then doubled down the left field line.

Johnson, the next batter, hit a grounder that shortstop Travis Jackson fumbled. Two runners on, still only one out. Then Earl McNeely hit what should have been an inning-ending double play ball to third baseman Fred Lindstrom, but the ball hit a pebble and bounced over Lindstrom's head. Ruel scored with the winning run, and Johnson had his first World Series win, in one of the most emotional moments in baseball history.

The next year, the Senators won another pennant, the first and last time in their history they would win back-to-back flags, and Johnson won 20 games for the last time in his career.

The World Series that year seemed to have his name on it. He won the first game, 4–1, the fourth game, 4–0, over the Pittsburgh Pirates. When the Series went to the seventh game, Washington manager Bucky Harris handed Johnson the ball once again.

But Johnson's—and the Senators'—luck had run out. The game was played in a steady downpour, but Commissioner Landis was reluctant to postpone it because it was already October 15, and more rain could be expected the next day.

Johnson was battered throughout the game, giving up 15 hits. He twisted his leg pitching in the mud early in the game and pitched in pain the rest of the way.

In the eighth inning, he gave up back-to-back doubles which tied the score at 7–7. A walk to George Moore followed, but with two outs, Johnson got Max Carey to ground to shortstop for what should have been the final out. Shortstop Roger Peckinpaugh threw high to manager/second baseman Harris, pulling Bucky off the bag. It was the eighth error of the Series for Peckinpaugh, and the Pirates were still batting.

Johnson got two strikes on the next batter, Kiki Cuyler, and then threw a fastball he thought was the third strike. It was ruled a ball, though, and on the next pitch, Cuyler doubled to right, scoring two runs. The game ended that way, 9–7 for Pittsburgh.

Billy Evans had been the umpire when Johnson had won the dramatic seventh game the year before. In 1925, he was not assigned to the umpiring crew, so he was writing for a newspaper syndicate. As he left the press box that day, tears were streaming down his cheeks. Walter Johnson had that kind of effect on people.

5. The 50-Year Field Boss

Nobody in baseball has ever approached Connie Mack's longevity, and probably nobody ever will. Mack was in professional baseball for 72 years, and he managed the same club for an astounding 50 years. Of course, he had a job security other managers lacked: He owned the club.

Mack won nine pennants and five World Championships, and managed two of the best teams in American League history, the 1910–14 and 1929–31 Philadelphia Athletics. He also managed some of the worst, finishing last 17 times.

He was an excellent judge of talent, chiefly responsible for building the good and great A's teams. As a manager, his forte was dealing with players, and he had success with some problem players, most notably Rube Waddell.

He was not known as a great strategist, as John McGraw was; nor did he have Casey Stengel's great gift for using just the right player at the right time. Mack's trademark was the use of a scorecard to motion outfielders into position, but it seems likely that those outfielders would have gotten into position without that help. And Mack managed into his dotage: By the time he retired, at nearly 88, he was calling the names of retired stars to pinch-hit, and his coaches were actually running the club.

But Mack's importance to baseball in general and the American League in particular is undeniable. He imparted a dignity to a game which was barely a step above the carnival in sophistication, and his mere presence changed the game for the better.

Even his manner of dress was dignified. So thin at 6'1" and 150 pounds that he had been called "Slats" during his playing career, Mack knew he did not look good in a baseball uniform. So, he dressed in a dark suit, with high collar and tie, and wore a hat—sometimes a straw hat, sometimes a derby.

In a era when profanity was common, Mack seldom swore. He seldom got in an argument with an umpire and was not thrown out of a game in 50 years. He never even used nicknames. To Mack, Chief Bender was always "Albert" and Waddell "Eddie." The players, awed by his dignity, called him "Mr. Mack."

As the years went on, Mack became more and more venerated. Probably

Connie Mack gave baseball dignity and managed for a half century, a record that will never be approached. *(George Brace)*

the best example came in 1930, when he was given the Edward Bok award (established by the famous editor of *Ladies Home Journal*) as the man who had done the most for Philadelphia. The award, which had a cash prize of $10,000 and a gold medal, had never before gone to anyone in sports.

Inevitably, Mack's reputation became that of a saint, which probably did the man a disservice. He was much more interesting than that. Behind that facade of dignity was a highly competitive man, and one who did not hesitate to pull tricks to gain an edge.

He was a catcher, for instance, in an era when a caught tipped strike was an out with less than two strikes on the batter, and he simulated the sound of a tipped ball with his hand and glove.

Later, he developed a technique of tipping the hitter's bat with his glove, just enough to deflect the swing. He was finally discouraged in that when a batter swung directly at Mack's hand, smashing his fingers and sidelining him for a period.

When he first got the Philadelphia franchise, he raided the National League teams for players, offering them more money, a move heavy with irony in light of his later problems.

He got Eddie Collins to play under the assumed name of Sullivan while

Collins was still a student at Columbia, breaking the rules against professionalism. On other occasions, he was fined for breaking league rules in transferring players.

Though he had great patience, it was not inexhaustible, as he proved when he finally shipped Waddell off to St. Louis. He seldom argued with umpires, but when he did, it was a lulu; he didn't speak to Silk O'Loughlin for years after a call went against the A's one day.

His frugality was legendary. He twice broke up dynasty teams, the first time because of Federal League competition, the second time because of the Depression, claiming he could not afford to pay the salaries the players were asking. The second time he did that, a bitter sportswriter wondered if he intended to sell the Bok award, too.

None of this detracts from his contribution to baseball. It does suggest that Mack was a more complex man than those blinded by a cloying sentimentality are willing to admit.

Mack was born Cornelius McGillicuddy on December 22, 1862, in East Brookfield, Massachusetts. It was said later that he changed his name to Connie Mack so his last name could fit into the box scores without being mangled by apostrophes, and that may be true. But in his childhood he was also known as Connie Mack by his friends who were unwilling to try to get their tongues around his legal name.

By the time he was nine, he was working in the town's cotton mill. His father died when he was young, leaving his mother to rear the family, and Connie quit school at 16 to take a job at a shoe factory.

Meanwhile, he was also playing ball. Probably, it was town ball, a game from which baseball descended. Similar in many ways to baseball, town ball's one big difference was that runners were put out by being hit by a thrown ball. Some baseball historians think Mack may not have played baseball until his late teens.

By 1883, though, Mack was catching for the East Brookfield team, and he became more enthusiastic about the game when Cap Anson brought his team to town for an exhibition game.

One year later, Mack signed to play professionally for the first time, with Meriden of the Connecticut State League, a minor league. By September 1886, he was in the National League with Washington.

Mack played with Washington through 1889, then jumped to Buffalo of the Players League, investing his life savings in the club. He lost his money when the club folded after a year, and he joined Pittsburgh of the National League the next year, lasting through 1896.

Mack was apparently a good defensive catcher, especially when pitching changed from underhanded to overhanded; he was one of the first to move into a crouch just behind the batter. In earlier days, catchers had played as much as 15 feet behind the plate.

He was constantly talking to hitters, trying to get them off balance, and his high, squeaky voice was a great distraction. But he was never much of a hitter—.247 lifetime in 711 games—and a broken ankle in 1893 reduced his mobility. He was quite happy to retire from playing and become a full-time manager when the opportunity came.

Mack actually had managed while he was still playing with Pittsburgh. Appointed in the last month of the 1894 season, he finished seventh and sixth in the next two full seasons and was fired.

But then Ban Johnson, a friend of Mack's, asked him to manage the Milwaukee team in Johnson's Western League, and Mack did for the next four seasons. When Johnson made his league the American League and expanded into the east, he awarded Mack the Philadelphia franchise. Mack owned 25 percent and got most of the rest of the backing from Benjamin Shibe.

The team that Mack assembled that year, 1901, was a collection of former National League players and unknowns. John McGraw, managing the Baltimore club, feared the A's would hold the rest of the league down. "White elephants!" he snorted, in reference to the former National Leaguers.

But one of them who jumped was Nap Lajoie, who hit an incredible .422 and won the Triple Crown, while playing impeccably at second base on defense. One of Mack's finds was Eddie Plank, fresh off the Gettysburg College campus, who won 17 games. The A's finished fourth, and the white elephant was their symbol and substitute nickname for many years.

Lajoie had jumped the Phillies to play for the A's, and the National League club got a court injunction to prevent him from playing American League games in Pennsylvania. So, Mack had to trade Lajoie to Cleveland, after just one game in the 1902 season.

But Connie got a good replacement for Lajoie in Danny Murphy, who hit .313, one of six .300-hitting regulars. The others were Lave Cross, .339, Ossee Schreckengost, .324, Socks Seybold, .317, Harry Davis, .308, and Dave Fultz, .302.

The steady Plank won 20 games, the first of eight such seasons in a career in which he won 327 games. Mack picked up the irrepressible but talented Waddell, who did not join the club until May but still won 24 games with a league-leading 210 strikeouts.

And Mack had the first of the nine pennants which was a league record until Casey Stengel won ten. Since the leagues were at war, there was no postseason competition.

Mack's 1905 team was even better, because of the physical maturing of Waddell, Plank, and Andy Coakley, and the addition of Chief Bender. Some said Bender was as fast as Waddell and Walter Johnson. Mack later said that of all the pitchers he had had, Bender was the best when he really needed a win. Bender was plagued by illness—and sometimes a drinking problem—throughout his career, but he still won 210 games and made the Hall of Fame. In 1905, his third season, he won 16 games.

The others did better. Waddell had a great year, winning 26 games, seven of them shutouts, saving another four games in relief, striking out a league-leading 287 hitters, and posting an unofficial ERA of 1.48.

Plank was right behind Waddell with 25 wins and a league-leading 35 complete games. Coakley, who had pitched for the pennant-winner in 1902 but had won only two games, won 20 games for the first and last time in his career, with an unofficial ERA of 1.84.

But on September 1, as the A's were traveling by train from New York to Boston, Waddell and Coakley got into a senseless fight on the train. At that time, men wore straw hats in summer, discarding them on Labor Day, which fell on September 4 that year. When Waddell saw Coakley wearing a straw hat on the train, he decided the season had ended for those hats, and he tried to take it away. In the ensuing fight, Waddell landed on his left shoulder, and he did not pitch again until next season.

That fight cost Waddell an almost certain 30-win season because he lost at least seven starts. It also made the pennant race tighter than it should have been. On September 28, the A's were only percentage points ahead of the Chicago White Sox, but then took two out of three from the White Sox in a series in Philadelphia to all but clinch the pennant.

Waddell's absence certainly hurt the Athletics' chances in the World Series, though hitting, not pitching, was the A's primary problem in that remarkable Series in which each of the five games finished in a shutout. Bender got the only Philadelphia win, 3-0 in the second game. The A's got only 25 hits in the entire Series. Christy Mathewson shut them out three times, including in the climactic game, and Joe McGinnity once.

But the 1905 team, good as it was, was nothing compared to the team

Mack assembled in the following years, culminating in 1910 with a team which won four pennants in five years and is recognized as the first "dynasty" team in American League history. That team was the first in American League history to win three World Series, and it is still a shock that it lost in its fourth Series competition.

The A's had finished 3½ games behind Detroit in the 1909 season, and most of the experts thought they were still too young to win in 1910. But, after a 1–0 shutout by Walter Johnson on opening day, the Athletics' came on strong and quickly and ran away from the rest of the league, eventually winning 102 games and finishing a whopping 14½ games ahead of second-place New York.

The 1910 team had four future Hall-of-Famers—second baseman Eddie Collins, third baseman Frank "Home Run" Baker, and pitchers Bender and Plank. Herb Pennock and Stan Coveleski, each of whom also made the Hall of Fame, joined the pitching staff midway through the A's great stretch, though each did his best pitching for other teams later.

The most startling fact about this team, though, is that it could have been even better. "Shoeless Joe" Jackson—who got his nickname because he once took off his shoes during a minor league game to rest a sore foot—played for the A's when he first came up from the minors.

Jackson, an uneducated and unsophisticated man, is often called the best natural hitter in baseball history. Ty Cobb said that when he was in a batting slump, he tried to get a look at Jackson to see what a good swing looked like, and Babe Ruth, making the switch from pitching to the outfield, said he also studied Jackson's swing. In 13 major league seasons, Jackson hit .356; only Cobb and Rogers Hornsby ever did better.

Joe played a total of ten games for the A's in the 1907 and 1908 seasons, but he was uncomfortable in Philadelphia, which was vastly different from the small towns to which he was accustomed, and was unmercifully hazed by his teammates.

Aware of Jackson's problems, Mack reluctantly concluded that Joe could never play well in Philadelphia and traded him to Cleveland, where he averaged .380 and hit as high as .408 during the A's great years, 1910–14. They could have used him.

Despite all the Hall of Fame talent on the team, it was Jack Coombs who had the best year for the A's in 1910, winning 31 games, 13 of them shutouts.

Coombs, one of three college men on the A's roster (Collins and Plank were the other two), outpitched even Bender and Plank for three seasons, following with 28 wins in 1911 and 21 in 1912. But illness curtailed his effectiveness after that, and he finished his career with 158 wins, a respectable total but certainly far less than he would have obtained if he had stayed healthy.

Coombs went on to win three complete-game victories in the World Series, as the A's disposed of the Chicago Cubs in five games.

The next year, Stuffy McInnis, who had been a reserve infielder for two seasons, became the full-time first baseman, and the famed "$100,000 infield" was intact, with McInnis, second baseman Collins, shortstop Jack Barry, and third baseman Baker.

Barry's contribution was primarily on defense—he hit as high as .275 only once in his career and finished with a .243 average—but the others were excellent hitters as well as fine fielders.

Collins's exploits were described in an earlier chapter. McInnis, who has Hall of Fame credentials though he has not been voted in, averaged more than .300 for his first five seasons as a regular, had ten seasons in which he played more than 100 games and hit more than .300, and had a lifetime average of .308.

Baker hit more than .300 for five of his first six seasons as a regular, and ended with a .307 lifetime average for 13 years, but he is known primarily for the 1911 World Series in which he gained his nickname.

The Giants, behind Mathewson, had won the first game of the Series, 2–1. In the second game, the score was tied, 1–1, when Baker hit a two-run homer off Rube Marquard in the sixth, the game ending three innings later with that 3–1 score.

Marquard and Mathewson had both been hired by newspaper syndicates during the Series, with their names appearing over columns written by newspaper ghostwriters. That next day, Mathewson's column suggested that Marquard had been careless in pitching to Baker.

The next day, Mathewson had a 1–0 lead in the ninth when Baker hit another home run to tie the score. In the 11th, he had a run-scoring single, and the A's won, 3–2.

In Marquard's column the following day was the suggestion that Mathewson had been careless in pitching to Baker.

Baker went on to hit .375 in the Series, and he led both clubs with nine hits, seven runs, five RBIs, and, of course, his two home runs.

It is tempting to think that Baker's nickname was undeserved because he never hit more than 12 home runs in a season and only 93 for his career. But this, of course, was in the dead ball era. Baker led the league in home runs for four straight years, starting in 1911, and the league record was only 16 at that time.

Hampered by injuries and illnesses—most notably, that of Bender, who pitched only 171 innings and won only 13 games—the A's started slowly in 1912 and were never really in the race, finishing third, 15 games behind Boston.

The Red Sox had a well-balanced team, with perhaps the best defensive outfield of all time, Harry Hooper and Duffy Lewis flanking Tris Speaker. And they had "Smokey Joe" Wood, who had one of the best seasons a pitcher has ever had.

Wood, whose fastball was responsible for his nickname, won 34 games and lost only five, saving another game in relief. He completed 35 of the 38 games he started, struck out 258 batters, had ten shutouts and an ERA of 1.91. And then he won three games as the Red Sox beat the Giants in the World Series.

Wood celebrated his 23rd birthday just nine days after his seventh game win had nailed down the World Series for the Red Sox, and he had already won 81 big league games. He should have gone on to be one of the best in history, but he hurt his arm the next year and was never the same kind of pitcher, winning only 33 games after 1912. But, switching to the outfield, he hit well enough to last through 1922.

Bouncing back in 1913, the A's won their third pennant in four years, finishing 6½ ahead of Washington, and disposed of the Giants in five games. The next year was more of the same in the pennant race, as the A's beat Boston by 8½ games. The American League had not lost a World Series since 1909, and the A's were overwhelming favorites in the Series.

But there were two elements working against the Athleticss that year. One was that the Federal League had come into existence, and many of the star Philadelphia players had been approached to jump leagues.

Another, and probably more important, factor was that the A's were playing the miracle Boston Braves, who had come from last place on July 4 to the National League pennant. On paper, the Braves could not match up with the A's, but this was one of those cases where a team was playing on a level that seemed impossible, and they swept the A's in four games.

And so, the first American League dynasty ended on a sour note. The team was quickly broken up, first by Federal League inroads, then by Mack.

The Federal League grabbed off Bender and Plank. Mack sold Collins to the White Sox for $50,000 in a deal engineered by league president Ban

Johnson, and then disposed of Coombs, Pennock, Barry, and Bob Shawkey for lesser amounts.

Even had the team stayed together, it's doubtful it could have staved off the Boston Red Sox, who had a young pitcher named Babe Ruth reaching for stardom. With these losses, the Athletics sank to last place.

After the 1915 season, though the Federal League was no longer around as an excuse, Mack also sold McInnis, catcher Wally Strang, pitcher Joe Bush, and outfielder Amos Strunk. And the A's did not climb out of the American League cellar until 1922.

6. League Wars

Even before the great Philadelphia team was broken up, the American League had entered the roughest period of its existence, facing a series of problems that threatened to destroy the circuit.

The first difficulty, and the one which bore directly on the A's, was the presence of a third "major league," the outlaw Federal League, which was to cause a great deal of havoc in its two years.

There was special irony involved for the American League in the Federal League challenge, because it had been such a short time earlier that the American League was the "outlaw" circuit, refusing to honor the National Agreement and raiding an established league for players. The Federal League was even operating in a similar fashion by going from a minor league one year to a major league the next, in name if not in reality.

That didn't prevent American League president Ban Johnson and the A. L. team owners from railing at the Federal League owners for their tactics. Their statements were virtually the same as those of the N. L. owners when the American League declared itself a "major" in 1901. The irony was lost on the A. L. owners and executives; it doesn't take long for a reformed outlaw to feel at home with the Establishment.

The Federal League began in 1913, independent of organized baseball, with clubs in Chicago, St. Louis, Cleveland, Pittsburgh, Indianapolis, and Cincinnati.

Cy Young managed the team in Cleveland, where he had begun his marvelous pitching career 23 years earlier, but that was the Federal League's only major league connection. The league did not sign any established major leaguers that first year, relying on free agents and young players starting their careers.

The second year, Chicago businessman James A. Gilmore became league president, replacing John T. Powers. Citing the prosperity of the two established leagues, Gilmore was able to bring considerable financial backing to the new association.

The Federals expanded to eight teams for the 1914 season, dropping Cleveland but adding Buffalo, Brooklyn, and Baltimore, and Gilmore declared it a major league, putting it into direct competition with the two existing circuits.

The established leagues were operating under the reserve clause, which supposedly bound a player to a team even after his contract had expired. The Federal League owners did not try to sign any players operating under unexpired contracts, but they challenged the validity of the reserve clause and eventually signed 81 major league players whose contracts had expired.

But unlike the American League, which had captured many star players in its early raids on the National League, the Federal League was unable to steal away enough stars to make a serious impact with the fans.

In its first year, the Federal League got only the players who were past their prime, such as Detroit pitcher George Mullin and Philadelphia outfielder Danny Murphy.

The second year, the league lured away Eddie Plank and Chief Bender from the A's, but could get no other American League stars. Without the big names, the Federal League fooled nobody in its pretense to major league status.

American League owners and executives battled to keep stars from jumping by threatening not to take back players who jumped to the outlaw association.

"I will not take a single man back who steps over the line dividing the American and Federal League," said Ban Johnson. "I hereby tell one and all of them that I will not even talk to them."

Few stars seemed frightened. They were aware that in previous such skirmishes, players were always forgiven when the war was over. The issue was never joined this time, however, because owners kept their star players at home by raising salaries dramatically.

Ty Cobb, for instance, went from $12,000 to $20,000. We know that Eddie Collins and Walter Johnson both got big boosts. So did Tris Speaker. The owners, as one admitted anonymously to a newspaperman of the day, were "purchasing loyalty."

Meanwhile, the Federal League was cutting into American League attendance, though its own was faltering despite ticket prices which dropped as low as ten cents. Organized baseball had to make peace, which it did after the 1915 season—after the Federal League had withdrawn an antitrust suit.

The truce included payments of $600,000 to the principal Federal League backers. Phil Ball was allowed to buy the St. Louis club in the American League and Charles Weeghman the Chicago National League team. In both cases, the new owners were wealthy men who strengthened their franchises and leagues.

There is an important footnote to the Federal League story. The Baltimore club was left out of the settlement and subsequently sued. When the suit finally reached the U.S. Supreme Court in 1922, Justice Oliver Wendell Holmes spoke for a unanimous court when he said that baseball was exempt from antitrust statutes because it was not "trade or commerce in the commonly-accepted use of those words" and was not an interstate business. That ruling preserved the reserve clause until it was successfully challenged in 1976.

The established leagues had barely recovered from their battles with the Federal League when another and more serious kind of combat intruded—World War I. The war, of course, had been fought in Europe since 1914, but it was not until the United States entered in 1917 that it caused any problems for baseball.

On February 1, 1917, following the resumption of unrestricted submarine warfare by Germany, the United States severed diplomatic relations with Germany. It was obvious that Americans would soon be fighting.

Would baseball suspend operations? Not the American League, said Ban Johnson, noting that the National League had continued playing during the Spanish-American War, a conflict of somewhat shorter duration.

Johnson's statement was typical of baseball's response to the crisis. For the next year and a half, owners and executives fought a delaying action with the federal government, maintaining their public patriotism while struggling to keep the game going.

Both leagues passed resolutions calling for players to put in an hour of military drill daily, though the American League teams were more faithful in continuing it. Johnson even offered a $500 prize to the team that was best drilled. The St. Louis Browns won the prize, the last prize the Browns would win until the 1944 pennant in, ironically, another war year.

Clubs encouraged purchase of Liberty Bonds and regularly donated money to the Red Cross. Troops paraded before games. Military personnel were admitted free. Washington's Clark Griffith raised money to send 3,100 baseball kits (each valued at about $30) to military bases. The kits contained catcher's equipment, a first baseman's glove, three bats, three bases, a dozen balls, a dozen scorecards, and a rule book.

The war had relatively little effect on baseball in 1917, except for a decline in attendance. The first draft calls were not made until July, and few players were tapped.

In a postseason meeting of both leagues, Johnson suggested asking the government to exempt the first 18 men on a team's roster from the draft, but that was quickly voted down. The owners decided to continue with a 154-game season—but a month later, after heavy newspaper criticism, decided instead on a 140-game season.

The shorter season and lessened attendance cut into club revenues, obviously, but the owners had ways of compensating. The quickest way was by cutting player salaries, which most clubs did. Even more interesting was the way they handled the "war tax."

The government had leveled a ten percent "entertainment tax" on admissions. For baseball, this meant a three-cent tax on 25-cent tickets, eight cents on 75-cent tickets, and thirteen cents on $1.25 tickets. So they wouldn't have to worry about the odd cents, so they said, owners raised prices five, ten, and fifteen cents, respectively, thus making a few pennies extra on each ticket. After the war, the tax was dropped. Ticket prices were not.

Even with these accommodations, however, the 1918 season was a rocky one. On May 23, the government issued a "work-or-fight" order, which made it mandatory for men to get into essential work by July 1 or risk induction.

Johnson did a real flip-flop after this edict. At first, he advocated closing "every theater, ball park, and place of recreation in the country."

About a month later, though, he claimed baseball was an essential industry because it was delivering around $300,000 to the government through the war/entertainment tax. He also claimed that baseball personnel had bought more than $8 million worth of Liberty Bonds. "Where is there another class of men earning so much for the government?" he asked.

Baseball people resented the fact that actors were exempted from the order, supposedly because they raised morale. (That exemption was later eliminated.)

In late July, Clark Griffith appealed the drafting of his catcher, Eddie Ainsmith. He claimed: 1) Baseball was a business which would be made temporarily worthless because it could not be used for other purposes, unlike plants which could shift to making wartime materials; 2) Ballplayers did not have the skills which would enable them to enter new occupations which would make them as much money as they had in baseball—a strange claim coming from the penurious Griffith; and 3) Baseball was the national sport, and its suspension would inflict social harm.

Secretary of War Newton D. Baker refused to change the regulations, however, and major league teams were soon crippled as players left for essential jobs or military service. In all, 124 American Leaguers eventually joined the military, and the remainder of the 1918 season was played with teams who depended heavily on over-the-hill players and untested minor leaguers.

The rest of the season was chaotic. Johnson called for an immediate end to the season after Baker's announcement, but club owners ignored him, the surest indication that Johnson's day of iron-man rule was over.

Secretary Baker allowed a two-month extension of the July 1 deadline so the season could be concluded. The next question was whether the World Series should be played before September 1, which would have caused the season to be further shortened.

Owners finally decided to play through Labor Day, which fell on September 2 that year, and the teams in the World Series—the Boston Red Sox and Chicago Cubs—were given an extra two weeks extension by Secretary Baker.

Cleveland did not play that extra day. Its players had believed that there would be no games on Monday, and many of them were scheduled to begin work at wartime jobs on Tuesday morning. They refused to go to St. Louis for the games scheduled on Sunday, September 1, and Monday, September 2.

The Browns demanded the games be forfeited and that Cleveland pay a $1,000 penalty for each. The games did not affect the standings, and Johnson, no doubt reasoning correctly that he had bigger problems, took no action.

The owners, who had already cut player salaries, managed a further cut by "releasing" all their players after the season had ended, thus not paying the balance of their contracts. This apparently saved them about $200,000.

Theoretically, this made the players all free agents, but the owners had privately agreed not to sign anybody else's players. Some players sued, though only one—Brooklyn's Jake Daubert—is reported to have gotten anything; his suit was settled out of court.

Washington outfielder Burt Shotton sued for $1,400 and was waived out of the league, finally signing with the St. Louis Cardinals of the National League. It is an interesting indication of the temper of the times that one reporter said, "Something or other turned him Bolsheviki."

By the 1919 season, everything was more or less back to normal, with the war over and most players back with their teams again. The owners tried to recoup losses by putting club salary limits into effect and lowering team rosters from 25 to 21, but they failed to reinstate the 154-game season, which was the one thing that would have brought them the most money. Not realizing that the first year after the war is always a boom time for entertainment, they stuck with the 140-game season and drew more than 6.5 million, more than double the previous year's attendance. The longer season would have meant a total gate of 7 million, back to the prewar highs.

Meanwhile, a war of another sort had broken out inside the American League, between Johnson and a minority of the team owners, known as the "Insurrectionists."

In its early years, the American League was a model operation, with Johnson in charge. That couldn't last. Some strong-willed men owned American League clubs, and they chafed under Johnson's autocratic rule. It was inevitable they would rebel when his decisions went against them.

The first to break with Johnson was his old friend, Charles Comiskey, who had brought him into baseball.

The first rupture in the friendship occurred as early as 1905, at a time when Johnson and Comiskey were still sharing an office. Johnson upheld the suspension of Chicago outfielder James ("Ducky") Holmes after a dispute with an umpire—and Comiskey moved out of their shared office.

Charles Comiskey was first a player and later an owner, and it was his team that became the "Black Sox." *(George Brace)*

Yet another break came in 1907, when Johnson suspended Chicago playing manager Fielder Jones. But Johnson and Comiskey papered over their differences and remained friendly in public, though hardly as close as they had once been.

In 1918, the irrevocable break occurred. The historic case involved Jack Quinn, a remarkable pitcher who lasted in the major leagues through 1933, when he was 49.

Quinn had pitched that year in the Pacific Coast League, until the league disbanded in July because of the war. The White Sox signed him and he won five games, losing only one, for the remainder of the American League season. But in the meantime, the New York Yankees had purchased Quinn's contract from his old PCL club, and the matter was turned over to the National Commission.

The commission ruled that Quinn was the Yankees' property, and Comiskey never forgave Johnson for siding with the Yankees. The men remained bitter enemies until they died, only months apart, in 1931.

Johnson was also battling with Boston owner Harry Frazee, whom he accused of permitting gambling in his park, and the New York owners, Colonels Jake Ruppert and Til Huston, for reasons unknown. He wanted all three out of the league.

It was fitting, then, that the case which broke the league apart and eventually caused a sharp curtailment of Johnson's powers involved both Boston and New York.

The case involved Carl Mays, a pitcher who is now known primarily because his pitch killed Cleveland shortstop Ray Chapman in 1920, the only fatality in a major league game.

Mays was pitching for Boston on July 13, 1919, against Chicago. After two innings, he stalked out of the game, dressed and left for the east. His reasons remain obscure. Always a man of stormy disposition, Mays was thought by some to be angry because of his teammates' lack of support, and his disposition was not improved when a throw from catcher Wally Schang, who was trying to catch a base stealer, hit him in the back of the head. One sportswriter claimed to have seen a note from Mays after the game, claiming personal problems.

Boston did not suspend Mays, but when talk of a trade arose, Johnson announced that he did not want a trade made until Mays returned to his club.

When Mays was gone for two weeks, however, Frazee traded him to the Yankees. Johnson immediately suspended Mays. Colonel Ruppert asked that the suspension be lifted. Johnson refused, and the battle was joined.

The first salvo came in the form of a temporary court injunction secured by the Yankee owners restraining Johnson and the league from interfering with Mays's right to pitch for New York.

For some time after that, there was a series of inconclusive meetings. The league was hopelessly split. Johnson had the support of five of the eight owners—Jim Dunn of Cleveland, Clark Griffith of Washington, Connie Mack (and the Shibes) of Philadelphia, Frank Navin of Detroit, and Phil Ball of St. Louis.

But the league's board of directors consisted of Johnson, Dunn, and three "Insurrectionists," Comiskey, Ruppert and Frazee, so the rebels had the majority there.

As if there weren't enough complications, Navin added another at World Series time. Only the first three teams shared in the World Series pool that year. The Yankees, with Mays winning nine games for them, finished third, a half game ahead of Detroit. Navin argued that the games Mays won should not be allowed because he was under suspension. The matter reached the National Commission, which withheld the Yankees' World Series shares until it was resolved.

Late in October, New York Supreme Court Justice Robert Wagner announced that the court had granted the Yankees a permanent injunction, in essence ruling that the clubs had the right to regulate their business, without Johnson's "interference."

Johnson and his supporters fought back by holding a league meeting at which the three "insurrectionists" were replaced on the league's board by owners loyal to Johnson. Undeterred, Comiskey, Ruppert, and Frazee fought back with a series of minor but nagging legal actions against Johnson.

Finally, the Yankee owners sued Johnson for $500,000, alleging that he had tried to drive them out of baseball. This brought about a final meeting, on February 10, 1920, in which the two factions sought to settle their differences.

It was, understandably, a tumultuous meeting. There are reports of owners nearly coming to blows more than once. Not until 2 A.M. was a settlement finally reached.

The settlement stripped Johnson of most of his powers and ended his one-man rule, making the last seven years of his presidency anticlimactic. The Yankee owners were clear winners in the struggle, with Carl Mays reinstated in good standing and New York's third-place standing in 1919 upheld.

A two-man board of review was created for two years, with Ruppert and

Griffith as its members, to review penalties or fines of $100 or more or suspensions of more than ten days. If the board members could not agree, the issue would go to a federal judge in Chicago for decision.

It was a momentous day in American League history, but bigger news was on the way: The fix of the 1919 World Series was unraveling.

7. World Series For Sale

If ever there was a sport ripe for a big scandal, it was major league baseball in 1919.

Gambling was a fact of life in baseball. Gamblers hung around the parks and the lobbies of hotels where teams stayed. It was no secret to anybody close to the game that regular season games were being fixed; some gamblers even boasted about it.

There was usually some way a gambler could get to a key player. Perhaps the player needed money; perhaps he disliked his team's owner or manager and was looking for a way to get revenge; perhaps there was an incident in the player's background that lent itself easily to blackmail.

There were rumors that some players were on a "payroll," getting weekly bribes. Even the great American Leaguers, Ty Cobb and Tris Speaker, were alleged to be involved in a fixed game, as related in an earlier chapter.

It was easiest to fix a game, of course, if a gambler could get to a pitcher; just a couple of bad pitches at the right time could make the difference in a game, and it was impossible to tell whether those bad pitches were intentional. Even the best pitchers, after all, can have bad days.

Other players couldn't control a game so easily as a pitcher, but they could definitely have an influence. An infielder could be just a split second slow in making the double play relay. An outfielder could be a shade slow in chasing a fly ball, or he could dive for it and miss, letting it go beyond him for extra bases. Again, it was impossible for even a trained observer to know for certain what was happening.

Newspapermen might be suspicious, but they dared not write what they thought because of the libel laws. Did owners and executives know? Almost certainly, but they preferred to pretend otherwise. They discouraged talk of fixed games because they didn't want to undermine public confidence.

The only thing that hadn't been fixed was a World Series, but when the Chicago White Sox became involved in 1919, it became almost . . . well . . . a sure thing that the Series would be fixed.

All the ingredients were there. The White Sox were clearly the best team in baseball, which meant it would be easy to get money down on their opponents, the Cincinnati Reds. The White Sox were, relative to their ability, the poorest-paid team in baseball, which meant they could be easily tempted.

Finally, the atmosphere was right. In retrospect, the most startling aspect of the fix was that the players involved never expected to be punished. They were only doing what others had done before them, though their efforts came in the game's showcase. They were often blatant in their misplays, and they made no real attempt even to cover up their pre-Series meetings with gamblers.

There is no question the White Sox were a great team, perhaps the best in the American League to that point. Three members of that team later made the Hall of Fame, and three others probably would have except for the scandal.

The team had great balance: good hitting, fielding, and pitching. It had no real weaknesses. Here is the lineup at the eve of the 1919 World Series:

CATCHER: Ray Schalk, called by no less an authority than Ty Cobb the best catcher he had seen. Known primarily for his catching ability, Schalk hit .282 in 1919 and was always a good clutch hitter. He was named to the Hall of Fame in 1955.

FIRST BASE: Chick Gandil, another fine defensive player, who was said to have such big hands that he could have played without a glove. Gandil had twice hit more than .300 in his nine-season major league career, and he had hit .290 in 1919.

SECOND BASE: Eddie Collins, still regarded by many as the finest second

Eddie Collins played a record 25 years and may have been the best second baseman ever.
(George Brace)

baseman in American League history. Collins was a superb fielder, an excellent hitter, and a feared base runner.

SHORTSTOP: Charles "Swede" Risberg was just coming into his own at 24. He covered a lot of ground and had a strong arm.

THIRD BASE: Buck Weaver, considered the best third baseman in the American League since Jimmy Collins. Cobb didn't even try to bunt on him, because Weaver was so fast coming in. A solid hitter—.296 in 1919—Weaver would have certainly been elected to the Hall of Fame but for the scandal.

RIGHT FIELD: Nemo Leibold was a steady fielder who also hit .302 in 1919.

CENTER FIELD: Oscar "Happy" Felsch probably ranked second only to Speaker as a defensive outfielder, and he was a good hitter and base runner, too. He was just reaching his peak: In 1920, playing under a cloud, he hit .338 with 40 doubles, 15 triples, 14 home runs, and 115 RBIs.

LEFT FIELD: "Shoeless Joe" Jackson, long considered the best natural hitter in baseball history. Jackson had a career batting average of .356, second only to Cobb in American League history, and had three consecutive seasons, 1911–13, in which he hit .408, .395, and .373. Jackson had speed to go with his hitting ability. He stole more than 20 bases five times in his career, with a high of 41, and three times led the league with 20 or more triples, with a high of 26. He hit .351 in 1919, and would have been a cinch for the Hall of Fame.

PITCHING: Eddie Cicotte was the staff's ace, the best in baseball. He had

Buck Weaver, an outstanding third baseman, was barred from baseball because of the Black Sox scandal. *(George Brace)*

Joe Jackson, another Black Sox player, is considered the finest natural hitter in baseball history and was underrated as an outfielder. *(George Brace)*

Pitcher Eddie Cicotte was a key figure in the thrown World Series in 1919. *(George Brace)*

won 29 games in 1919, 28 in 1917 for another Chicago pennant-winner. He probably would have made the Hall of Fame, too.

Red Faber had an off year in 1919, winning only 11 games, but he followed with seasons of 23, 25, and 21 wins, eventually won 254 games in his career, and was elected to the Hall of Fame in 1964.

Claude "Lefty" Williams was just reaching his peak, and seemed on his way to a brilliant career. Known for his control, Williams won 17 for the 1917 pennant-winners, 23 in 1919, and another 22 in 1920.

Dickie Kerr, another left-hander (like Williams, just 26), reaching his peak. Kerr won 13 in 1919 and followed with seasons of 21 and 19 wins.

But the key man in all this was not a player but the Chicago owner, Charles Comiskey, known as the "Old Roman," a nickname shortened from the much more flowery one bestowed on him in his playing days: "The Noblest Roman of the National League."

Comiskey's place in baseball history is secure, and he was named to the Hall of Fame in 1939. He started as a player, usually at first base, and his playing career lasted 13 years.

He was a fair hitter, but known primarily for his defense and tactics. He developed a style of playing off the bag (first basemen of that era often stayed camped on the bag), so he could cover more ground. He worked with his fellow infielders on such things as shifting positions for hitters, cutoff throws, backing up throws, charging bunts, and executing double plays that are taken for granted now but were innovations then.

He became a manager in 1883 and managed a dozen years. He was, of course, the man who got Ban Johnson into baseball. Comiskey was granted the Chicago franchise when the American League formed, and his team won the first American League pennant—and two others later.

Comiskey was an imaginative executive, and his franchise became a successful one, so much so that he became a wealthy man. And, like many self-made men, he displayed glaring inconsistencies in his attitude toward money.

Early in his career, for instance, he resigned as manager of the St. Louis club of the National League to join the newly formed Players League in 1890, at a substantial cut in salary. It was a move of principle. "I couldn't do anything else and still play square with the boys!" he was reported as saying.

He had spent a great deal of money building the White Sox into a strong team. As related earlier, he had bought Eddie Collins for $50,000 from Connie Mack. He had paid $65,000 for Joe Jackson, then at Cleveland. For another $12,000, he had purchased Happy Felsch from Milwaukee. Those were impressive sums at that time. He had also spent $500,000 after the 1909 season to rebuild his park, expanding it to 33,000.

But Comiskey's generosity ceased when he dealt with his ballplayers. Collins had been able to work out a lucrative contract because of the Federal League competition, but other White Sox stars were terribly underpaid.

Cicotte, for instance, was being paid only $5,500 a year, Lefty Williams under $3,000. Gandil and Felsch got only $4,000. Jackson and Weaver got $6,000. As a comparison, for Cincinnati, Edd Roush got $10,000, Jake Daubert $9,000, Heinie Groh $8,000.

It wasn't just the low salaries that bothered the White Sox, either. Comiskey paid them only $3 a day meal money on the road; other clubs paid at least $4. He had promised Cicotte a $10,000 bonus if the pitcher won 30 games in 1917, but when Cicotte approached that figure, he was benched—to rest for the World Series, it was said.

During the 1918 season, when salaries were cut even further because of the war, the White Sox players had threatened to go on strike one day, though they had finally backed off.

The players had been seething because of Comiskey's penny-pinching, and they looked for ways to get the money they thought was due them. One player thought of a way: fixing the Series.

For years, it was thought that gamblers had approached the White Sox players, but Eliot Asinof, whose *Eight Men Out* is easily the most complete book on this subject, learned that it was a player who made the first move. Gandil approached a gambler, Joseph "Sport" Sullivan, and told him, "I think we can put it in the bag!"

Sullivan was a front man for Arnold Rothstein, and while he was consulting with Rothstein, Gandil talked to the players he thought would be receptive. He stayed away from Collins, Schalk, and Kerr, probably as much because they were in another clique as because he thought they wouldn't go for the scheme; the White Sox were split into two groups, as they had been for years, and players from one group seldom spoke to players from the other.

The key was Cicotte, since he would control so much of the play. Cicotte was 35, worried that each year might be his last and that he wouldn't have enough money when his career had ended. Gandil played on these fears. Finally, Cicotte agreed—if he got $10,000 before the Series started.

With Cicotte in, Gandil was able to recruit Williams, Felsch, and Risberg as active conspirators. Reserve infielder Fred McMullin overheard Gandil and Risberg talking and demanded in, but his role in the Series was a minor one.

These six, with Jackson and Weaver, met in Gandil's hotel room. The meeting appears to have been a casual, even jolly, one. The players, after all, were no strangers to this kind of thing. Asinof mentions an instance in 1917 which saw the White Sox assessed $45 each to bribe two Detroit pitchers to throw a double-header.

Jackson's role was a curious one. He apparently accepted $5,000, but he didn't play like a man in on a fix, hitting .375 with 12 hits during the Series. An unsophisticated man, it's likely he just went along with the others because they were friends.

Weaver's role is even more puzzling. There is no indication that he ever intended to take part in the fix. He neither asked for nor received any money, and he had no further conversations about the fix with his crooked teammates. He, too, had an outstanding Series, fielding with his usual skill and hitting .324. But that one meeting eventually knocked him out of baseball.

Supposedly, the players were supposed to split $80,000, payable before the first game. It didn't work that way. Cicotte got his $10,000, and so did the instigator, Gandil, but Sullivan stalled Gandil on the rest. Nevertheless, the players decided to go along with the fix.

Rumors of a fix were widespread as Cincinnati prepared for its first Series ever. This was not the first time such rumors had spread. In 1912, there was a rumor that the Series was fixed for the Giants—but the Red Sox won. But this time, the reports were true. Anticipating a great Series after a booming attendance year, baseball executives had expanded it to nine games for the first time since the first one in 1903. (The length returned to seven games in 1922.) Instead, they got a Series which nearly tore the game apart.

Cicotte threw the first game virtually by himself. With the score tied, 1–1, in the fourth, he quickly gave up five runs on six hits, including a triple by opposing pitcher Dutch Reuther. Cincinnati went on to win, 9–1.

That was not the way Rothstein would have chosen the game to go. He wanted the White Sox to win the first game, so he could get better odds. But he put more money down on the Reds, even though the odds had dropped to 5–7.

Williams was next for the White Sox. He made it closer, but the Reds still won, 4–2. The pitcher who was known for his fine control walked three men in the fourth and gave up a triple to Larry Kopf in a three-run inning for the Reds.

Kerr, who was not in on the fix, shut out the Reds, 3–0, in the third game, but then Cicotte lost the next game, 2–0. The two runs scored when he deflected an outfield throw to catcher Schalk. To those in the know, that was another tip-off to what was happening, because Cicotte was a fine fielding pitcher.

The White Sox lost again in the fifth game, 5–0. The Reds scored four times in the sixth off Williams, two of the runs coming on a long drive by Roush that Felsch dropped; it was scored as a triple. Felsch always insisted that he had tried to catch the ball, and perhaps he did.

Then, the Black Sox—as they became known later—got angry. They had been continually stalled when they asked for the money that was supposedly theirs, and they decided that, if they weren't going to get paid, they weren't going to throw any more games.

With Kerr pitching, the White Sox won the sixth game in Cincinnati, 5–4, with Gandil knocking in the winning run. The next day, Cicotte beat the Reds, 4–1, and now Cincinnati had only a 4–3 edge with the last two games shifting to Chicago.

And then Rothstein had a talk with Sullivan, the gist of which was that the Series should end the next day. Sullivan called on a hoodlum, who threatened Williams.

The next day, Chicago baseball writer Hugh Fullerton was making his way to the press box when a gambler he knew told him, "All the betting's on Cincinnati. It's going to be the biggest first inning you ever saw."

The gambler wasn't far wrong. Cincinnati got four runs in that first inning and the game was all but over. Eventually, the Reds won, 10–5.

And how did the conspirators fare, financially? According to Asinof, Risberg got $15,000, Cicotte $10,000, Felsch, Williams, Jackson, and McMullin $5,000 each.

The ringleader, Gandil, gathered $35,000 for himself, a grand sum then, and retired to California. The others, though they did not know it yet, were only a year away from enforced retirement.

First, though, came an attempt by Comiskey to cover up. He announced the next day after the end of the Series: "There is always a scandal of some kind following a big sporting event like the World Series. These yarns are manufactured out of whole cloth and grow out of bitterness due to losing wagers. I believe my boys fought the battles of the recent World Series on the level, as they have always done. And I would be the first to want information to the contrary—if there be any. I would give $20,000 to anyone unearthing any information to that effect . . ."

In fact, Comiskey had no intention of investigating the mess. He had been told after the first game by gambler friends exactly what was happening. Jackson had told friends he would talk about it, and Comiskey knew that, but made no attempt to talk to Jackson.

Joe Gedeon, second baseman for the St. Louis Browns, talked to Comiskey and implicated Risberg. It wasn't enough for Comiskey. Harry Redmon, a St. Louis theater operator, told of conversations with Abe Attell, who was in on the fix. That, too, wasn't enough.

Except for Gandil, all the White Sox players returned for the 1920 season, and the team was still the best in the American League. But it didn't always play that way. The players who had been in on the Series fix were still throwing games, just often enough to keep the race with Cleveland close.

Finally, on August 30, the White Sox started a three-game series in Boston, half a game ahead of Cleveland. They lost all three in so obvious a manner that second baseman Collins went to Comiskey and insisted the three games had been thrown. That was hardly news to Comiskey, but he could not—or would not—do anything.

But Comiskey's lack of effort was not enough to keep the lid on. Newspaper articles hinted at the fix; Ban Johnson, trying to embarrass his one-time friend, was conducting his own investigation. When a Chicago grand jury started an investigation, Johnson gave them names of gamblers to talk to. The fix was unraveling.

The final blow came on September 27, when Jimmy Isaminger, in *The Philadelphia North American,* reported an interview with Billy Maharg, a gambler, which implicated the Black Sox. The players then confessed, and indictments followed.

The case did not come to trial until June 27, 1921, though the players had been suspended since late September of the previous season.

By then, the confessions had been either lost or stolen, and the players had repudiated them. The players were represented by some top attorneys—Ben Short, Thomas Nash, and Michael Ahearn—and they were apparently paid most of their fees by Comiskey.

The case was a curious one. The players' attorneys based much of their defense on an attack on Ban Johnson, pictured as the mastermind of the prosecution. Much was made of the fact that Rothstein, who engineered the fix, was not on trial, and that the players were scapegoats. The jury agreed; on August 2, they acquitted all eight players.

The players celebrated with a party which lasted long into the morning hours. Even as they were coming out of their party, early editions of Chicago morning papers were coming out with a statement by baseball commissioner, Judge Kenesaw Mountain Landis:

". . . Regardless of the verdict of juries, no player who throws a ball game, no player that undertakes or promises to throw a ball game, no player that sits in conference with a bunch of crooked players and gamblers where the ways and means of throwing a game are discussed and does not promptly tell his club about it, will ever play professional baseball!"

Cicotte, Williams, Felsch, Jackson, Risberg, McMullin, and Weaver thus joined Gandil in retirement from baseball.

Baseball mythology has painted Judge Landis as honest and fearless while ignoring his less honorable qualities: a narrow, vindictive mind and an unquenching thirst for the spotlight. He was known as the "grandstand judge," and Heywood Broun wrote, "His career typifies the heights to which dramatic talent may carry a man in America if only he has the foresight not to go on stage."

He meted out justice with a meat ax. In a 1907 case, Landis, then a U.S. district court judge in Illinois, fined Standard Oil of Indiana $29,240,000. The decision was later reversed by a higher court. In 1917, he sentenced labor leader William Haywood to 20 years in prison. That decision was reversed by the U.S. Supreme Court.

In his job as baseball commissioner, Landis had finally found a position where his decisions could not be reversed.

His supporters have argued that his decision to ban the Black Sox players was necessary to restore public integrity to baseball, but, in fact, that did not end the practice of thrown games, several instances of which came to light in the following years. And Landis was not always so diligent in pursuing action when it involved popular players. The Cobb-Speaker case is just one example. Johnson thought there was enough there to suspend both players, but Landis dismissed the allegations almost as an afterthought.

In banning the seven Black Sox players, Landis did not take into account the atmosphere of the day, nor did he differentiate between those who actively participated and Weaver, who did nothing but listen to what was said.

Cicotte, Williams, and Risberg, whose actions were the ones which affected the games, should have been banned. It would have been more equitable, however, to suspend the others for a year, with a clear warning that any connection with a fixed game in the future would mean banishment.

But that, of course, would not have been nearly so dramatic.

Meanwhile, Gandil, who had instigated the fix and gotten nearly half the money, was out of Landis's jurisdiction. So were the gamblers, who had engineered the fix and made money on it. And Comiskey, whose penuriousness made it all possible and who tried to cover it up, went unpunished.

Largely as a result of this case, Landis's reputation grew over the years, and he was often referred to as the "savior of baseball."

Uh, uh. The savior of baseball was already on hand before Landis arrived, an ignorant, uncouth, but marvelously talented man named George Herman "Babe" Ruth, whose soaring and frequent home runs were soon to transform baseball and make everybody forget about the Black Sox.

THE BIG BAT ERA

8. A Man Named Ruth

There has never been another player like Babe Ruth. Some may argue that Ty Cobb was the better player, but there is one significant difference between the two: Cobb played the existing game better than anybody else, but Ruth completely changed the game. Baseball was not the same after Ruth.

First, a minor caveat: Strictly speaking, the lively ball predates Ruth. In 1910, both major leagues had experimented with a new, cork-centered ball which had far more resiliency than the old ball, using the new ball in some regular season games and in the World Series.

The next year, the ball was used for all games, and the results were obvious in the batting averages: 35 American Leaguers batted over .300, while Cobb hit .420 and Joe Jackson .408.

But the game had not changed. Teams still played for one run at a time, by bunting, stealing, and using the hit-and-run. The home run, though it came with more frequency with the new ball, was still not considered a major weapon.

Then, in 1919, Ruth shattered all existing records by hitting 29 home runs for the Boston Red Sox. Though the Red Sox were a mediocre team, finishing in a tie for fifth, large crowds came out to see Ruth throughout the league.

The correlation was not lost on baseball owners. Before the next season, they banned all trick pitches (although those pitchers who had used the spitball in the majors before 1920 were allowed to continue), and the ball was juiced up again. "They fixed up a ball," wrote Ring Lardner in disgusted exaggeration, "that if you don't miss it entirely it will clear the fence. . . ."

Meanwhile, Ruth had been traded to the New York Yankees, and he hit 54 home runs in 1920, twice what anybody else had ever done and more than any other *team* but the Yankees. Attendance went to 1,289,422 for the Yankees, nearly 380,000 more than the previous major league club record, though the team finished only third.

Others tried to emulate Ruth, and a pitcher's game became a hitter's game, as it has remained since. Teams started playing for the "big inning," in which they would score enough runs to win a game even if they were shut out for the rest of the game. Owners looked for strong players who could hit the ball over the fence. Pitchers had to pitch much more carefully, aware that one bad pitch could now beat them. It was a very different game.

Not all the changes have been good. Now, we see 150-pound players swinging for the fences. The subtle skills of the game are often ignored: Few players know how to bunt properly, and for a long period, hardly anybody tried to steal a base. Sluggers willingly accept 170 strikeouts in a season (Ruth himself never struck out as many as 100 times) in exchange for 30 homers.

But, good or bad, it is Ruth's game we are watching now, as even Cobb acknowledged, however bitterly. And nobody has ever played that game as well as Ruth did.

Ruth's statistics are remarkable enough now; in the context of his times, they are simply incredible. As Robert Creamer noted in his superb biography, *Babe,* Ruth owned the home run. He was the first to hit 30 home runs, the first to hit 40, the first to hit 50, the first to hit 60. The year he hit 60, 1927, he again had more homers than any team other than the Yankees.

Before Ruth, the career home run record was only 136, a figure he surpassed in 1921. When he hit his 700th home run, only two others had surpassed 300. When he retired with 714 home runs, he had more than twice as many as anybody else.

From 1920 through 1931, he averaged nearly 47 homers a season. Some great sluggers—Lou Gehrig, Ted Williams, Joe DiMaggio—have never hit 50 home runs in a season; Ruth *averaged* more than 50 home runs a season for six years, 1926–31.

Inevitably, his home run heroics overshadowed the rest of his game, but the Babe was a natural, skilled at every phase of the game. That graceful swing also produced a .342 lifetime average, and he hit as high as .393 in one season.

In his youth, he was a finely conditioned athlete with good speed; he twice stole 17 bases in his first four seasons in New York. The potbelly he acquired over the years slowed him down, but he was always an alert, aggressive base runner. He was also a surprisingly graceful outfielder.

Babe Ruth revolutionized baseball with his incredible home run hitting feats. *(New York Yankees)*

But people didn't come to see Ruth field or run the bases; they came to see him hit, and he seldom disappointed them. He did everything with a flourish, even striking out. And when he hit the ball . . . well, everywhere he went around the league, people pointed to spots where Ruth's monstrous home runs had hit. Just as nobody else had ever hit as many home runs as Ruth, nobody else had ever hit them as far, towering drives that sometimes landed outside the park.

In 1920, he had the best year any hitter had ever had, leading the league with 54 home runs, 158 runs, 137 RBIs, 148 walks, and a slugging percentage of .847, which is still the major league record. He also had 36 doubles, 9 triples (99 extra-base hits), and a batting average of .376.

But the next year, he had an even better year. He fell just short of 1920 in slugging percentage, at .846, and in walks, with 144, but surpassed his 1920 figures in every other department. Read them and gasp: 204 hits, 44 doubles, 16 triples, 59 home runs (109 extra-base hits, more than half his total), 177 runs, 171 RBIs, and a .378 batting average.

One year before the turn of the century, walks had been counted as base hits, and Tip O'Neil had averaged .493. If the same rule had been in effect for Ruth, he would have hit .509 in 1921, .528 in 1920!

But perhaps the most significant fact is this: Ruth's 1927 season, in which he hit 60 home runs, was only the third best of his career.

Ruth was a charismatic figure, the most popular player baseball has ever known. People flocked to him, at the park or away from it, and he loved the attention; a trip to Paris in one off-season was cut short when Ruth discovered that few people recognized him.

He was a man of gargantuan appetites. When he first came to the Yankees, Frank "Ping" Bodie (who became his roommate) was known as the club's eating champ, but Bodie voluntarily relinquished his title after seeing Ruth down three steaks at one sitting.

His gluttony was probably the cause of the ailment which sidelined him for the first part of the 1925 season, his only bad one until late in his career (though his '25 figures of .290 and 25 home runs would cause modern players to ask for a raise).

Coming home from spring training, Ruth had to be hospitalized when abdominal pain caused him to faint. He was operated on and played only 98 games that year, and his teammates thought he came back too early even so.

That incident caused a wild spate of rumors. One writer, W. O. McGeehan, imagined it to be a result of Ruth eating too many hot dogs, and it was billed as "The Bellyache Heard 'Round the World." Players thought Ruth had a venereal disease, a reasonable enough assumption for anyone familiar with Ruth's habits.

But the scar on Ruth's stomach when he returned testified to his surgery, which seems to rule out the venereal disease theory, and the hot dog story was more imagination than fact.

Babe was a man of action, not introspection. He enjoyed any physical acts—eating, drinking, playing baseball . . . and sex. Women were readily available to him, and he took full advantage of that, but he seems not to have boasted about it or even given the matter any real thought.

In *No Cheering in the Press Box,* sportswriter Richards Vidmer told of the times he had played bridge with Ruth in a hotel room when a woman would call from the lobby and Babe would invite her up. "Up she'd come and interrupt the bridge game for ten minutes or so. They'd go in the other room. Pretty soon they'd come out and the girl would leave. Babe would say, 'So long, kid,' or something like that. Then he'd sit down and we'd continue our bridge game."

It was fortunate for the Babe that there were no night games then, because he liked to be out and around at night. Bodie once quipped, "I don't room with Babe. I room with his suitcase."

Ruth's nocturnal ramblings inevitably got him into trouble with managers. When he was with the Red Sox, Ed Barrow fined and even suspended Ruth for breaking curfew. Eventually it must have occurred to Barrow that Ruth's escapades didn't seem to hurt his playing, and that suspending him hurt the club. So, Barrow made an agreement with Ruth: Nothing would be done to him so long as Ruth left a note in Barrow's box telling the manager what time he had come in that night—or morning.

The Babe swept through life like a hurricane, sampling everything and conserving nothing. After his rookie season in the American League, he married Helen Woodford, a South Boston girl, but she was only 17 and he 19 (and emotionally even younger), and the marriage did not change Ruth's living patterns.

His first wife died in 1929 in a fire—she and Ruth were separated by then—and he then married Claire Hodgson, a widow he had known for some time. She was able to exert a civilizing influence on Ruth at least part of the time, but not all; you cannot entirely tame a force of nature.

Ruth often battled authority figures, not because he was unnaturally contentious but because he simply did not recognize any restrictions on his behavior; the laws that govern other men did not apply to him, or so he thought.

He was often caught speeding in one of his cars (at one point, he owned nine luxury automobiles). Often, the policeman would recognize him and let him go. One policeman who did not know Ruth brought him into court, and he was sentenced to a "day" in jail. It was the practice of that time to consider 4 P.M. the end of the day in jail, so Ruth waited in his cell until that time, with his uniform on under his street clothes. Promptly at 4 P.M., he was released and given a police escort to the park, and he got there in time to play the last three innings of the game, which had started at 3.

Early in his career, he had frequent run-ins with umpires. The best known battle was joined on May 23, 1917, in a game against the Washington Senators.

Ruth was still a pitcher then, but he lasted for only four pitches in this game. All of them, to Ray Morgan, were called balls by plate umpire Brick Owens. Ruth came storming off the mound after the fourth ball and confronted Owens, who threw him out of the game. Ernie Shore came on in relief and pitched a perfect game. Morgan was caught stealing, and Shore retired the next 26 men in order.

In 1922, Ruth was twice suspended by American League president Ban Johnson for protracted squabbles with umpires; during one, he threw sand in the umpire's face. That appears finally to have taught Ruth a lesson, and he never quarreled seriously with umpires for the rest of his career.

In 1925, he learned another lesson. That was the year of his abdominal surgery. When he came back, he was not the player he had been. Weakened by his surgery and convalescent period, he aggravated his problems by eating and drinking too much and staying out all night at times.

Manager Miller Huggins imposed a $1,000 fine on Ruth at one point because of his late-night ramblings, but then reconsidered and dropped the fine. Nevertheless, it was obvious something had to be done. The club was going bad, riding along in seventh place. Ruth was not hitting, and he was openly contemptuous of the tiny Huggins.

Finally, after a game in Chicago in which Ruth had twice disobeyed Huggins's instructions, the manager fined him $5,000 and suspended him indefinitely.

Ruth blustered at first, confident that he could force Huggins to back down. But Yankee owner Jake Ruppert stood firmly behind his manager. The money didn't hurt as much as the suspension. Depriving Ruth of the chance to play baseball was the worst thing anyone could do to him. Finally, he went to Huggins and apologized profusely, and he was then reinstated.

From that point, Ruth was much more conscientious. Though his weight remained high, he worked on his conditioning, and the results showed. By the next season, 1926, he was already 31, an age at which most players are at least beginning to slow down, and many baseball experts thought his great years were behind him. But in the next six seasons, Ruth hit .372, .356, .323, .345, 359, and .373, with home run totals of 47, 60, 54, 46, 49 and 46. Some slowdown.

In 1921, he had had an even more serious confrontation with authority, this time with the commissioner of baseball, Judge Kenesaw Landis, and he was fortunate that he was not suspended for the entire season.

The major leagues had had a rule for several years prohibiting players who had competed in the World Series from going on barnstorming tours after the season, the reasoning being that these tours would detract from the importance of the Series.

But, as usual, Ruth figured the rules did not apply to him. He made plans for a barnstorming tour, signing up outfielder Bob Meusel, catcher Wally Schang, and pitchers Carl Mays, Bill Piercy, and Tom Sheehan. At worst, he reasoned that Judge Landis would fine him the equivalent of his World Series share, and he thought he could make much more than that on tour.

From the start, nothing went right with the project. Yankee owner Til Huston, after speaking with Landis, publicly spoke out against the tour and privately tried to dissuade Ruth, to no avail. Landis warned that the penalty for disobeying the rule would be severe; it was still early in Landis's career as commissioner, and he knew he would have to take a firm stand or his authority would be seriously undermined.

Mays and Schang immediately backed out. Meusel, who generally followed Ruth's lead, remained in and so did Piercy and Sheehan, who reasoned they had little to lose.

The tour did poorly, and Colonel Huston persuaded Ruth to call it off early. And then, everybody waited for Landis's decision.

The Yankees feared that the commissioner might suspend Ruth and Meusel for the whole season. Ed Barrow, who had been Ruth's manager in Boston but by now was general manager for the Yankees, talked to Landis. The Yankees, of course, had been one of Landis's early supporters because of their feud with Ban Johnson, and that weighed in their favor.

Finally, on December 5, 1921, Landis announced his decision: Ruth, Meusel, and Piercy were fined the equivalent of their World Series checks and would be suspended for the first six weeks of the 1922 season. Sheehan was not punished because he had not pitched in the Series and did not come under the provisions of the antibarnstorming rule.

Though Ruth was limited to 110 games because of that suspension and later, shorter ones by Johnson, the Yankees repeated as American League champions in '22. Ruth hit "only" 35 home runs and failed to win the home run title for the first time in five years (St. Louis's Ken Williams had 39). The fine? It probably didn't bother Ruth. It was literally easy come, easy go for him.

The same year he had been suspended, Ruth's salary was boosted to $52,000, a truly incredible figure at the time. The second-highest salary on the Yankees was Frank "Home Run" Baker's $16,000. Bob Shawkey, a three-time 20-game winner, was making only $8,500; first baseman Wally Pipp, going into his ninth season, was at $6,500.

Eventually, Ruth's salary was to go to $80,000, higher than the president's. With irrefutable logic, he pointed out: "I had a better year."

This, remember, was at a time when the value of the dollar was much higher than it is today, and when income taxes took very little out of Ruth's salary. Ruth unquestionably had more purchasing power with his salary than the highest-paid players have today.

But the money went out almost as fast as it came in. Ruth spent lavishly on the things that gave him pleasure, and he was an incredibly generous tipper; witnesses have told of him leaving $100 bills as tips.

Later, business manager Christy Walsh and his second wife, Claire, helped him manage his money. Ruth could never have done it alone, because it simply went against his nature to plan and conserve. He remained remarkably childlike to the end, with all that implied. He could hurt people—living with (and without) him was a crushing experience for his first wife, and manager Huggins suffered through many indignities before establishing control—but it was never done with malice. The Babe loved people, indiscriminately, and they loved him back.

That was true even in baseball. Even those who quarreled with Ruth liked him. It was impossible to stay angry with him; how can you sustain a grudge against a child?

Ruth actually had two careers, the first, abbreviated one as a pitcher and the second as the greatest power hitter in the game's history.

It is easy to forget, in light of his hitting accomplishments, just how good a pitcher Ruth was, but he probably would now be regarded as the best left-hander in American League history if he had stayed with pitching.

Strong words? Of course, but consider a few points. At the age of 22, Ruth had already won more than 20 games in two seasons and had a total of 67 major league wins. Eddie Plank, the American League's winningest left-hander with 327 career wins, was not even in the majors at 22; neither was Lefty Grove, who won 300 games in his career. Both Plank and Grove were 28 by the time they had won 67 major league games, which means that Ruth had six full seasons on them.

In his first full season, 1915, Ruth won 18 games and lost only eight. The next year, he was 23–12 with a 1.75 earned run average and nine shutouts; in 1917, he was 24–13 with an ERA of 2.01. But perhaps the most telling statistic was the fact that in those two years, he allowed only about 6½ hits per nine innings.

Some thought he was the best pitcher in the league, better even than the legendary Walter Johnson, and Ruth's pitching in two World Series, 1916 and 1918, bears that out: He was 3–0 and had a stretch of 29 ⅔ scoreless innings that lasted more than 40 years as a World Series record.

Ruth's hitting ability was obvious even at this stage of his career. He was used as a pinch hitter when he wasn't pitching, and he had batting averages of .315, .272, and .325 in his first three full seasons. But his first two managers, Bill Carrigan and Jack Barry, were surprisingly conservative, batting Ruth in the traditional pitcher's spot, ninth, and never using him at another position.

That finally changed in 1918, though Barrow, by now the team's manager, made a change reluctantly. Though Ruth's hitting was already talked about in baseball, Barrow felt he would be regarded as a fool if he used the best left-hander in baseball at another position, risking injury.

One of Barrow's coaches that year was Harry Hooper, who had been a great outfielder for the Red Sox. Hooper was the one Barrow relied on for strategic advice, and Hooper constantly advised Barrow to use Ruth at another position, to take advantage of his hitting and as a gate attraction (Barrow had money invested in the club).

Finally, Barrow gave in and used Ruth in the field, first as a first baseman, then as an outfielder. Ruth loved it. He quickly came to enjoy hitting far more than pitching. As his hitting improved, his pitching fell off; at one point, he was 4–5. He went to Barrow and said he wanted to concentrate on the outfield, and Barrow agreed—for a time.

Ruth went on to play 95 games that year. His season statistics look puny alongside his later accomplishments, but they were enough to get him billing as the finest power hitter in the league: a league-leading 11 home runs,

26 doubles, and 11 triples among his 95 hits. His average was an even .300.

But his pitching career was not quite over. When a series of sore arms hit the staff, Barrow begged Babe to return to the mound, and Ruth pitched down the stretch as he had before, winning 9 of his last 11 games for a 13–7 season mark.

In the Series, Barrow surprised everybody by starting Ruth in the first game, instead of 21-game winner Mays. Ruth blanked the Chicago Cubs, 1–0, in that game, and added a second win later as the Red Sox won the Series in six games.

But that was the effective end of Ruth's pitching career. He pitched enough to notch a 9–5 record in 1919 and later pitched five widely scattered games for the Yankees, winning all of them, but 1919 was his first great hitting year, and the switch from pitcher to hitter was complete.

As Ruth came roaring through that 1919 season, statisticians dug up home run record after home run record to pass. The first to go was the American League record of 16, set in 1902 by Ralph ("Socks") Seybold. Ruth tied that on July 29 but went more than two weeks before hitting the record-breaker.

Next was the modern major league record of 24, by Gavvy Cravath of the Phillies, set in 1915. The pre-1900 record was Buck Freeman's 25, for Washington in 1889. And there was one final fluke: 27 home runs by Edward Williamson of Chicago in 1884. Williamson's team had played that year at a field which had a right field foul line of only 215 feet; a truer test of his power was that in the preceding and following seasons, played in bigger parks, he had hit 2 and 3 home runs, respectively. In 1884, when Williamson hit 25 of his 27 homers at home, teammates Fred Pfeffer, Abner Dalrymple, and Cap Anson had 25, 22, and 21, respectively.

On September 20, in Chicago, Ruth tied Williamson's record with an impressive home run to left field off Claude ("Lefty") Williams, of Black Sox notoriety. A few days later, against the Yankees in New York, he hit his 28th over the Polo Grounds roof, the longest ever hit in that park. Finally, in Washington on the last weekend of the season, Ruth hit his 29th, accomplishing the first-ever feat of homering in every park in the league.

After that season, though he had hit only 49 homers in his career, Ruth was called the leading power hitter in history. Much more was to come.

Boston owner Harry Frazee completed the demolition of a fine Red Sox team, which had won pennants in 1915, '16 and '18, by selling Ruth to the Yankees after the 1919 season. Fans were so bitter over Frazee's selling of stars that in the 1930s, when Tom Yawkey first bought a star player, newspapers headlined it as a "Man Bites Dog" story.

With the Yankees, Ruth extended the home run record to 54 in 1920, 59 in 1921, and 60 in 1927. In later years, every time an assault was mounted on the 60-homer mark, hysteria would build for months, but there was relatively little in '27. Perhaps it was the fact that Ruth hit 17 homers in September; before that, it had not seemed he would come close to matching his best of 59. More likely, it was just that his hitting feats had benumbed the public. They expected the unbelievable.

Ruth's World Series exploits were as dramatic as you would expect from the man. In 1918, he set the pitching record already mentioned. In 1928, he hit .625, a record. And in 1932, he hit the last of 15 Series homers, the "called shot."

Ruth was batting against Charley Root in the fifth inning of the third game. With two strikes on him, he stepped out of the box and gestured. Some said he pointed to the center field bleachers, saying in effect to the bench jockeys in the Cubs' dugout that he was going to hit the next pitch there. Others claim he was saying that he had one strike left.

The truth will never be known. Ruth himself never gave a clear explanation of what he was thinking. But at any rate, he hit the next pitch into the center field bleachers, and another legend was born.

Ruth's years after 1932 were not happy ones. When he fell to 22 homers and a .288 average in '34, the Yankees sold him to the Boston Braves of the National League. Fat and 40, he played only 28 games for the Braves and hit only six home runs. But three of those came in one last bit of drama in a single game against the Pirates in Pittsburgh. The third homer went over the Forbes Field roof and, of course, nobody had ever done that before.

Babe always said he wanted to manage when his playing career was over, but the closest he ever got in regular season play was a job as coach for the Brooklyn Dodgers in 1938, and that was a job given him only to boost attendance. He was given no responsibility.

The Yankees—and other clubs—reasoned that Ruth could not control himself, let alone the players, which is true enough. But a scrutiny of managers, past and present, indicates that requirements for the job are not high.

Many managers have been hired for their names, while coaches have made the strategic decisions. It seems strange that was not tried with Ruth, especially by a club which needed an attendance boost. Perhaps no club wanted to be the one which fired him, and thus, nobody hired him.

And so, Ruth remained out of baseball after 1938. Eventually he contracted throat cancer and died on August 16, 1948. But, more than 30 years after that his name means more than those of most contemporary stars.

More than just a player, he has remained a symbol of American sports. It has been told many times, for instance, how Japanese soldiers in World War II, seeking to ire their American counterparts, would yell, "To hell with Babe Ruth!"

His name is often evoked as the ultimate comparison. Some that Creamer mentions, for instance: Willie Sutton, "the Babe Ruth of bank robbers"; Enrico Caruso, "the Babe Ruth of operatic tenors"; Chuck Stearns, "the Babe Ruth of water skiing."

There will never be another like him.

9. Window Breakers

For the first 20 years of the American League, the New York Yankees did not win a pennant, but they have corrected that oversight since. No team in any sport has ever dominated as the Yankees have in baseball for the last six decades.

The Yankees have won 32 pennants, more than twice the 14 won by the New York/San Francisco Giants, who have the second-best record in baseball. The Yankees have won 22 World Series; the second-best showing is eight, by the St. Louis Cardinals.

Twice the Yankees have won five straight pennants, 1949–53 and 1960–64; no other team has won more than four in a row. The Yankees have won five straight Series, 1949–53, and four straight, 1936–39; no other team has won more than three straight.

Their great success started a year after Babe Ruth's arrival, which was hardly a coincidence, as they won three straight pennants, 1921–23. But it was later in the decade that they fielded the first of the great teams which have not only won pennants but terrorized their opponents.

The arrival of that great team was as swift as it was unexpected. In 1925, the year of Ruth's surgery and subsequent suspension by manager Miller Huggins, the Yankees had finished seventh, with their fourth-worst record ever. Question marks hovered over the future of Ruth and the club.

The question marks were soon resolved. Ruth bounced back with a .372 average and 47 home runs, and a young first baseman named Lou Gehrig started to show what a great hitter he would become, hitting .313 and knocking in 107 runs.

Mark Koenig became the starting shortstop, plugging a hole. Tony Lazzeri, who had hit 60 home runs and knocked in 222 runs in a 200-game Pacific Coast League season in '25, became the second baseman and plugged another hole, while knocking in 114 runs.

The Yankees got off to a good start and led the league by ten games in mid-August. They faded in the stretch, but still managed to win the pennant by three games over Cleveland. In the World Series that fall, one of the most dramatic in history, Ruth hit four home runs, but he was no match for

40-year-old Grover Cleveland Alexander. In the twilight of a brilliant career, Alexander won two games as a starter and then came on in relief to save the seventh game, striking out Lazzeri with the bases loaded in the seventh. The final out came when Ruth rashly tried to steal second and failed with two outs in the ninth.

But the Yankees were only warming up. Everything fell into place in 1927, and that team is still considered by most experts the best in baseball history. It had everything, great hitting, solid pitching, and a tight defense. The Yankees had the best pitching staff ERA, 3.20. Their club hitting average of .307 was the league's best, and their power was such that they became known as the "Window Breakers."

Three regulars and two pitchers from that team eventually made the Hall of Fame. The catching—split between Pat Collins, Johnny Grabowski, and Benny Bengough—was only average, but the rest of the lineup was virtually an all-star team. Consider it, position by position.

FIRST BASE: Gehrig, often considered the best first baseman in baseball history, had an awesome year, hitting .373, with 47 home runs, 18 triples, 52 doubles, 175 RBIs.

SECOND BASE: Lazzeri was known for his clutch hitting and nicknamed "Poosh 'em Up, Tony" because of his ability to hit with men on base. He averaged .309, with 18 homers and 102 RBIs.

SHORTSTOP: Koenig was an outstanding fielder and a solid hitter, averaging .285.

THIRD BASE: Injuries limited Joe Dugan to 111 games and held his average to .269, but he was a fine fielder and a better hitter than that average indicated.

LEFT FIELD: Bob Meusel was an outstanding player who suffered only in comparison to Ruth. In the field, he was known for his outstanding arm. He was an excellent hitter (.309 lifetime average), with good power; he had led the league with home runs and RBIs in 1925, 33 and 138. In '27, his power production was off but he still had his highest average, .337, and knocked in 102 runs. And he stole 24 bases.

CENTER FIELD: Earle Combs is in the Hall of Fame with Ruth and Gehrig, and 1927 was unquestionably his best season. An outstanding fielder, he was an equally good hitter that year, leading the league with 231 hits and 23 triples, and also scoring 137 runs while batting .356.

RIGHT FIELD: Ruth, who hit 60 home runs that season.

PITCHING: There were two future Hall-of-Famers on the staff, Herb Pennock, who was 19–8, and Waite Hoyt, who led the staff with 22 wins, against only seven losses.

Waite Hoyt was a star pitcher on the great '27 Yankees and later made the Hall of Fame *(George Brace)*

But the real standout on the pitching staff that year was a balding right-hander named Wilcy Moore, a 30-year-old rookie who was 19–7. Six of those wins came as a starter, but it was as a relief pitcher that Moore was most effective, winning 13 games and saving another 13. His ERA of 2.28 led the league.

Any great team usually owes its success to the top players having great years, and that was certainly true of the Yankees in '27. Combs, Gehrig, and Koenig had their best years. Lazzeri and Meusel had representative years. Ruth's season paled in comparison only to his incredible back-to-back years in 1920 and '21. On the pitching staff, Hoyt had one of his two best years ('28 was a virtual repeat), Pennock had a good year, and Urban Shocker had his last good year, with 18 wins. But the most remarkable story was Moore's.

Moore had knocked around the minors for years without conspicuous success. In 1926, though, he won 30 games and lost only 4 for Greenville of the Sally League. The Yankees bought him, and for one year, the sinkerball specialist was the best in the league. He appeared in 50 games for the Yankees, and stood first in a stable of remarkable Yankee relievers.

Moore's magic disappeared as quickly as it had appeared. Though he lasted through the 1933 season, he was never again a mystery to the league's hitters, winning only 32 and losing 37 in his last five seasons. But for one glorious year, he was an integral part of a great team.

There was no American League pennant race in 1927. The Yankees were never out of first place, and they won the pennant by a league-record 19 games. Their totals of 110 wins and a .714 percentage were the best in league history and remained that way until the Cleveland Indians won 111 in 1954.

Though their pitching and fielding were excellent, it was the Yankees'

Wilcy Moore had only one good year, 1927, but he was sensational for a Yankee team that many consider the best in history. *(George Brace)*

Earle Combs was a great
center fielder and leadoff
hitter for the '27 Yankees.
(George Brace)

hitting that awed the other teams. Harry Heilman of Detroit won the batting championship with a .398 mark, and George Sisler of St. Louis led the league with 27 stolen bases, but in every other offensive department, it was a Yankee who was on top. Combs led in at bats, hits, and triples; Ruth led in home runs, runs, walks, and strikeouts; Gehrig led in doubles and RBIs.

Often, too, the Yankees not only had the best marks but the second and even third best. Gehrig was second in the league with 47 home runs, and Lazzeri third, at only 18. Ruth was second in RBIs, at 164. Gehrig was second in runs scored, at 149, and Combs third, at 137.

Ruth and Gehrig were especially awesome. Gehrig had 117 extra-base hits and Ruth 97; in slugging percentage, they were one-two in the league, with Ruth at .772 and Gehrig at .765. Al Simmons of Philadelphia was a distant third at .645.

Ruth hit more home runs than any other American League team, Gehrig more than four other teams. Apart from the Yankees, American League teams hit only 283 home runs that year; Ruth and Gehrig combined for 107.

With the pennant race decided so early, fans followed the home run race between Ruth and Gehrig with great excitement. It was the first time Ruth had truly been involved in a competition since he had started his record-breaking run in 1920. He had won five titles in that stretch, and nobody had been close. Twice he had relinquished the title, in 1922 and '25, but in each case, he played much less than a full schedule and was never really in the race.

In 1927, Ruth got off to a very fast start, hitting 22 homers in his first 55 games. Then, he fell off, hitting only 14 in his next 58 games. Meanwhile, Gehrig was hitting at a steadier pace, behind Ruth early but catching up as the season wore on. By August 15, Gehrig was ahead, 38 to 36.

But then Gehrig slowed down, hitting only seven the rest of the season. Ruth got hot again and quickly pulled out in front, ending that race.

Few thought the Babe would seriously challenge his record of 59, though. He entered September with 43, far behind his own pace of 1921. But when Ruth was hot, he was capable of incredible feats. One of those was approaching.

The home runs were coming in bunches now. In three games, September 6–7 (a double-header the first day), he got five homers, and 49 for the season. He went three days without a homer, then hit one a day in three successive days. Perhaps he had a chance to break his record. But then he hit only one homer in six games, which left him with 53 and only nine games remaining. No chance.

But once again, Ruth fooled everybody. It actually took him only eight games to reach 60. He hit a homer in each of the next three games to reach 56, then went homerless in the next two games. The next day, he hit number 57, a grand-slam off Lefty Grove. The next day he hit two more. Finally, on September 30, in the 153rd game of the year, he got number 60.

Ruth failed to get another in the final game of the season, but his stretch run was incredible: 17 homers in the month of September, 24 in his last 42 games. Time after time in the years to come, one slugger or another would match Ruth's early 1927 pace, only to wilt under the impossible strain of trying to match the Babe's stretch run.

And so the Yankees and Ruth came barreling into the World Series that fall. The Pittsburgh team they met was a good one, led by the Waner brothers, Paul "Big Poison" and Lloyd "Little Poison," and the great third baseman, Pie Traynor, but nobody really gave the Pirates a chance. Brooklyn manager Wilbert Robinson got in trouble for saying what everybody thought—the Yankees were the best team ever. Robinson backtracked and said he thought the Pirates would win the Series, but even the Pirates didn't believe that.

The World Series was virtually over before it started. Before the opening game, the Pirates came out as the Yankees were taking batting practice and, according to accounts of the day, were awestruck. They were watching first-hand for the first time what they had only heard about. Tanks never look so big as when they are about to run over you, and that must have been the feeling the Pirates had.

Ruth was taking his swings when the Pirates first came out, and he hit four balls in succession into the stands. Then, he looked over at the Pirates and, pointing to the bleachers, said, "Okay, sonnies, if any of you want my autograph, go out and collect those balls in the bleachers. I'll sign 'em for you."

Gehrig, Meusel, and Lazzeri followed Ruth in the batting cage, and they nearly duplicated Ruth's shots. The Pirates had never seen anything like it. Before that year, nobody else had, either.

The Yankees went on to sweep the Pirates. The first and last games were close, 5–4 and 4–3; the middle two were not, 6–2 and 8–1. It didn't make any difference to the Yankees, who could win them either way.

The Waner brothers did well in the Series, hitting .400 and .333, and their combined 11 hits were one more than Ruth and Gehrig got. But the Pirates were playing with popguns and the Yankees had cannons. Ruth had two homers among his six hits and seven RBIs to go with his .400 average.

Gehrig had two doubles and two triples, a .308 average and five RBIs.

Joe Devine, then with Pittsburgh but later a Yankee scout, had sat in on Pittsburgh club meetings and knew how awed the Pirates were.

"If they had played a hundred games," said Devine later, "I honestly believe the Yankees would have won them all. That's how scared the Pittsburgh club was."

The Yankees started the 1928 season just as they had concluded in 1927. By July 1, they had a 13½ game lead. But the team was starting to deteriorate, despite superlative seasons by Ruth and Gehrig. Lazzeri had a bad shoulder and missed 40 games. Dugan had a bad knee and missed 60. Koenig was not as sharp in the field as he had been. Meusel was also hurt and, though only 32, beginning to slip; he had only two seasons left.

Hoyt had another excellent year, winning 23, and George Pipgras saved the club by winning 24, by far the best season he had ever had. But Pennock, though he won 17, had arm trouble late in the season and was never again a topflight pitcher, and Moore was no more than an average pitcher, then and for the rest of his career.

And, the biggest problem of all was the Philadelphia Athletics, a young team that was beginning to come together, with ominous portents for the Yankees' future.

The A's started their rush with a 25–8 record in July, and they steadily gained ground on the Yankees, who seemed to be fading. By September 8, the A's actually pulled into first place.

But the Yankees still were champions, and they had just enough left to fight off their challengers. On September 9, the A's came to New York for a Sunday double-header, and a record 85,264 fans poured into Yankee Stadium. The Yankees won both games, 3–0 and 7–3, captured the third game of the series the next day, and were never again headed. They won the pennant by 2½ games.

As the World Series approached, however, Yankee manager Miller Huggins was worried. He had reason to be. His great center fielder, Combs, was injured (accounts vary on whether it was a sprained wrist or broken finger) and out of the Series, except for one pinch-hitting appearance. Pennock could not pitch at all. Lazzeri's shoulder bothered him so much that a weak-hitting infielder named Leo Durocher was replacing him in the late innings of every game. Durocher could do the job in the field, but the Yankees missed Lazzeri's bat.

So, all the poor, lame Yankees could do was to walk out there and blast the Cardinals off the field in four straight. Naturally, it was the first time a team had swept two consecutive Series. There is no record that the Cardinals were as awed as the Pirates had been the year before, but they went down even easier. The Yankees took the lead in the very first inning of the Series and won each game with ease, 4–1, 9–3, 7–3, and 7–3.

The Yankees needed only three pitchers. Hoyt won the first and last games, Pipgras and a left-hander named Tom Zachary, who had won only three games during the season, won the middle games. All the wins were complete games. (The year before Zachary, then pitching for Washington, had yielded Ruth's record 60th homer.)

But the story of the Series was the unparalleled hitting of Ruth and Gehrig. No two hitters have ever had such a Series. Ruth hit .625, a record which still stands, and Gehrig .545. Gehrig had four home runs, Ruth three. Ruth scored nine runs, Gehrig five. Gehrig knocked in nine runs, Ruth four. Together, they outscored the Cardinals, 14–10.

In the first game, they got five of the Yankees' seven hits. Ruth scored two of the four runs, Gehrig knocked in two.

In the second game, Gehrig hit a three-run homer off Alexander which started the rout; he added two more homers in the third game, and a fourth in the final game.

Ruth didn't hit a homer in the first three games, but he burst through with three in the final game, tying a record he had set two years earlier and which has not been surpassed since.

Ruth was also involved in an incident in the fourth game which was a precursor to his controversial "called home run" in the '32 Series—and probably a more legitimate one.

The Cardinals were leading, 2–1, in the seventh when Ruth came to bat with the bases empty. Cardinal left-hander Bill Sherdel got two quick strikes on Ruth, and then fired in another strike before Ruth got set. This maneuver, called a quick pitch, had been legal but was not allowed in the Series. The umpire ruled it no pitch.

This was exactly the kind of decision that would have enraged Ruth in his pitching days, but this time, he was on the right side. He watched in amusement as the Cardinal players surrounded the umpire and protested the call.

When Sherdel returned to the mound, Ruth jibed at him and Sherdel reacted in kind. "Put one in here again," said Ruth, "and I'll knock it out of the park for you."

Which he did. Sherdel threw two balls, then came in with a fastball, and Ruth hit it out, tying the score. Gehrig followed with another homer, and the Cardinals' last chance had disappeared.

Ruth and Gehrig continued their great hitting the next season—and beyond—but it was no longer enough. Athletic success is a fleeting thing, and age and injury had made too many inroads on that great Yankee team. They were a badly beaten second in 1929 and another dynasty team, the Philadelphia A's, took their place. But the Yankees would be back, many times.

10. Connie's Last Glory

After Connie Mack sold off the best players from his 1910–14 Philadelphia Athletics' dynasty team, the A's finished last the next seven years and in the second division for the three seasons after that.

But slowly—very slowly—and surely, Mack was building another great team. He shuttled players in and out at a rapid pace in those years, searching for the good ones. Jimmy Dykes, one of the good ones who stayed, estimated that one season, there were 50 players who came and went. "At one point," Dykes told Donald Honig for *The Man In the Dugout,* "we used to say we had three teams: one playing that afternoon, one coming in that night, and one leaving the next morning . . . Sometimes when you shook hands with a guy you were saying hello and goodbye at the same time."

By the mid-'20s, Mack had built the team into a contender. The A's finished second in 1925, third in 1926. In 1927, they were good enough to win 91 games, which would win a lot of pennants. That year, all it got them was a distant second, 19 games behind the great Yankee team. The next year, they made it very close and even led at one point before falling back before the last great surge of that Yankee team.

But by 1929, all the pieces were in place, and the A's swept to three straight pennants by margins of 18, 8 and, 13½. For comparison, the 1926–28 Yankees won by 3, 19, and 2½.

The A's of that streak were a very settled team. The only changes in the starting lineup came at shortstop and third base. Sammy Hale was the nominal regular at third in 1929, though he played only 91 games; Dykes, who played a lot of third base and shortstop that year, became the regular at third for the final two years of the streak. Joe Boley played the first two years at shortstop, then yielded to Dib Williams, at 21 an important 13 years younger than Boley.

Otherwise, the lineup remained intact: Mickey Cochrane, catcher; Jimmie Foxx, first base; Max Bishop, second base; Al Simmons, left field; Mule Haas, center field; Bing Miller, right field.

The top three pitchers for the three years were Lefty Grove, George Earnshaw, and Rube Walberg, and Ed Rommel played an important role on all three teams, too.

As with all dynasty teams, the A's were solid in every department. Even more than the '27 Yankees, whose catching was a minor problem, the A's had no weaknesses. They were a solid hitting team, averaging .296, .294 and, .287 in the three years. Their pitching staff had the league-leading earned run average in two of the three years. And their fielding was excellent, with Cochrane and the Simmons-Haas-Miller outfield particularly outstanding.

And they had some great players. Foxx, Cochrane, Simmons, and Grove all later made the Hall of Fame. Grove is generally considered the best left-hander in American League history, and Cochrane gets a lot of votes as the best catcher in major league history.

Foxx was a more complete player than many fans who did not see him play realize. He had good speed and was a good-fielding first baseman, assets which were overshadowed by his hitting; he was the best right-handed power hitter in league history. But as talented as Foxx was, he was forced to shift positions before he could become a starter with that A's team. He had come up as a catcher, but Cochrane was already there.

Cochrane was a gifted athlete who probably could have excelled at another position, too, because he had the kind of speed that is very rare among catchers. In fact, he became a catcher almost by accident: When the first minor league team he played for, Dover of the Eastern Shore League, developed a vacancy at catcher, Mickey volunteered to play there, and he stayed there for the rest of his career.

At Boston University, Cochrane was a multi-sport star, participating in baseball, track, football, basketball, and boxing. He played halfback in football and also was the team's place-kicker, with a 52-yard field goal the highlight of his career.

But baseball was his first and abiding love. Even in high school he had dreamed of both playing and managing major league baseball—both goals he realized later.

After graduating from Boston University in 1923, Cochrane entered professional baseball with Dover under an assumed name: Frank King. His reasoning was that if he failed there, he would try another team under his real name.

He didn't fail. Cochrane batted .322 in 65 games and impressed Tom Turner, owner of the Portland club in the Pacific Coast League. More important, Cochrane also impressed Mack.

Turner could not raise the kind of money that Dover was asking for

Mickey Cochrane was a great catcher for the A's and then led Detroit to consecutive pennants as a playing manager. *(Detroit Tigers)*

Cochrane. So, Mack invested $150,000 to get operating control of the Portland team, and then purchased Cochrane's contract for another $50,000. Considering how closely Mack watched his dollars, that is an impressive tribute to Cochrane's ability.

It's possible Mickey was ready for the A's even then, but Mack wanted to give him another year of minor league ball to build his confidence. After Cochrane hit .333 for Portland in 1924, he was brought to the A's to stay.

Still only 22 in 1925, Mickey immediately replaced Cy Perkins as the A's catcher and batted .331 as a rookie. It was the first of nine .300 seasons for the left-handed-hitting Cochrane.

Mickey hit his peak as a hitter as the A's hit their peak as a team, batting .331, .357, and .349 in the 1929–31 stretch. But even if he'd hit 100 fewer points, he would have been an extremely valuable player because of his defense and leadership. Defensively, he was compared to Ray Schalk, the feisty (and honest) little catcher from the Black Sox team. His leadership was such that in, 1928, when he hit only .293, 27 points below his career average, he was named the league's Most Valuable Player.

Cochrane was later traded to the Detroit Tigers and also managed the Tigers, but his best years were with the A's.

Al Simmons was an interesting case, a player who succeeded though he apparently did everything wrong. Simmons's hitting style was characterized by a stride by his left (lead) foot in the direction of third base, instead of toward the pitcher. Ballplayers call that "hitting in the bucket," apparently a reference to water buckets which used to be placed near the dugout for drinking purposes.

Theoretically, that style robs a hitter of power, because his body is facing toward the pitcher, instead of moving directly into the ball. But that didn't seem to bother Simmons. He was an outstanding hitter, averaging .334 in his 20-year career, with 307 home runs and an RBI total of 1827.

He was also a very confident player from the start, though he had some difficulty convincing others of his ability. He wrote a letter to Roger Bresnahan, then managing at Toledo of the American Association, asking for a tryout but never got a reply. He also apparently wrote to Mack, saying he would come to Philadelphia for the price of a train ticket, but Mack declined the offer, a move which would cost him in later years.

So, Simmons started his career in semipro ball, with the Juneau, Wisconsin team (Simmons was a native of Milwaukee). His strong play was noticed by the Milwaukee Brewers of the American Association, and they signed him to a contract in 1922, when he was 19. Milwaukee farmed him out to Aberdeen of the Dakota State League, where he hit .365. In 1923, he hit .360 in 144 games for Shreveport of the Texas League and then .398 for the Brewers in the final 24 games of their season.

The Brewers probably made a mistake in not keeping Simmons for the entire 1923 season, because he certainly could have helped them. But they had made no mistake in signing him earlier, because, after 1923, they were able to sell him to Philadelphia for a considerable sum; estimates ran from $40,000 to $70,000.

Simmons had a good rookie season, hitting .308, but it was in his second year that he started the kind of hitting that eventually landed him in the Hall of Fame, as he hit .384 with 243 hits, only four fewer than the major league record which had been set by George Sisler of the St. Louis Browns just five years before. Simmons hit for power, too, with 43 doubles, 12 triples, and 24 home runs. He scored 122 runs, batted in 129.

Simmons's career can be divided into two parts: the first nine years with the Athletics, the final 11 with several other teams. Even in the latter part of his stay in the big leagues, Simmons was a solid hitter capable of excellent seasons: .331 with 119 RBIs in 1933; .344 with 104 RBIs in 1934; .327 with 112 RBIs in 1936.

Al Simmons was one of the greatest hitters ever and a key man in the A's dynasty of 1929-31. *(George Brace)*

But his reputation really rests on an eight-year stretch he had with the A's, 1925–32. Consider some of these averages, for instance: .381 in 1930; .384 in 1925; .390 in 1931; .392 in 1927. In a five-year span, 1927–31, he averaged about .375! In a four-year stretch, 1929–32, he hit more than 30 homers three times—34, 35, and 36. And he was a great run-producer. He scored more than 100 runs in five of his nine years with Philadelphia, going as high as 152 in 1930. He knocked in more than 100 runs every year he played for the Athletics, and his last four-year totals were 157, 165, 128, and 151.

Simmons was only 30 his final year with the A's, but he was never again that kind of hitter. His decline—relatively speaking, of course—is surprising, because hitters with that kind of ability usually continue well past their 30th birthday.

Ty Cobb, for instance, hit over .400 once and more than .380 three times after he was 30. Joe Jackson hit .382 at 33, his last season because of the Black Sox scandal. Ted Williams hit .356 at age 37 and .388 at age 39.

Simmons, in contrast, fell to .267 when he was 33, .279 when he was 35, .274 when he was 37, the last season in which he played more than 100 games. Thus, on a career basis, he cannot be ranked with hitters like Cobb and Williams, but for his nine years with the A's, he was a great, all-round hitter.

The most interesting character on that great A's team was the star of the pitching staff, Robert Moses Grove, called "Lefty" by everybody but Mack, who invariably called him Robert.

Grove had an explosive fastball and a temper to match. He was notorious for tearing his locker apart after a tough loss, although when Grove was in his prime, there weren't many losses, tough or otherwise.

Dykes recalled a time when Grove lost a game in relief against the White Sox in the 11th inning, came into the locker room and tore up everything he could find, then jumped into his car and drove home to Lonaconing, Maryland, and didn't return until his next turn, four days later. "When he showed up," said Dykes, "nobody said anything. We were all familiar with Lefty's moods."

Nobody crossed Grove in those days. He was mean . . . what managers euphemistically call a great competitor. He would throw at batters during games, which was no surprise. What was surprising was that he would throw at his own hitters in batting practice if they dared to hit one up the middle at him.

Grove is generally considered the fastest left-hander in league history, and for the early part of his career, the fast ball was virtually his only pitch. Not until 1923, his fourth year in professional baseball, did he learn to throw a curve, and by his own admission, that curve broke so little it would be considered a slider today. Not until his great years were behind him, when he lost his fastball, did he finally learn to throw a good curve.

Control was also a problem for Grove in his early years. His first four years in the minors, for instance, he averaged six and seven walks a game. His first year in the majors, he averaged better than six walks a game and

Lefty Grove was as mean and talented a competitor as baseball has seen. *(George Brace)*

led the league in walks. But by his third season, Lefty had conquered his control problem. His walk totals were never high after that, and he knew where his pitches were going, and he was devastating.

Grove did not come to the majors until he was 25, but that was less because he wasn't ready than because of the way baseball was structured those days.

After a brief stint with Martinsburg of the Blue Ridge League in 1920, Grove was purchased by Jack Dunn of the Baltimore Orioles of the International League.

Baltimore was an independent team, known for developing stars: Babe Ruth had played there before being sold to the Boston Red Sox. Grove had some excellent years for Baltimore, winning 25, 18, 27, and 26 in the 1921-24 stretch. But there was no major league team which had a claim on Grove, and because Lefty was an excellent draw, Dunn was content to keep him on the team, instead of selling him.

It didn't bother Grove. Playing for Baltimore had a lot of advantages. It was an excellent team, winning seven straight pennants, including the five when Grove was there. And the players got along very well, off the field and on.

Dunn was a generous owner. Grove was making $750 a month by his final year with the Orioles, more than many big league owners were paying. There was always extra money from exhibitions with major league clubs and from the Little World Series, a playoff between the International League and American Association champions.

As an example of Dunn's generosity, in 1920, the first year of the Little World Series, Dunn told his team that if they won, they'd get the owner's share as well as their own. They won, and each player pocketed $1,800.

But after the 1924 season, Dunn got an offer from Mack he couldn't refuse: $100,600 for Grove. The odd sum was because Dunn wanted more than the even $100,000 he had gotten for Ruth.

Considering the money paid for him and the strong seasons he had had with Baltimore, Grove's rookie season was a disappointment. His control problems (he walked 131, a league high) contributed to a 10–12 year and a 4.75 earned run average.

His second season was a marked improvement, though he won only three more games and lost as many as he had as a rookie. He brought his ERA down to 2.51, the first of nine times he would lead the league in that department. He struck out 194, for one of his seven league-leading marks in that area. Most important, he was getting his pitches under control. As a rookie, he had averaged better than six walks a game. His second season, he averaged under four, and he would improve on that.

In his third season, Grove won 20 games, starting a streak of seven seasons in which he won at least that many. And when the A's won their three straight pennants, Grove was dynamite, improving with each year until he exploded with a season in 1931 that is probably the best in the American League since Babe Ruth changed the game in 1920.

In 1929, Grove won 20 games, lost only six, with an ERA of 2.81 and a strikeout total of 170. The last two figures, and his percentage, led the league, but Grove was only warming up.

In 1930, Grove won 28 games and lost only five, with an ERA of 2.54 and 209 strikeouts. His ERA was especially remarkable because that was the year the ball was really souped up; the runner-up that year was Wes Farrell, at 3.37.

But even that year was only a prelude for Grove. In 1931, he won 31 games and lost only four, with an ERA of 2.06 and 175 strikeouts. He led the league in wins, percentage, complete games (27), ERA, and strikeouts. He won 16 straight games, tying the league record of Walter Johnson and Joe Wood. The four games he lost were by 7–5, 4–3, 2–1, and 1–0. Not surprisingly, he was the league's Most Valuable Player.

The famed Grove temper flared again when he lost in his attempt for a 17th straight win, 1–0 to Dick Coffman and the St. Louis Browns. After the game, he came into the locker room, tore steel lockers off the wall, ripped up his uniform, and threw everything he could get his hands on.

Grove was especially angry with Simmons because, for a reason never fully explained, Simmons had left the team to go home to Milwaukee that day. In his place, Jim Moore misjudged a fly ball which went over his head and allowed the one St. Louis run to score. The sure-fielding Simmons would have caught the ball, Grove felt, and Lefty blamed Simmons, not Moore, for the mishap.

Grove went on to win 300 games, the second American League left-hander to do so. The first was Eddie Plank, whose greatest years also came with the A's. They were elected to the Hall of Fame a year apart, Plank in 1946, Grove in 1947. Fittingly, Grove's battery mate in the great years, Cochrane, made the Hall the same year.

Because the A's won their pennants so easily, most of the drama in their pennant years came during the World Series, and the most dramatic of the three they played was the first, in 1929.

The Chicago Cubs had won almost as easily in the National League that year as the Athletics had in the American, finishing 10½ games ahead of Pittsburgh.

The Cubs had good pitching, led by Pat Malone (22 wins), Charlie Root (19), and Guy Bush (18), but there was no question that their strength was in their hitting. As a team, the Cubs had hit .303, and they had such individuals as Rogers Hornsby, who had hit 39 home runs, knocked in 149 runs, and hit .380; Kiki Cuyler, who had batted in 102 runs with a .360 average, while also stealing 43 bases; Hack Wilson, who had hit 39 homers, with 159 RBIs and hit .345, tuning up for a 1930 season in which he would set a National League record with 56 home runs and a major league record with 190 RBIs; and Riggs Stephenson, who had hit .362 with 110 RBIs.

All of those hitters were right-handed. Of the eight Chicago regulars, indeed, only first baseman Charley Grimm was a left-handed hitter. Noting that fact, Mack decided he would start only right-handers against the Cubs and keep his southpaws in the bullpen, though Grove had won 20 games and Rube Walberg 18 that season. In Grove's case, at least, that was not as strange a strategy as it might seem. Throughout his career, Lefty was effective when used in relief. He won 33 games in that role and saved another 55 in his career.

The A's had an outstanding right-handed starter in George Earnshaw who had won 24 games and who, Grove thought, might have been as fast as Walter Johnson. Because the A's had won so easily, Earnshaw was well rested for the Series, and it was assumed, because of the preponderance of Chicago right-handed hitters, that Earnshaw, and not Grove, would start the first game. But he didn't.

About a month before the end of the season, Mack had assigned a seldom-used pitcher, Howard Ehmke, to scout the Cubs. Legend has it that he also told Ehmke to stay in shape because he would start the first game against the Cubs.

Ehmke had been in the American League for 13 years. He was the kind of pitcher who is usually the third or fourth starter in the rotation, a solid but hardly spectacular pitcher. Some managers call them .500 pitchers, and that's precisely what Ehmke was. Even in his best years—when he won 20 and 19 games in 1923 and '24 for Boston—he had barely been over .500, with 17 losses each year. For his career, he was 167–166, and he would be forgotten by everybody today but for the '29 Series.

In 1929, Ehmke was used in only 11 games, pitching 54⅔ innings, for a 7–2 record. He pitched only in those stretches when the double-headers piled up and depleted the pitching staff, and his absence was hardly noted when he left to scout.

When he went out to warm up before the opening game of the '29 Series at Wrigley Field in Chicago, hardly anybody could believe it, including Ehmke's teammates. Simmons rushed up to Mack and said: "Mr. Mack, are you going to pitch him?"

"Why, yes I am, Mr. Simmons, if it's all right with you," answered Mack. Simmons protested no more.

Mack had his reasons. He knew that the Cubs were a fastball hitting team, and he thought they would have trouble with Ehmke's slow breaking pitches. And at that time, it was often hard to pick up the ball because of the white-shirted fans in center field. Ehmke threw sidearm, and his motion would make it even more difficult for the Cub batters.

Mack's strategy worked perfectly. Ehmke's slow stuff had the Cubs continually off-balance. They not only couldn't hit it, they couldn't even make contact; at one point, five consecutive Cub batters struck out.

The game was scoreless until the seventh, when Foxx blasted one into the left field seats. The A's lead went to 3–0 with two runs in the ninth, unearned because of two errors by the usually reliable Chicago shortstop, Woody English.

Ehmke already had 12 strikeouts, tying Ed Walsh's 1906 Series mark, when the Cubs came to bat in the bottom of the ninth. He knocked down a Wilson line drive and threw out Hack for the first out but lost his shutout when Dykes made a two-base wild throw on a Cuyler grounder and Stephenson followed with a single. Then, Grimm followed with another single.

Mack didn't lose his faith in Ehmke, though, and the 35-year-old right-hander got pinch hitter Footsie Blair to hit into a force play and another pinch hitter, Chick Tolson, to strike out. That gave the A's the win and Ehmke a strikeout record.

The A's won the next game, too, 9–3, with Grove pitching 4⅓ innings of scoreless relief to save it. When the Series shifted to Philadelphia, the Cubs got their first win as Bush outdueled Earnshaw, 3–1. That set the stage for the fourth game, certainly one of the most dramatic in World Series history.

Sticking with his policy of right-handed starters only, Mack selected Jack Quinn for the fourth game. If Ehmke was a gamble, what about Quinn? In his 21st big league season, Quinn was 45, and his 1929 statistics were hardly overwhelming. He was 11–9, but with a 3.97 ERA, and he had allowed 182 hits in the 161 innings he had pitched.

Little is ever mentioned about Mack's starting Quinn, though. Perhaps that's because Quinn turned out to be less than an inspired choice, yielding seven runs (five earned) in five innings plus, before being relieved by Walberg.

Going into the bottom of the seventh, the Cubs had an 8–0 lead and seemed to be on their way to evening the Series. In fact, they were just one incredible half inning away from being taken right out of it.

Simmons started the inning with a home run to left, which seemed meaningless, but then Foxx, Miller, Dykes, and Boley followed with singles to score two more runs. George Burns popped up as a pinch hitter, but Bishop followed with another single, and the A's trailed by only four.

Chicago manager Joe McCarthy took out starter Root and brought in the left-handed Art Nehf to pitch to Mule Haas, a left-handed hitter. Haas lined one to center which should have been caught, but Wilson lost it in the sun. By the time Hack could run it down, Haas had circled the bases for an inside-the-park home run, and the A's trailed by only 8–7.

Nehf walked Cochrane, and McCarthy brought in Sheriff Blake. But nothing was going to stop the A's now. Simmons singled and so did Foxx, tying the score. Malone came in as the fourth Chicago pitcher of the inning. He hit Miller to load the bases, and then yielded a double to Dykes, making the score 10–8, before finally getting the side out.

Grove came on in relief for the A's in the eighth and ninth and had no trouble protecting the lead, striking out four of the six batters he faced in a scoreless stint.

To their credit, the Cubs didn't collapse in the next game. Indeed, they led for most of the contest. Mack went again to Ehmke, but Howard, without the advantage of the white shirts in center field, wasn't so successful this time. The Cubs knocked him out with a two-run rally in the fourth and carried a 2–0 lead into the bottom of the ninth.

The A's had only two hits off Malone in the first eight innings, but in the ninth, Bishop singled and Haas followed with a homer to tie the score. Simmons doubled, Malone walked Foxx intentionally, and Miller singled to score Simmons and end the Series.

What of Mack's pitching strategy in the Series? Ehmke had started two games, pitching brilliantly in one and getting knocked out in the second. Earnshaw had pitched one complete game, which he had lost, and had to be lifted in the other. Quinn was derricked in the one game he started.

Meanwhile, the Chicago right-handed hitters hadn't bothered left-handers Grove and Walberg a bit. Each pitched 6⅓ innings of scoreless relief, and each yielded only three hits. Walberg got one win, Grove two saves. Grove struck out ten, Walberg eight.

Would the A's have done as well if Mack had started Grove and Walberg instead of Ehmke and Quinn? Probably, but it wouldn't have made as good a story.

Mack went against the book in his pitching strategy in the 1930 World Series, too, though it didn't get as much notice.

That one, in which the A's met the St. Louis Cardinals, was a tough Series for the A's, though they won the first two games easily, 5–2 behind Grove and 6–1 behind Earnshaw. The Cardinals bounced back to win the next two, beating Grove in the fourth contest, and it was obvious the fifth game would be the key to the Series.

Earnshaw and Burleigh Grimes battled through seven scoreless innings before Mack took out Earnshaw for a pinch hitter in the eighth. Connie then brought in Grove, though Lefty had pitched nine innings the day before.

Going into the ninth, it was still scoreless. Cochrane walked to start the inning, and then Simmons popped up. But then Foxx hit the most famous, though not the longest, of his home runs, into the left-center seats for a 2–0 lead that Grove protected in the bottom of the inning.

After a travel day, the teams took the field in Philadelphia for the sixth game, and Mack had Earnshaw starting again. He was determined he was going to go with his best the rest of the way, and let them rest over the winter. If Earnshaw couldn't do it in the sixth game, Grove would be ready for the seventh.

Lefty wasn't needed. Staked to a two-run lead after the first inning, Earnshaw stopped the Cards on just five hits and won easily, 7–1, and the Athletics were two-time World Champions.

In many ways, the 1931 season was the A's best. They won 107 games for a .704 percentage, a record surpassed in league history only by the '27 Yankees and '54 Indians. Grove won 31 games, Simmons led the league with a .390 average.

Though the Cardinals had won 101 games to take the National League pennant by 13 games (the A's winning margin was 13½), they weren't given much of a chance against the Athletics. It was expected that Philadelphia would win their third straight World Championship.

But the brevity of the World Series and the unusual pressures often produce surprising results and heroes, and the 1931 Series is a classic example of that. A good but not great player named Pepper Martin, known more for his weird off-field stunts and the way he stopped line drives with his chest than for anything else, had as good a Series as any player has ever had, and he led the Cardinals to an upset win in seven games.

For the Series, Martin batted an even .500, with 12 hits, including four doubles and a home run. He stole five bases against the great catcher, Cochrane. And he seemed to always be in the middle of Cardinal victories.

For example: In game two, Martin singled and doubled, stole a base and scored both runs in a 2–0 Cardinal victory; in game three, he got a single and a double and scored two runs as the Cards won, 5–2; in game five, he got three hits, one a homer, scored one run and knocked in four as the Cards won, 5–1; in game seven, he went hitless but stole another base in the 4–2 St. Louis win.

Grove had won two games in the Series—in the three years, he won four games and saved two, with an ERA of 1.75—but it wasn't enough to overcome Martin.

The A's dynasty ended with the last pitch of that Series. The Athletics were still a very good team in 1932, winning 94, but the rebuilt Yankees were better, taking 107 games and the pennant.

Once again, too, economic circumstances were overwhelming Connie Mack. The Great Depression had hit the land, and baseball teams were feeling it; American League attendance had dropped to about 60 percent of what it had been in the glory days in the '20s. Once more Mack had to sell his stars to survive. Simmons, Haas, and Dykes went first, to the White Sox for $150,000. The A's slipped to third without them in '33.

Next, Cochrane went to Detroit for $100,000, and Grove, Walberg, and Bishop to Boston for $125,000. The next year, Foxx also went to the Red Sox, for $150,000.

Mack went on to manage the A's through the 1950 season, completing 50 years as a field boss. Those close to him, though, said he'd been touched by senility. He could not remember names—Hank Majeski was "Majestic," for instance—and first baseman Ferris Fain told of getting the take sign with two strikes.

The team was consistently terrible. In the last 15 years Mack managed, the A's finished last ten times and were in the first division—fourth—only once.

It would be more than four decades from the time the A's won in 1931 to their next pennant, in 1972, and by that time, the franchise had moved twice and was under the control of a man light years from Mack in personality—the erratic, bombastic Charles O. Finley.

11. They Carried Heavy Lumber

From its very beginning, the American League had been known as a great hitter's league. Nap Lajoie had hit a thundering .422 in the first season. Ty Cobb, who had the highest average ever, was an American Leaguer. So was "Shoeless Joe" Jackson, always considered the best natural hitter in baseball history. And, of course, so was Babe Ruth, who had changed the game so dramatically.

In the wake of Ruth's revolution, there were several other outstanding hitters who gravitated to the American League. Hitting behind Ruth on the Yankees was Lou Gehrig, and there has never been a more devastating one-two punch; with Bob Meusel and Tony Lazzeri added, that Yankees' lineup became known as "Murderer's Row."

Al Simmons was a great hitter for Philadelphia, both in average and power. Heinie Manush bounced around the league but hit wherever he

Charlie Gehringer was known as the "Mechanical Man" for his smooth defensive play at second base and great hitting for the Detroit Tigers. *(Detroit Tigers)*

went, averaging .330 lifetime. Sam Rice and Goose Goslin formed a potent pair for Washington, and both later made the Hall of Fame. Charley Gehringer, the "Mechanical Man," stroked his way to a .320 lifetime average with Detroit, while playing a virtually flawless second base.

Even in this great company, there were some who stood out. George Sisler was one. Sisler never got the attention he deserved because he played for a St. Louis Browns' team which never won a pennant, but he was a marvelous hitter.

Only a ruling by the National Commission made Sisler an American Leaguer, because the Pittsburgh Pirates of the Senior Circuit had claimed to own Sisler's contract.

While he was still in high school, at Akron, Ohio, Sisler had signed a contract with the Akron team in the Ohio-Pennsylvania League. He never took any money from the club and decided to go instead to the University of Michigan, but the Akron club still considered him its property.

Sisler soon became known as the best college player in the country, and Akron transferred its contract with Sisler to Columbus, which in turn, sold the contract to Pittsburgh.

Branch Rickey was Sisler's coach at Michigan, and also a scout for the Browns. Rickey helped Sisler bring the matter before the National Commission, and George and his father testified that he had been a minor when he had signed the contract.

The National Commission ruled the contract void, and Sisler eventually signed with the Browns, by that time managed by Rickey.

Like Ruth, Sisler started as a pitcher, though he wasn't in Babe's class. He had a 4–4 record in 15 games, with a 2.83 earned run average, as a rookie in 1915. But Rickey quickly realized that Sisler's future was as a hitter, not a pitcher. He used George in 81 games that year, including 37 as a first baseman and 29 as an outfielder, and the next year, Sisler was a full-time first baseman.

Sisler adapted so well to his new position that he is often considered, with Hal Chase, one of the two best-fielding first basemen in baseball history. Even so, it is as a hitter that he is best remembered. Had it not been for an eye problem he suffered in his prime, he would probably now be ranked with Cobb as a hitter.

Those are strong words but, after he had warmed up with consecutive years of .353, .341, and .352, Sisler had a streak of three consecutive seasons, 1920–22, that even Cobb would have been proud of.

In 1920, for instance, Sisler hit .407 with 257 hits, a major league record

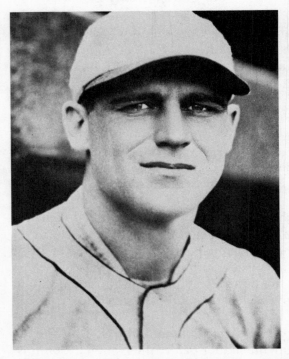

George Sisler set a major league record with 257 hits in a season and hit more than .400 twice before an eye ailment curtailed his effectiveness. *(George Brace)*

which still stands. He had 49 doubles, 18 triples, and 19 home runs, second in the league (to Ruth, of course) that year. He knocked in 122 runs, scored 136, and went hitless in only 23 games the entire season. For good measure, he stole 42 bases.

In 1921, he "slumped" to .371, with 216 hits, 38 doubles, 18 triples, 11 home runs. He knocked in 104 runs, scored 135, and stole a league-leading 35 bases.

Sisler capped his three-year string with a .420 mark in 1922, leading the league in hits (246), triples (18), runs (134), and stolen bases (51). He set a league record with a 41-game hitting streak, batted in 105 runs, and struck out only 14 times all season! Though his team finished second, he was fittingly named the league's Most Valuable Player.

Had he stayed healthy, Sisler no doubt would have had more superlative seasons, because he was only 29 in his last great year. But he developed sinusitus in the off-season, which gave him double vision. He missed the entire 1923 season, and when he returned, though he was still a good hitter, he was not the great one he had been.

In his remaining seven seasons after his return, Sisler hit .305, .345, .290, .327, .331, .326, and .309. He finished with a lifetime average of .340, which was good enough to get him into the Hall of Fame, but it is not unreasonable to think that he would have posted a lifetime mark 15–25 points higher if he had not had vision problems.

Another remarkable hitter whose career paralleled Sisler's was Harry Heilmann of Detroit, a fearsome line drive hitter who nearly became the first hitter to have four .400 years.

Heilmann's value was strictly as a hitter. He was slow and a weak fielder, though he had a strong arm. And early in his career, he was not a great hitter, either; it was not until his fifth season with the Tigers that he hit over .300, .320 in 1919.

The turning point in Heilmann's career came when Ty Cobb was named manager of the Tigers in 1921. Heilmann was one of the few players who ever got along with Cobb, perhaps because he appreciated the help Ty gave him as a hitter. The transformation was immediate, as Heilmann hit .394 in 1921.

That was the first of four American League batting titles for Heilmann. Each time, his average was truly remarkable; he hit .403, .393, and .398 the other three years he led his circuit. And consider this: He was only four hits shy of a .400 mark the year he won his first title, another four hits shy when he won his third championship, and only one hit shy of .400 in his fourth championship year. Had Heilmann been of only average speed, he would probably have had enough leg hits to bat .400 in each of those years.

Heilmann won his titles in odd years—1921, '23, '25, and '27. Joking about that later, he said he was on the last year of a two-year contract each time and was making a salary drive. Unfortunately, some fans took that remark seriously, but Heilmann hardly had to apologize for his interim averages of .356, .346, and .367.

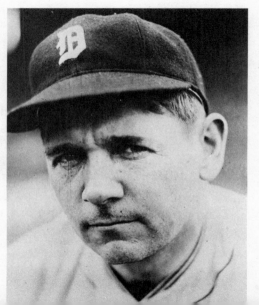

Harry Heilmann benefited from Ty Cobb's advice in winning four batting titles in the '20's, once beating out Cobb. *(Detroit Tigers)*

Cobb may have regretted helping Heilmann so much when Harry beat out his teacher for the batting title in 1921. At first, the story seemed different. Unofficial league averages at the end of the year credited Cobb with a mark of .391 and Heilmann with .390. But when the official averages came out, Heilmann was at .394 and Cobb at .389. Ty reportedly called up the statistics bureau and gave a tongue-lashing to an employee there, but that didn't change the results.

The 1925 championship also came hard. In fact, Tris Speaker had a lead of approximately fifteen points going into the final month. But Heilmann came on strong that last month, going six-for-nine in a double-header on the last day, and finished four points better than Speaker.

But Heilmann gave his most dramatic performance in 1927, though it was overshadowed by Ruth's 60 home run performance. Heilmann and Simmons were locked in a tight duel for the batting title, with Simmons ahead by two points going into the final day.

Simmons and the A's were playing a single game in Washington that day. Heilmann was playing in a double-header for the Tigers in Cleveland. Because of the time difference, Heilmann knew midway through his first game exactly what he had to do to win the title.

In his first two times up, Heilmann doubled each time. Then, he heard that Simmons had gone two-for-five in Washington, finishing at .392.

His third time up, Heilmann attempted a bunt and was thrown out. His fourth time, he tried the same thing, and this time the surprise worked. At that point, Heilmann knew he could win the batting title by sitting out the rest of the day—the games had no bearing on the standings for either team—but he refused, and in his final time at bat in the first game, he hit a home run.

Even then, he would not sit down, and in the second game, he came back with a single, double, and home run in four trips. For the day, he had a remarkable seven hits in nine at bats, and he won the title by six points over Simmons, .398 to .392.

But though Sisler's and Heilmann's batting performances were remarkable, the long ball still belonged to Ruth. For a 14-year span, 1918–1931, Ruth won or tied for every home run title, except in 1922, when he was suspended for the first part of the season, and 1925, when illness sidelined him for a third of the season. Three times he had hit more than 50 home runs; nobody else had done it once. Not until the '30s was his home run supremacy challenged, as first Jimmie Foxx and then Hank Greenberg made serious runs at his magic mark of 60 homers in a season.

Two men more different than Foxx and Greenberg could hardly be imagined. They had in common only an ability to hit the ball enormous distances from the right-handed side of the plate.

Foxx was naive, an easygoing, always-smiling man who was liked by everybody. What Jimmie liked was a good time; his outlook on life was much like Ruth's. He drank heavily and, inevitably, dissipated his talents. He was through as an effective ballplayer at only 34, though a man of his ability should have had another 5–6 good years left. In retirement, he learned that many of his "friends" had disappeared when his talents did, and he had one disappointment after another in business. He suffered a heart attack in his mid-50s and died when he choked on a piece of meat in July 1967, three months short of his 60th birthday.

But as a player, Foxx was a wonder, perhaps the strongest man ever to play the game. He hit the ball tremendous distances, once even out of Chicago's spacious Comiskey Park. Sometimes, it was said, the balls he hit were crushed out of shape.

Foxx was a natural athlete, blessed with speed as well as power, and he was only 16 when he began his professional baseball career, playing for Easton of the Eastern Shore League. The team was managed by Frank "Home Run" Baker, who had played on the great Philadelphia teams, 1910–14.

Jimmie Foxx hit 30 or more homers in twelve consecutive seasons, a mark the Babe never matched. *(George Brace)*

When Foxx had a respectable season, catching 76 games and batting .296 with ten home runs, several major league teams became interested, but Baker felt an allegiance to Connie Mack, for whom he had played with the A's, and Mack was able to swing a deal for Foxx.

Foxx hit well in very limited appearances for the Athletics in his first three seasons, but the problem was finding a position for him. Catcher was out, because the A's had Mickey Cochrane there. He was tried at third base and first base, and also caught occasionally when Cochrane needed a rest, but it was not until 1929 that Foxx was made a regular at first base. He responded with the first of his great seasons, hitting .354 with 33 home runs and 118 RBIs. It was the first of 12 consecutive seasons in which Foxx would get at least 30 home runs, a mark even Ruth never achieved.

Foxx and Simmons were the main power hitters for the A's as they swept to three straight pennants, 1929–31, but Jimmie achieved his best years after that stretch. And the best of all was 1932, when he hit 58 home runs, just two short of Ruth's mark.

Two things stopped Foxx from at least equalling Ruth's record. He lost two homers in rained-out games and three more because of a wire netting above the regular fence in St. Louis. That netting, which had not been there when Ruth had set his record in 1927, caught three Foxx drives and reduced them to ground-rule doubles.

Nevertheless, even though he had been stopped short of the record, Foxx had the kind of year that only Ruth had been known to have before. Along with his home runs, Foxx led the league with 151 runs and 169 RBIs and had 213 hits, while batting .364. He also won the Most Valuable Player for the first of three times.

That batting average was especially significant. Like Ruth, Foxx was not just a slugger, as so many power hitters of today are. He was a high average hitter for most of his career, finishing with a lifetime record of .325. Twice he led the league in hitting—.356 in 1933 and .349 in 1938—and only twice in his first 12 years as a regular did he fall below .300 for the season.

Foxx's 1933 performance was nearly as good as it had been the previous year; he hit 48 home runs, scored 125 runs, and batted in 163 with a .356 average. Once again, he was the league's Most Valuable Player.

His reward for all this? A pay cut. His $16,333 salary of 1933 was cut to $16,000 for 1934. Money was tight in Philadelphia.

Foxx lasted two more years in Philadelphia, continuing his superb play though the team was deteriorating around him as Mack was forced to sell off his stars. In '34 he hit 44 home runs, in '35, another 36; oddly, the latter, lesser total led the league, while the former one did not.

Finally, Mack had to sell Foxx, too, to the Boston Red Sox after the 1935 season. It was a blessing for Foxx. Fenway Park, with its short left field fence, was an inviting target for Jimmie, who went on to hit 220 of his lifetime 534 home runs for the Red Sox.

And, for a change, he was well paid for his efforts. Millionaire Tom Yawkey, who owned the club, was a generous man to those who produced, and Foxx's top salary in Boston was $32,000, nearly double his best in Philadelphia.

Foxx hit 41 homers his first year with the Red Sox, and another 36 in his second year. He had one great season left, rivaling 1932 in many respects.

In 1938, Foxx smashed 50 home runs—35 of them at Fenway—knocked in 175 runs, the top mark of his career, hit .349, and had a slugging percentage of .704. The last three marks all led the league, and Foxx won his third MVP award. But his home run total was second in the league, because that was the year Greenberg hit 58.

Unlike Foxx, Greenberg was not a natural athlete, lacking both speed and grace. His only asset was the strength he could generate from his 6'3½", 210-pound frame. In his youth, he played basketball better than baseball because of his size. He was often teased because of his awkwardness, and when he played baseball, he was stationed at first base, where his awkwardness and lack of speed would not be great drawbacks.

Hank Greenberg made a great run at Babe Ruth's season home run record before falling just short with 58 in 1938. *(Detroit Tigers)*

Greenberg never became a graceful player. Pictures of his batting swing look like the "before" panels of a television commercial offering relief for lower back pain. But he worked until he made himself into the most feared right-handed hitter in the league.

In his youth, Greenberg would take batting practice swings until his hands bled. He scattered sawdust over the lawn in front of his house to practice sliding. He didn't stop working even when he made the majors. One time, when he was having trouble hitting at night, he stayed out after a night game to take additional batting practice.

Greenberg was also a courageous player. In the 1935 World Series, he fractured his wrist in a collision at home plate with Chicago Cubs' catcher Gabby Hartnett. He sat out the next three games, as the Tigers moved to a 3–2 lead. Before the sixth game, though, he decided he wanted to play in what could be (and was) the clincher for the Tigers. He had trainer Denny Carroll tape the wrist tightly, and then he played catch with batboy Joe Rogin. He told Rogin to throw as hard as he could. As the ball slammed into Greenberg's glove, he turned white with the pain. He couldn't play, but he had tried.

Greenberg was also a much more worldly man than Foxx. He was the son of Rumanian-Jewish immigrants, but his father quickly learned the ways of American business, and the senior Greenberg's success in the garment district of New York enabled him to buy a 16-room house in the Bronx while Hank was still in high school.

Hank always made certain he was paid commensurate with his performance, and he invested wisely. By the end of his career, he was secure enough financially that he said he would retire when the Tigers traded him to the Pittsburgh Pirates after the 1947 season—until the Pirates made him an offer he couldn't refuse, reputedly $100,000. He played one more year and retired.

Like most stars of his era, though, Hank had to fight for what he got. After his 58-homer year, for instance, Detroit owner Walter Briggs wanted him to play for the same salary the next year. "He said he didn't have the money to give me a raise because he needed it to paint the stadium," remembered Greenberg many years later. Hank held out for a $5,000 raise instead.

When he fell off from 58 homers to 33 in 1939, the Tigers tried to cut his pay $10,000. But Greenberg learned that they were trying to get him to move to left field to make room for young slugger Rudy York at first base. He agreed to the move—but not until he got a $10,000 raise.

The best that could be said of Greenberg as an outfielder was that he was adequate, and York's fielding was such that somebody termed him "half Indian and half first baseman."

But the two were dynamite at the plate that year, 1940. York hit .316 with 33 home runs and 134 RBIs. Greenberg was even better, hitting .340 and leading the league in home runs (41), doubles (50), and RBIs (150), which earned him the Most Valuable Player award.

And the Tigers won the pennant. The race came down to a three-game series between the Tigers and Indians in Cleveland in the last week of September. The Tigers needed to win only one of the three.

Detroit manager Del Baker decided he would hold back his best pitchers—"Schoolboy" Rowe (16–3) and Bob Newsom (21–5)—for the final two games and throw a sacrificial lamb against Bob Feller, who was overpowering that season. Feller had already won 27 games, losing only 10, and had thrown an opening day no-hitter.

The pitcher Baker selected was Floyd Giebell, a right-hander who was nearing his 31st birthday (for some reason, some accounts placed his age at 25), who had bounced around the minors for years without distinction. He had been brought up late in the season and had won the only game he had pitched. The year before, he had split two late-season games for the Tigers.

That day, Giebell pitched the game of his life, blanking the Indians on six hits. Feller yielded only three, but one of them was a two-run homer by York. The Tigers were champions. Giebell? He never won another game in the major leagues.

As a youngster, Greenberg never thought seriously of being anything but a ballplayer, but he had to fight against his family and friends, who were horrified that he would even think of such an unintellectual occupation.

"I'll sum it up this way," Greenberg said, years later, in an interview with Ron Bergman of *The Oakland Tribune.* "Our neighbors in the Bronx used to ask my parents, 'Why does he have to grow up to be a bum?' They all wanted their sons to be a doctor or a lawyer.

"I was a disgrace. My sister and two brothers all graduated from college. One, Ben, became a lawyer."

It wasn't until Hank was offered bonuses to sign that his parents changed their minds. "My family finally realized that baseball must have required some exceptional talent. They subsequently became proud of my achievements."

Greenberg had grown up as a fan of the Giants, and he would have been a natural for them, because they were always looking for Jewish players as a lure for the large Jewish population of the city. But John McGraw watched Greenberg play and thought he was too awkward to be a major league player. It was one of the few mistakes McGraw ever made in judging a player.

Meanwhile, the Yankees had offered Greenberg $7,500 to sign, but Hank never considered them. He thought that, with his physical limitations he would have to play first base, and the Yankees had Lou Gehrig there.

Detroit offered Greenberg $9,000. Washington went higher, to $12,000. But there was another consideration. David Greenberg, Hank's father, still wanted him to go to college. When the Tigers agreed to that, his father allowed him to sign a contract.

Hank didn't even last a full year in college. In the spring of 1930, he dropped out of NYU to play minor league ball; three years later, he was up to stay with the Tigers.

Though he was a free-swinger by the standards of the day, Greenberg was also a good average hitter until late in his career. He hit .300 or better in each of his first seven full seasons and averaged .318 for his career.

But it was his power that brought Greenberg the most notice, although that power didn't show itself fully in his rookie year when he hit only 12 home runs. The next year he hit 26 homers and an astounding 63 doubles, only 4 below the major league record which had been set four years before by Earl Webb of the Red Sox.

He also started his run of big RBI years. Even more than his home runs, Greenberg loved to see his RBI totals grow. Years later, Gehringer told how Greenberg would urge him to move runners along to third—so Hank could knock them in.

In 1935, Greenberg hit 36 homers, tying Foxx for the league title, and knocked in a league-high 170 runs, on a .328 average. But that was the year he broke his wrist in the World Series, and the next season, he broke it again in a collision with Jake Powell of the Yanks. He played only 12 games in 1936, and there was a question whether he'd ever be a topflight hitter again.

He answered that question in 1937, when he hit .337 with 200 hits, 49 doubles, 14 triples, and 40 home runs, for a total of 103 extra-base hits. He scored 137 runs and knocked in 183, only one below Gehrig's league record. It was his finest all-round season.

But that year, good as it was, lacked the drama of Greenberg's run at Ruth's record in 1938.

Greenberg reached 58 with five games remaining in the season, and the pressure was enormous as baseball fans across the country waited to see what he could do.

The Tigers had two games left in Detroit against the St. Louis Browns and then three in Cleveland. For the first game in Detroit, the Browns started a wild left-hander named Howard Mills who walked Greenberg four times. In the next game, Newsom, who had always given Hank trouble, held him to a single in four at bats.

Then, it was on to Cleveland. At that time, the Indians were dividing their games between old League Park and the lakefront Municipal Stadium. Both were enormous parks. At League Park, it was 375 feet down the left field line, 415 feet to the "power alley" in left center. Distances were comparable at Municipal Stadium (eventually, the Indians installed inner fences to cut down the distances), and it was even worse when the wind blew in off Lake Erie.

Greenberg went hitless against Denny Galehouse in the Friday game at League Park which opened the three-game series. The Cleveland management then rescheduled the Saturday game as part of a Sunday double-header at Municipal Stadium, knowing they could get a huge gate.

Cleveland started the 19-year-old Feller in the first contest, and Feller fanned 18 Tigers. Greenberg struck out twice and went hitless. It was down to the final game.

In the second game, Hank doubled twice off Johnny Humphries. One of the doubles, which would certainly have been a home run in any other park, bounced to the fence, 420 feet away.

But it was getting darker and darker. Finally, in the sixth inning, umpire George Moriarty (once a Detroit player) called the game, apologizing to Greenberg. "I'm sorry, Hank. This is as far as I can go."

"That's okay," said Greenberg. "This is as far as I can go, too."

In many ways, Greenberg's career was a series of what-might-have-beens. He lost 4½ years to military service (he actually was in uniform for most of 1941, before the United States was at war) and another full season because of his broken wrist. In effect, he played only the equivalent of ten full seasons.

As a result, his homer total of 331 is far down on the career list, but no right-handed hitter has ever surpassed what he did in that one magnificent year of 1938.

12. The Pride and the Tragedy

The story of Lou Gehrig is well known thanks to *Pride of the Yankees,* one of the very few good movies ever made about a sports hero. Gehrig was the classic tragic hero, cut down in the prime of life by a disease so rare it was named after him following his death. What isn't always remembered, though, is that it wasn't until Gehrig fell victim to the disease that he got the acclaim he truly deserved.

Lou Gehrig was a great hitter. His lifetime statistics are awesome: .340 batting average, 493 home runs, 1,888 runs scored; 1,991 runs batted in, 1,508 walks, a slugging percentage of .632.

Only Babe Ruth and Hank Aaron have ever knocked in more runs; only Ruth and Ted Williams have a higher lifetime slugging average. In his prime, Gehrig could match the singles hitters for percentage, the home run hitters for power.

Those statistics don't tell the whole story, either. He was only 34 when the first stage of his fatal disease struck. Had he remained healthy, he could have been expected to hit perhaps 600 home runs and knock in far more than 2,000 runs.

As it was, when he retired, only Ruth had hit more home runs and collected more RBIs. But that was the problem, of course: Ruth played on the same team.

Ruth's presence was both a blessing and a curse for Gehrig. It meant success; the two played on four pennant-winners, and Gehrig was undoubtedly helped as a hitter by the fact that Ruth was immediately ahead of him in the batting order. But it also meant that Gehrig played nearly his entire career in Ruth's shadow.

This was inevitable, in part because of the difference in personality between the two. Ruth was a flamboyant, charismatic personality. Gehrig was quiet, withdrawn.

Gehrig, in fact, was the quintessential Eagle Scout, a man of truly noble character. He was unfailingly courteous to everybody, and kind to all but opposing pitchers. Except for a latter-day feud with Ruth, he never seems to have quarreled with teammates, and he didn't dispute umpire's calls.

He never held out, never battled authority figures. He worked hard to perfect his play, and he was a man of exemplary personal habits.

The one flaw in his character was that he was very close with his money, the last of the dime tippers. But he was not a greedy man and, in fact, once turned down an opportunity to make money on a cigarette commercial because he thought that would be a bad influence on youngsters.

Gehrig didn't marry until he was 30, and his marriage came as a shock to those who knew him because he was known to be terribly shy; he stuttered and stammered when a woman asked him for an autograph.

Until his marriage, Gehrig lived with his parents, and it was his mother who was the dominating personality in his life. Sometimes, she even went on Yankee road trips to be near her son. Four children had been born to the elder Gehrigs, who had come to the United States from Germany in 1900, but Lou was the only one who survived infancy. Lou's father had suffered a head injury working in the steel mills, which had somewhat diminished his mental capacities, and it was Ma Gehrig who ran the household.

For a long time, Gehrig and Ruth were close friends. Ruth patronized Gehrig, but Lou didn't mind; he felt Ruth was the bigger star and was content to follow his lead. Ruth also helped Gehrig financially, because he arranged exhibition tours on which Gehrig also played. Following the 1927 season, in fact, the exhibition tour on which they both played apparently brought Gehrig more money than he had made in regular season play for the Yankees.

The relationship couldn't last that way indefinitely. Even as mild-mannered a man as Gehrig couldn't have been content playing second fiddle forever, especially since he was a star in his own right.

The first fissure appeared in 1929. Ruth approached Gehrig and proposed that they hold out together, reasoning that this would put great pressure on the Yankee management. Gehrig refused. It was not his style, which is one reason his top salary, $39,000, was just under half of what Ruth made at his peak. Club managements talk enthusiastically of loyalty, but they don't reward it.

Still, the two remained close. Ruth often visited Gehrig's home for some of Ma Gehrig's German cooking, and he once brought her a Chihuahua pup, which she named "Jidge," which was one of Ruth's nicknames.

It was Gehrig's mother who was at the center of the incident which caused the final break between the two. One time after Ruth had married Claire Hodgson, he visited Ma Gehrig, with his daughter, Dorothy (from his previous marriage), and Claire's daughter, Julie. Dorothy was no more than 12, and Julie was 5 years older. Julie dressed like a young lady, while Dorothy was still in the tomboy stage.

Ma Gehrig commented that it was a shame Claire didn't dress Dorothy as well as she did her own daughter. That remark got back to Claire, who became very angry. She communicated her anger to Ruth, who said something to Gehrig about telling his mother to mind her own business.

That was it. Nobody criticized his mother in Lou's hearing. He stopped speaking to Ruth off the field, and the two were never close again.

There was, of course, a reason apart from personality why Ruth overshadowed Gehrig: He was the better player. That was no knock on Lou, of course; Ruth was better than everybody.

Their styles emphasized the difference. Ruth did everything with a flair, striking out or hitting 600-foot home runs. Gehrig had a compact, economical swing. He struck out rarely for a power hitter; in the '30s, he had a string of six consecutive seasons in which he struck out fewer than 50 times. His home runs went 400 feet, not 600. As somebody remarked at the time, a Gehrig home run was just a home run; a Ruth home run was an event.

With his flair for the dramatic, Ruth always seemed to one-up Gehrig's most impressive accomplishments. In 1927, for instance, Gehrig had an incredible year, hitting .373 with 218 hits, 52 doubles, 18 triples, 47 home runs (a near-record 117 extra-base hits), 149 runs scored, 175 RBIs. He was the league's Most Valuable Player. But that was the year Ruth hit 60 home runs.

In the 1928 World Series, Gehrig hit a remarkable .545, but Ruth hit .625, a record which still stands. In the 1932 Series, Gehrig led everybody with a .529 average. But that was the year Ruth hit his famous "called shot" home run off Charlie Root of the Cubs.

And so it went. Whatever Gehrig did, Ruth did better—or so it seemed. Not until 1934, when Ruth was 39 and over-the-hill, did Gehrig hit more home runs in a season than Babe. He should have done it three years earlier, in 1931, but a fluke robbed him of a home run. With Lyn Lary on base, Gehrig had hit the ball into the stands, but for some reason, Lary lost the flight of the ball and thought it had been caught for the third out of the inning; so he ran on into the dugout. Gehrig, head down, didn't see Lary leave the base paths, and he was declared out for passing a runner. His home run was reduced to a triple, and he and Ruth ended the season with 46 homers each.

Gehrig's success with the Yankees was no surprise. In his teens, he had been a big star for Commerce High in New York, and was considered probably the best high school player in the country. When Commerce

Lou Gehrig set a record of 2,130 consecutive games before being cut down by a rare disease. *(New York Yankees)*

played Lane High of Chicago in an unofficial battle for the country's championship, Gehrig's grand-slam homer in the ninth won the game.

Lou's parents wanted him to go to college before he played ball, but John McGraw signed him to a contract to play for Hartford of the Eastern League. McGraw convinced Lou and his parents that he could play under the assumed name of "Lou Lewis" and still go to college (Columbia) in the fall.

Gehrig hit only .261 at Hartford, and the subterfuge was quickly discovered. He could not play as a freshman at Columbia, but he somehow regained his amateur status and played both football and baseball as a sophomore. He was a hard-running fullback in football, and he pitched and played first base and the outfield too, in baseball.

The contract with the Giants had been abrogated, apparently because Gehrig was underage when he signed it, so the Yankees offered him $1,500 to sign and $3,000 for the remainder of the 1923 season. His parents still wanted Lou to finish college, but the money was too good to pass up, so he signed. Ironically, he was again assigned to Hartford, because the Yankees had negotiated a working agreement with the club.

Gehrig played a partial season with Hartford in '23 and a full one the next year. In only 59 games in 1923, he hit .304 with 24 homers and 40 extra-base hits. In 1924, he hit .369 in a full season, with 37 homers, 13 triples, and 40 doubles.

Each year, he was brought up at the end of the season to the Yankees, and he hit .423 in 26 at-bats in 1923, .500 in 12 at-bats in 1924.

In 1925, he was brought up to stay, but even then he was not a starter early in the season. The Yankees had a good first baseman in Wally Pipp, who had hit .295 with 113 RBIs in 1924 and .304 with 108 RBIs the season before. Pipp was only 31, and he obviously had some good years left.

So, Gehrig played little the first six weeks of the season, occasionally pinch-hitting and playing half a dozen games in the outfield. Then, on June 1 (the day before Ruth returned to the lineup following his operation), Pipp went to manager Miller Huggins and said he'd like to take the day off because he had a headache. He should have taken an aspirin and played.

Gehrig started that game at first, and Pipp never again got into the Yankee starting lineup; he was traded to Cincinnati before the next season started. Gehrig went on to compile the record for which he is best known, 2,130 consecutive games played.

He was understandably proud of that record, which is one that is certain never to be broken. Once, during the 1934 season, he was in such pain from a sore back that it seemed he would have to come out. Manager Joe McCarthy put him in the lineup as leadoff hitter and nominal shortstop. Gehrig batted in the top of the first and, despite the sore back, hit a double. McCarthy then took him out of the game and put in Frank Crosetti at shortstop, and Gehrig's string was preserved.

His first year as a regular, Gehrig was almost literally an average hitter; he hit .295, and the league hitters averaged .292. The next year he improved to .313 and started to show his power; though he hit only 16 homers, he had 20 triples and 47 doubles, and he knocked in 107 runs.

But it was in the 11-year stretch, 1927–37, that Gehrig gave his best performances. In those seasons he blasted homer totals of 47, 27, 35, 41, 46, 34, 32, 49, 30, 49, and 37. He hit as many as 52 doubles in a season and as many as 18 triples. His RBI totals five times led the league. In order, they were: 175, 142, 126, 174, 184, 151, 139, 165, 119, 142, 159.

He was known as the "Iron Horse" for his durability and consistency. Day in and day out, he was the one Yankee who was always there, getting his hits, knocking in his runs. It seemed he would go on forever. But, of course, he didn't.

The first sign of trouble showed itself in the 1937 World Series against the

Giants. The Yankees won in five games, without much help from Lou, who hit .294 and had only one homer and three RBIs. For any other player, those totals would have been quite respectable. But Gehrig had been an extraordinary Series competitor, averaging .361 in 34 games during his career, with 10 home runs and 35 RBIs. He knew something was wrong. He complained mildly of "lumbago."

The next year, Lou had his weakest year since he was a rookie, averaging .295, with 29 homers and 114 RBIs. Again, these were respectable figures, but not by Gehrig's standards. For the previous 11 years, he had averaged about .350, with 39 homers and 153 RBIs. He was only 35 and had never abused his body; he should have had several seasons left.

As it happened, he had none. The next season, when he came to spring training, his physical deterioration was shocking. He had lost weight, and his uniform hung on him like a sack. His coordination and strength had left him. He played eight games at the start of the season, hitting only four singles in 28 at bats. He was having so much trouble in the field that when he handled a routine play without error, his teammates praised him. More than anything else, that convinced Gehrig that he had to take himself out of the lineup.

He had a talk with manager McCarthy, and McCarthy bluntly told him that he had to sit down. McCarthy felt he could not mince words with Gehrig. "His reflexes were shot," McCarthy told Donald Honig many years later. "I was afraid of his getting hit with a pitched ball. He wouldn't have been able to get out of the way. . . ."

Gehrig was the team captain, and it was his job to take the starting lineup card to the umpire. When he did it that day, the public address announcer told the crowd that Gehrig was ending his consecutive-game streak.

The crowd gave Gehrig a standing ovation. Too late, they realized what he had meant to the team, and to them. On the bench, Lou wept unashamedly. Some of his teammates did, too.

Finally, Lefty Gomez came over and kidded Gehrig. "Now you know how pitchers feel when they're knocked out of the box," he said. Gehrig smiled, and the tension in the dugout was broken.

That was May 2, 1939. Gehrig never played another game, though he remained in uniform for the rest of the season. Shortly after that, Gehrig went to the Mayo Clinic in Rochester, Minnesota, for a complete examination. Doctors discovered he was suffering from amyotrophic lateral sclerosis, a progressive paralysis that was incurable. He was told he had two years to live, a chillingly accurate prediction.

On July 4, Lou Gehrig Day was held at Yankee Stadium. It was a sad and memorable day. Gehrig told the crowd that, despite the doctors' predictions, "I can say on this day that I consider myself the luckiest man on the face of the earth."

Ruth was present for the ceremony, and he impulsively hugged Gehrig, ending the feud. Their presence together was a reminder of how much the two had meant to the Yankees in the '20s and '30s. In less than ten years, they would both be dead.

Gehrig did youth work for the city until a month before his death, on June 2, 1941. Before he died, he was elected to the Hall of Fame, and the Yankees retired his uniform. He was the first Yankee so honored. Finally, he had outdone even Ruth.

13. The Best Team There Ever Was

Any serious discussion of the best baseball teams in history inevitably comes down to which of the great Yankee teams was the best.

The 1926–28 Yankees had Babe Ruth, and probably no team has ever been better in one season than the 1927 Yankees. The 1960–64 Yankees, led by Mickey Mantle, won five straight American League pennants. The 1949–53 Yankees of Casey Stengel won five consecutive World Series championships, a feat which will probably never be equalled.

But the best team of all may have been the 1936–39 Yankees, who won everything in sight with awesome ease.

That team was the first American League team to win four consecutive pennants, and the first team in baseball to win four straight World Series.

More impressive, though, was the ease with which they won. Their four pennants came by margins of 19½, 13, 9½, and 17, an average of nearly 15; the 1936 pennant was clinched on September 9, earliest date in American League history.

The Yankees lost only three games in the four World Series, sweeping the final two, matching the 1927–28 Yankees; nobody else has done that since. Only in '36 were they extended at all, to six games, and they won one game that Series, 18–4!

For the first three years of their run, the Yankees were a team without a serious weakness, which had not been true of the '27 Yankees, a team with mediocre catching. The '36–39 Yankees had Bill Dickey, often regarded as the best catcher in history.

Dickey was a Yankee only because of the alertness of the Yankee front office, always a significant factor in the team's success.

In 1928, he was playing for Little Rock, and most major league clubs assumed he would go to the Chicago White Sox, who had a working agreement with Little Rock. But the Yankees learned that Dickey was the property of Little Rock, and they made an offer for him, which was accepted.

Dickey came up for the final month of the '28 season and caught ten games. The next year he caught 130, starting a streak of 13 years in which he caught at least 100 games.

Bill Dickey was an outstanding catcher and hitter for the great Yankee teams of the '30's. *(New York Yankees)*

At 6'1½" and 185 pounds, Dickey was considered big for a catcher, but he was very quick, had excellent baseball sense, and had a great throwing arm. He was valuable for his defensive ability alone, but he was also an outstanding hitter.

Though playing a position which weakens players and usually detracts from their offensive abilities, he hit better than .300 in 10 of his first 11 seasons as a starter. He hit as high as .362 in 1936, and his lifetime average was .313. He also hit for power, with 102 home runs and 460 RBIs during the four straight championships.

At first base, the Yankees had Lou Gehrig for the first three championship years. His replacement, Babe Dahlgren, was a mediocre player, though he managed 89 RBIs in 1939.

At second base, the first two teams in that era had Tony Lazzeri, who had also been a key man on the championship teams of 1926, '27, '28, and '32. When Lazzeri was sold to the Chicago Cubs after the 1937 season, he was replaced by Joe Gordon, which even improved the team. Gordon was an acrobatic second baseman and a powerful hitter who had a total of 53 home runs and 208 RBIs in his first two seasons.

Frankie Crosetti, a superb fielder, was the shortstop. As with most teams, the Yankees were willing to sacrifice offense for defense at shortstop, and Crosetti—though he hit .288 in 1936—seldom hit for good average. But he had an ability to draw walks, so he was often on base for the Yankee sluggers, and he scored 486 runs in those four years.

At third base was the underrated Red Rolfe, an excellent fielder and a strong hitter. Rolfe hit .300 or better in three of those years; his best year was 1939, when he led the American League with 213 hits, 46 doubles, and 139 runs, with a batting average of .329.

In the outfield, the Yankees had several good outfielders—George Selkirk, Tommy Henrich, Jake Powell, Charlie Keller, and Ben Chapman—during that period. They also had one great outfielder, Joe DiMaggio. It is no coincidence that their pennant string started the first year DiMaggio played.

DiMaggio was a manager's dream, a superb player who always gave his best. He could do it all. In the field, he roamed the great distances of the Yankee Stadium center field to make great catches effortlessly. As a hitter, he had both power (as many as 46 home runs in a season) and consistency (as high as .381). On the bases, he was a brilliant runner, often taking the extra base but seemingly never getting caught in a foolish move.

The '30s were not an era of good pitching; the Yankees' staff earned run average of 4.17 was enough to lead the league in 1936. But the Yankees had three pitchers who deserve special mention, two starters and one relief pitcher.

The first starter was Red Ruffing, the Yankees' best during that stretch. Ruffing had a career which, to understate it, was very unusual, as he went from the losingest pitcher in the league to the winningest.

Ruffing had become a pitcher almost by default. A power hitter as a youngster, he had been forced out of a possible career as an outfielder by a mining accident which cost him four toes on his left foot. He found that his foot problem did not prevent him from pitching, so he turned to that.

He pitched two years in the minor leagues and then was brought up to stay in 1925 by the Boston Red Sox, who had purchased his contract from Danville, the first minor league club for whom he had played.

The Red Sox of that era were a model of consistency; they finished last in each of Ruffing's five full seasons with them. Accordingly, Ruffing's personal statistics were dismal. He was 9–18, 6–15, and 5–13 his first three seasons, and then it got worse. In 1928, he was 10–25; in 1929, 9–22. In each of those years, he was the losingest pitcher in the league.

But there is a saying in baseball that it takes a good pitcher to lose 20 games—because a bad one simply won't get the opportunity. Ruffing showed signs of ability: 25 complete games in 1928, for instance. The Yankees wanted him. The only question was whether they could get him. They had already gotten so many good players from the Red Sox—Babe Ruth, of course, but also Carl Mays, Herb Pennock, and Waite Hoyt, among others— that the Red Sox should have been leery of dealing with the Yankees.

But, early in the 1930 season, the Yankees were able to deal with the Red Sox, sending to Boston outfielder Cedric Durst and $50,000 for Ruffing. Presumably, the money helped the Red Sox. Durst didn't. He hit only .245 in 110 games and retired.

Meanwhile, Ruffing began a series of excellent years with the Yankees that eventually got him into the Hall of Fame. His turnaround was immediate; 0–3 at Boston in the first month of the 1930 season, he was 15–5 for the Yankees for the rest of the year.

His peak coincided with the Yankees, as he won 20, 20, 21, and 21 in the 1936–39 period. Eventually, 236 of his career 273 wins came with the Yankees.

Ruffing's bat was a factor in his success, too. He was an exceptional hitter for a pitcher, and he was even used as a pinch hitter at times. His career average was .269, and he had 36 home runs and 273 RBIs. That RBI figure is especially significant because Ruffing had only 1,937 at bats in his career, not much more than three full seasons for a regular.

The Yankees' top left-handed starter in that era was Lefty Gomez, although Gomez's best year came before the pennant string, when he was 26–5 in 1934. His best year during the championship era was 1937, when he was 21–11.

When Gomez first came up with the Yankees, he was primarily a fastball pitcher, and he three times led the league in strikeouts. Later, he developed a slow curve which was a big aid when he had arm trouble. But the thing which really set Gomez apart from other players was his wit.

After his retirement, Gomez became a very effective banquet speaker with a stock of funny baseball stories, some of which may even be true. In 1978 he was sent around the country by Gillette to speak to groups to publicize the All-Star game.

During his career, Gomez was able to joke even in the most tense moments. Once, with Jimmie Foxx at the plate, Dickey signaled for a fastball. Gomez shook him off. Dickey signaled for a curve. Gomez shook him off. Dickey signaled for a change. Gomez shook him off.

Dickey came out to the mound. "What do you want to throw this guy?"

Lefty Gomez was known for his wit, but his pitching was good enough to get him into the Hall of Fame. *(George Brace)*

he demanded. "To tell you the truth, Bill," said Gomez, "I don't want to throw him anything at all."

Once during a World Series game, Gomez stopped pitching to watch a plane flying overhead. Talking to a teammate one time, he said he planned to invent a rotating goldfish bowl, so the goldfish wouldn't have to do all the work. His nickname of "Goofy" was not without merit.

Gomez suffered from arm trouble periodically throughout his career, which held him to a total of 189 wins. But when he was healthy he was an outstanding pitcher, winning 26 games, 24, and 21 twice. There are other indications of his ability; twice he pitched 25 complete games in a season, for instance. In a hitter's era, he had three seasons in which his ERA was under 3.00 and in 1934 and '37, he had identical ERAs of 2.33. And he was best in the clutch, with a 6–0 mark in World Series games.

Lefty always liked to direct his humor at himself. One of his favorite lines was that he had made relief pitcher Johnny Murphy famous, the obvious implication being that Murphy had saved him many times. In truth, Gomez needed help less than most pitchers; when his arm was sound, he completed a high percentage of his starts. But Murphy certainly did become famous.

Murphy was the first Yankee relief pitcher who was successful over a period of time. Wilcy Moore had one great year in 1927 but wasn't effective after that. Murphy never had a year as spectacular as Moore's in 1927, but he was an effective reliever for the Yankees from 1935 through '43.

Murphy's Yankee career actually started in 1932, when he pitched 3⅓ innings in two games. He was returned to the minors the next season and came up to stay in 1934. But he appeared in half of his 40 contests that first year as a starter, and he had 10 complete games.

The next season, he was made into a reliever and was used only sporadically as a starter after that. In fact, he started only 20 more games during the rest of his career.

His most effective years were 1937–39, when he saved a total of 40 games (it should be noted that the rules defining "saves" were considerably stricter then). He was also a big factor in the 1941 and '42 pennants when he had 15 and 11 saves respectively. Those two totals led the league, as did his marks of 11 in 1938 and 19 in '39.

Five members of that team—Ruffing, Gomez, DiMaggio, Gehrig, and Dickey—were later voted into the Hall of Fame. So, fittingly, was the team's manager, Joe McCarthy.

McCarthy is one of the great managers of all time. In 24 years, with the Chicago Cubs, Yankees, and Red Sox, he never finished out of the first division. Eight times, his teams won pennants; six times, World Series. In 1926, he took over a Chicago team that had been last the year before; that first year, he brought them back to fourth, and by 1929, the Cubs were in the World Series.

McCarthy's reputation suffered somewhat during the Yankee years because of a remark made in jest by Jimmy Dykes, then the manager of the talent-starved Chicago White Sox.

Noting with envy the ability of the Yankee management to bring up good players from the farm system, Dykes commented that McCarthy had it easy, because if one player failed, he had only to push a button and another jumped up.

McCarthy's critics then labeled him a "push button manager," which probably bothered Dykes as much as McCarthy. Dykes had never intended the remark as criticism of McCarthy's managerial ability because he respected McCarthy.

To be sure, McCarthy had the players, but he also knew what to do with them. On a team of stars, no player got special privileges; it helped, of

Joe McCarthy became the first manager to win four straight World Series with the Yankees of 1936-39. *(New York Yankees)*

course, that Gehrig, DiMaggio, and Dickey, the biggest stars, did not demand anything extra.

McCarthy never let his team play less than its best. Psychological pressures make it difficult for a championship club to repeat. Once men have played on a team that wins a championship, there is a natural tendency to relax the next year, thinking the championship will come automatically. It is more difficult to win the second pennant than the first, and much more difficult to win a third straight pennant for that reason.

The premier example of that is probably the Philadelphia dynasty team of 1910–14. Connie Mack always felt the 1912 squad was the best in that era, but it was the only one which did not win a pennant. The players were overconfident and didn't give their all until it was too late.

That malaise didn't strike this Yankee team because McCarthy wouldn't let it. He kept the pressure on. Consequently, the fourth pennant in the string, which should have been the toughest, came as easily as the first. The Yankees won it by an incredible 17 games.

McCarthy also had the ability to recognize talent and know when changes had to be made. Gordon, for instance, was originally a shortstop, but Mc-

Carthy was convinced he could be switched successfully to second and, indeed, worked long hours with Gordon to facilitate the move. (McCarthy had been a minor league infielder in his playing career.)

Rolfe, too, was a shortstop, but McCarthy thought he lacked the arm to make the long throw from the hole. He talked to Rolfe about making the switch to third, telling him that all the talk about hot smashes down the line was ridiculous because Rolfe had the glove to stop them. In his first game at third, Rolfe had his eye blackened when a drive hit him there. "You gave me some bad advice, Joe," he said when he came back to the bench, but he stayed to become an excellent third baseman—and a great admirer of McCarthy.

When Charlie Keller came up to the Yanks, he hit the ball to all fields. In the International League of that time, fences were short all the way around, and Keller got a lot of home runs to left field, the off-field for a left-handed hitter. As a rookie with the Yankees in 1939, he hit .334—but with only 11 home runs. His drives to left were staying in the park.

McCarthy took him aside and talked to him of the virtues of pulling the ball at Yankee Stadium, where the right field fence was only 296 feet down the line. When Keller took batting practice, McCarthy had his pitchers throw him nothing but inside pitches, so Keller would get confidence in his ability to pull the ball. In his next five full seasons, Keller hit 141 home runs and, obviously, became much more valuable to the Yankees.

McCarthy had an almost unbelievable memory, too. Tommy Henrich told an interesting story in Donald Honig's, *Baseball Between the Lines,* concerning a player named Jimmy Wasdell.

Henrich had played with Wasdell in the minors in 1935 and knew him both as a friend and a good hitter. Wasdell came up with Washington in 1937, the same year Henrich came up with the Yankees. The first time he appeared against the Yankees, Ruffing was the pitcher, and Ruffing wondered aloud what to throw Wasdell.

McCarthy had seen Wasdell once, in an exhibition game in the spring. "He can't hit a change-up," he told Ruffing. Although Ruffing usually threw mostly fastballs, he threw a lot of change-ups to Wasdell, and McCarthy was right: Wasdell went oh-for-four.

McCarthy set the tone for the club. The Yankees were supposed to be dignified, and they were. They were expected to win, and they did. Players who didn't fit in were soon gone. When he moved to the Cubs, McCarthy got rid of Grover Cleveland Alexander because he knew he couldn't discipline others if Alexander was going his own way. For similar reasons, he got rid of Ben Chapman and Johnny Allen with the Yankees.

McCarthy was no fool, though, and he did not value conformity above talent. He talked Chicago owner William Wrigley into getting Rogers Hornsby before the 1929 season because he thought the Cubs could win with Hornsby. Wrigley did get Hornsby, and the Cubs did win the pennant, though Hornsby caused so many problems the next year that McCarthy was fired in September.

Finally, McCarthy was a very sound, fundamental manager. Theoretically, every manager should be. Actually, few are. McCarthy realized that physical errors are inevitable, but he constantly stressed the importance of being mentally alert. The Yankees did not throw to the wrong base, or disregard coach's signals. Any player who did came out of the game.

The Yankees were looking for a manager after the 1930 season, and McCarthy's availability made their choice easy. Joe won the pennant in 1932, and he got revenge when his team beat the Cubs in the World Series. That was the last Yankee pennant with Ruth, and it was in the Series that year that Ruth had his "called" home run. McCarthy later insisted that Ruth had pointed into the Cubs' dugout to silence hecklers, not at the center field bleachers where his subsequent home run landed.

Despite that pennant and World Championship, McCarthy's early seasons with the Yankees were frustrating; he finished second three years in a row. That may not seem like a long time to most managers and most clubs, but to McCarthy and the Yankees it seemed like eternity itself.

He had a lot of trouble with Ruth, who had wanted to be the Yankee manager. Ruth was still a good hitter, but his great years were behind him; his homer totals slipped to 34 and 22 in 1933 and '34, and his batting average to .301 and .288. He had slowed greatly in the field and on the base paths, and McCarthy was no doubt relieved when Ruth left the club in 1935.

The team was in transition from the glory days of the late '20s, but by 1936, most of the pieces were in place. The last one arrived that year, when DiMaggio came from the Pacific Coast League.

The year before, the Yankees had finished two games behind pennant-winning Detroit. In 1936, they finished 19½ games ahead of Detroit. DiMaggio wasn't the only reason for the turnaround, but he was probably the biggest one.

That was a big year for a lot of Yankees. Gehrig hit 49 home runs and knocked in 130 runs, both league highs, and was Most Valuable Player.

Tony Lazzeri was known as "Poosh-em-up, Tony" because of his ability to knock in runs for the Yankees. *(George Brace)*

Lazzeri, in his last big year, knocked in 109 runs. Dickey and Selkirk each knocked in 107. Ruffing won 20 games, Monte Pearson 19.

But it was DiMaggio who was the big story. Check these numbers: 206 hits, 44 doubles, 15 triples, 29 homers (88 extra-base hits), .323 average, 132 runs, 124 RBIs. Remember that he was a rookie, and remember also that he replaced Ben Chapman, who had hit .289 with only eight home runs and 74 RBIs the year before. Chapman couldn't field with DiMaggio, either.

In the World Series that fall, the Giants seemed able to make it interesting when Carl Hubbell, the famed "Mealticket," beat the Yankees, 6–1. The game was a tight one until the Giants scored four times off Ruffing in the eighth.

But the Yankees sent the Giants into shock with a 17-hit, 18–4 shellacking that set a Series record. There was really no question who would win after that. The Yankees won the third game, 2–1, and Hubbell was knocked out as the Yankees won Game Four, 5–2, to take a 3–1 Series lead.

The Giants hung in to win the fifth game, 5–4, but then the Yankees rolled out the big guns again in Game Six, winning 13–5, on another 17-hit explosion. It was awesome.

DiMaggio improved in the second year, as the great ones often do, hitting .346 with 46 homers, 167 RBIs, 151 runs scored. Gehrig had his last great year, with 37 homers, 159 RBIs, and a .351 average. (Neither of them was the Most Valuable Player, though; Detroit's Charley Gehringer, who hit .371, was.)

That was the year Henrich came to the Yankees, too, in an unusual deal. Just as DiMaggio and Gehrig symbolized one type of Yankee player, the superstar, Henrich symbolized another. One of the big factors in the Yankee success, in the '30s and at other times, too, has been their ability to get players who, though lacking spectacular ability, always seemed capable of making a big play when it counted. Henrich was a solid outfielder and a clutch hitter. His nickname was "Old Reliable," which says it all.

Henrich had been signed originally by Cleveland, and he had spent three years in the Cleveland organization, hitting .326 in D ball, .337 in C, and .346 in AA. But Cleveland general manager Cy Slapnicka thought more highly of another outfield prospect, Jeff Heath, than he did of Henrich.

Heath was brought up to Cleveland at the end of the 1936 season and went on to have a fine career, slightly better statistically than Henrich's. Meanwhile, Henrich was sold to Milwaukee, which was in the Cleveland organization.

After that sale, Henrich read stories saying that Milwaukee might sell him to the Boston Braves and that Cleveland might trade him to the St. Louis Browns. The latter story was an indication that Cleveland still had control of his destiny, which was a clear violation of baseball law—though not an uncommon one.

Henrich wrote a letter to baseball commissioner Judge Kenesaw Landis, describing what was happening. Eventually, he had a hearing with Landis

Tommy Henrich was known as "Old Reliable" for the Yankees because of his clutch hitting and fielding. *(George Brace)*

and was declared a free agent, apparently as much because Landis disliked Slapnicka as because Cleveland had violated a baseball rule.

Eight clubs made offers to Henrich. The Browns pursued him the hardest, but he didn't want to sign with them because they were perennial also-rans. Though he was from Ohio, he had always been a Yankee fan, and he wanted to play for the Yankees. His dad asked him if he thought he could make the club. Henrich's reasoning was that if he wasn't good enough, it didn't make any difference where he went, but if he was good enough, he wanted to play for the Yankees. He signed with them.

Henrich divided his time that year between the Yankees and Newark, their top farm club, hitting .320 in 67 games for the Yankees. He lasted through the 1950 season.

For the second straight year, the Yankees won 102 games, and for the second straight year, it was a subway World Series, as the Giants won in the National League. But the Giants were not as strong as they had been the season before, mainly because Bill Terry, a fearsome hitter and good first baseman, had become strictly a bench manager. His replacement, Johnny McCarthy, didn't scare pitchers as Terry had.

Nobody gave the Giants much chance in the Series, and the official line was correct. This was the Series in which Gomez paused on the pitching mound to watch a plane fly overhead. As it turned out, that was the highlight of the Series.

The Yankees smashed their way to 8–1 wins in each of the first two games and then took a 3–0 lead with a 5–1 win. Hubbell slowed the onslaught briefly with a 7–3 victory in the fourth contest, but then Gomez put the Giants away with a 4–2 win in the fifth game.

The Yankees had won easily, and with relatively little help from their best hitters. DiMaggio had batted only .273, Gehrig .294, with only three RBIs. Dickey, who had hit .332 and knocked in 133 runs during the season, had a Series high six RBIs, though he hit only .263. Lazzeri, sold to the Cubs after the Series, went out in high style for the Yankees, hitting .400.

McCarthy has said that he thought the 1938 team was the best he managed. Certainly it had a strong, well-balanced lineup. Gordon played his first year at second and added power with 25 homers; Henrich was a starter in right field. The pitching was probably the soundest of any of the championship teams, with Ruffing winning 21, Gomez 18, Pearson 16, and Spud Chandler 14, and Murphy having his first big year in relief, saving 11 games.

Curiously, though, that team was the only one in the stretch that failed to win 100 games, stopping at 99. That was good enough for a 9½ game bulge over the Red Sox.

In the World Series, the Yankees swept by the Chicago Cubs, 3–1, 6–3, 5–2 and 8–3. The only real drama came in the second game. A sore-armed Dizzy Dean, relying on soft curves because his great fastball was gone, took a 3–2 lead into the eighth inning. Then, Frankie Crosetti hit a two-run homer.

As Crosetti circled the bases, a defiant Dean said, "I wish I could call back one year, Frank. You wouldn't get a loud foul off me."

"You're so right, Diz!" Crosetti yelled back over his shoulder. "You're so right!"

The Yankees seemed vulnerable in 1939. Gehrig's shocking inability to do anything in spring training and the very early season affected the other players, though they didn't realize Lou was ill. They only thought he was through as a player. He ran as if the base paths were all uphill, and he could manage only four feeble singles in eight games before he took himself out of the lineup.

Until May 11, the Yankees bounced back and forth between first place and second. In early July, just before the All-Star break, the Red Sox came into Yankee Stadium and won five straight, including a couple of double-headers. Boston was tremendous at the plate that year with Ted Williams, in his rookie season, batting .327 with 31 homers and a league-leading 145 RBIs, Jimmie Foxx hitting .360 with 35 homers and 105 RBIs, Joe Cronin at .308 with 107 RBIs, Bobby Doerr hitting .318 and Doc Cramer .311.

A loss in Detroit immediately after the All-Star break extended the Yankees' string to six, but then McCarthy got them back on the track and they breezed the rest of the way, winning 106 games—the most in the four-year stretch—and burying the Red Sox, who finished 17 games back.

The Yankees had some great individual performances that year—DiMaggio hit .381, his lifetime best, and Ruffing won 21 games—but McCarthy had to juggle this team more than his previous ones, especially the pitching staff. Gomez's arm problems limited him to 12 wins; though he wasn't even 30 years old until after the World Series that year, his great seasons were behind him. McCarthy had no real number 2 starter behind Ruffing, but he had a lot of good pitchers: Atley Donald won 13 games, including his first 12; Gomez, Bump Hadley, and Monte Pearson all won 12; Steve Sundra was 11–1; Oral Hildebrand won 10 games.

Balance was also the story offensively. The Yankees had five .300 hitters, including Keller in his rookie season. They had four hitters with 20 or more home runs and 100 or more RBIs—MVP DiMaggio, with 30 homers and 126 RBIs; Gordon, 28 and 111; Dickey, 24 and 105; and Selkirk, 21 and 101.

In the Series, the Yankees again swept, this time over the Cincinnati Reds, 2–1, 4–0, 7–3, and 7–4. The last game went ten innings, but the key to the Series was the first game, between Ruffing and Cincinnati ace Paul Derringer, a 25-game winner in the regular season.

Going into the bottom of the ninth, the score was tied, 1–1. Keller led off with a triple, putting the winning run on base with DiMaggio, Dickey, and Selkirk coming up.

The baseball "book" called for the Reds to walk both DiMaggio and Dickey to load the bases and then pull the infield in, so a ground ball could result in a home-to-first double play. Instead, Cincinnati manager Bill McKechnie walked DiMaggio but then pitched to Dickey, always known as a good clutch hitter.

McKechnie was worried about pitching to Selkirk because George was a low-ball hitter, and Derringer would have to pitch to his strength, trying to get a ground ball. Because Dickey was slow, McKechnie thought the Reds had a chance to get a double play on a ground ball while still holding Keller at third.

Watching from the dugout, Henrich knew better. When he saw that the Reds were going to pitch to Dickey, he picked up his glove and prepared to go into the clubhouse. He knew Dickey would get the run in and Bill didn't disappoint him, hitting a ground ball past second baseman Hal Frey.

The amazing thing about that Yankee team was how close it came to winning eight consecutive pennants. Only a third-place finish in 1940 stopped them, and they almost pulled that one off, too.

That was a curious year, for the Yankees and for the American League. Bob Feller had a great year, winning 27 games, but his accomplishments were overshadowed by the "Cry Baby" reputation his Cleveland teammates got because they tried to get rid of manager Oscar Vitt. Detroit had great hitting, with Hank Greenberg and Rudy York. But it was the Yankees' decline that made it a race.

The Yankees fielded exactly the same lineup that had swept to an easy pennant and World Championship the year before, but the performances were vastly different. They spent two weeks in May in last place and were no better than .500 as late as early August.

Then, they streaked, winning 16 of 19. After the first game of a double-header in Cleveland on September 11, they were in first place. They were ready to take command again, it seemed, but it didn't happen. The Indians won the second game, and the Yankees never regained the lead, though they finished just two games back of the Tigers.

Perhaps the Yankees were getting old. Ruffing, after all, was 36, Dickey 33, Selkirk 32, Rolfe and Gomez 31. But that age didn't seem to matter the next year, when DiMaggio's 56-game hitting streak helped power his team to 101 wins and a remarkably easy pennant, by 17 games over second-place Boston.

This was practically the same team that had finished third the year before. Henrich was the starting right fielder, replacing Selkirk, but statistically, the change was hardly noticeable: Henrich hit .277 with 85 RBIs, Selkirk had hit .269 in 1940 with 73 RBIs. At first base, Johnny Sturm replaced Babe Dahlgren, but the offensive production actually fell off there, from Dahlgren's .264 and 73 RBIs to Sturm's weak .239 and only 36 RBIs.

In the 1942 and '43 seasons, the draft materially weakened the Yankees, as it did everybody, but enough quality players remained for the Yankees to win two more pennants and again by impressive margins, 9 and 13½ games, respectively.

It was an incredible period of mastery for the Yankees, seven pennants in eight years and only one World Series loss. Casey Stengel's Yankees would later have an even more impressive record, wresting nine pennants in ten years, but Stengel's teams usually had a battle to win. McCarthy's teams never did. There was never any suspense after midseason in any of their pennant years. That's dominance.

THE TRANSITION PERIOD

14. A Schoolboy Mows 'em Down

It was a meaningless exhibition game between the St. Louis Cardinals and Cleveland Indians in July of 1936, and a young right-hander, walking with the bouncing stride of a farmboy, took the mound for the Indians in the fourth inning. His warm-up pitches sounded like the crack of a whip as they hit the glove of Steve O'Neill, catcher and manager of the Indians.

Watching in the opposite dugout, Cardinal playing manager Frankie Frisch was suddenly glad that he was only a manager and not a player in this particular game. "That kid's the fastest pitcher I've ever seen," he mused.

"The "kid" was Bob Feller. He was so unknown then that the public address announcer added an *s* to his name, and Dizzy Dean after the game called him "Fellows." But his debut was one of the most spectacular in major league history, and it would not be long before his name was very well known, indeed.

Feller was strictly a thrower, not a pitcher. He couldn't field his position; he knew nothing about holding runners on base; and his curve was such a tentative pitch that O'Neill had told him to forget it for this game and use only his fastball.

But what a fastball! Very quickly, he was compared to Lefty Grove and Walter Johnson, and the plate umpire for Feller's first game, Red Ormsby, called him faster than Johnson.

The first major league batter Feller faced, Cardinal catcher Bruce Ogrodowski, realized the futility of trying to hit that fastball. Ogrodowski bunted and was thrown out.

The first two pitches to the next batter, Leo Durocher, went whizzing over his head to the backstop. "Keep the ball in the park, busher," yelled Durocher.

The next two pitches were strikes, and then O'Neill said, "You'd better be careful, Leo. He's liable to put this next one in your ear."

Durocher pretended to be frightened, and no doubt his fright was not all pretense. He ran back to the dugout and hid behind the water cooler. Umpire Cal Hubbard yelled at him to come back because he had another strike coming.

"The hell with you, Hubbard," yelled Durocher. "You take it for me." On the Cardinal bench, those players who were not in the game were laughing. Those who knew they'd have to step in against Feller didn't see the humor in the situation.

Durocher finally came back to take his third strike. He might as well have let Hubbard take it; Leo missed the pitch by a foot. That was the first of eight strikeouts in three innings for Feller, two against Durocher.

But that was only an exhibition. What would he do in a league game? The baseball world soon found out.

The Indians used Feller only occasionally in relief until August 23. They were playing the St. Louis Browns that day at League Park in Cleveland. By this time, they were well out of the pennant race, and O'Neill thought the seventh-place Browns would be a good team to start Feller against.

Again, Feller stuck strictly with his fastball, and that was all he needed. After five innings, he had struck out ten batters. After seven, he had 14 strikeouts. The American League record, set by Rube Waddell in 1908, was only 16.

Feller didn't quite make it. He didn't get any strikeouts in the eighth inning and only one in the ninth, as Lyn Lary became the last out in Feller's 4–1 win, his first in the big leagues.

But those 15 strikeouts were an amazing achievement for a rookie in his first start. Nobody has ever done better. Strikeouts were not nearly so common then as they are now, either, because batters used thicker-handled bats and cut down their swings when they had two strikes.

Some sluggers now feel it is a fair exchange to strike out four or five times as often as they hit home runs. In 1936, it was quite different. Lou Gehrig, for instance, hit 49 home runs and struck out only 46 times. Joe DiMaggio had 29 homers, 39 strikeouts; Hal Trosky, Feller's teammate on the Indians, had 42 homers, 58 strikeouts. The only hitter who had more than 100 strikeouts in the American League that year was Jimmie Foxx, at 119. The pitcher with the most strikeouts was Detroit's Tommy Bridges, with 175.

Thus, Feller's 15 strikeouts created quite a stir, but he was soon to do even better. On September 13, he faced the Philadelphia Athletics, again at Cleveland, and his fastball was never better.

Even the fastest of pitchers needs something more than sheer speed, because eventually, the batters will time the pitches and hit them. The strikeout pitchers always have a fastball that "moves," either rising or sinking, and Feller was no exception. His fastball was a rising one, and on his best days it also moved in on right-handed hitters. That's exactly what was happening when he took the mound against the A's.

Because his fastball was so active, Feller had even more trouble than usual in controlling it, and he walked nine men. He also gave up nine stolen bases–to a team which stole only 59 all season. But none of that mattered, because Feller was striking out A's even faster than he was walking them.

By this time, Feller had also developed a curve and, though still not the great pitch it would become, he had enough confidence in it to use it in critical situations, though the fastball was still his primary pitch.

After eight innings, Feller had tied Waddell's league record with 16 strikeouts. He was tiring, though. He got Frankie Hayes on a pop fly to start the ninth inning but walked pinch-hitter Les Moss. That brought up George Puccinelli, who had struck out twice before. The count went to 3–2, and then Feller, figuring Puccinelli would be looking for a fastball, threw a curve that broke across the plate. Puccinelli watched it for Feller's 17th strikeout.

That strikeout, Feller's last in his 5–2 win, set a league record and tied Dizzy Dean's major league mark. Feller had struck out every A's player at least once. He had struck out the side twice and had missed a strikeout in only one inning, the fourth. It was an amazing performance.

And then, he went back to school. He was only 17, and had his senior year in high school ahead of him.

Feller's success came as no surprise to his father, who had planned it that way. The senior Feller had been an excellent semipro pitcher in his youth, but playing baseball was not a very profitable career in those days, so he had stuck to farming.

But his dream lived on in his son, and he started preparing Bob for a baseball career very early. Bob first thought of himself as an infielder or outfielder and a powerful hitter, but it soon became obvious that his future was in pitching.

Father and son spent many hours playing catch on the farm near Van Meter, Iowa. In the summer, it would be outside the barn; in the winter, they would go inside.

When Bob was 12, he and his father built their own baseball field, leveling land and clearing trees. The senior Feller started his own team—with Bob as the pitcher, of course—and even charged 35 cents admission for the games. Feller later remembered crowds of as many as a thousand people at those contests.

Building a field for your son is admittedly a little extreme, but in his other actions William Feller was not a great deal different from thousands of other American fathers. Many fathers have played long hours of "catch" with their sons and have been just as confident as William Feller that their sons would be major league players. Very few of them ever were. The difference in Feller's case was not his father's dedication but his own talent.

By 1933, that talent made it obvious that Bob had outgrown the Van Meter competition, and so he joined an American Legion team in Des Moines. Soon, he was attracting notice there, too, and an anonymous umpire wrote letters to Cleveland general manager Cy Slapnicka, raving about Feller.

Quickly, Feller had outgrown American Legion ball, too; by 1935, he was pitching semipro ball in Des Moines. On July 21, 1935, he was working in the wheat fields with his dad when Slapnicka came walking through the fields to meet him.

Slapnicka was in the neighborhood primarily to take a look at Claude Passeau, who eventually signed that year with Pittsburgh and went on to have a fine major league career. Since Feller was pitching in the same league, Slapnicka decided he might as well have a look at him, too. What the Cleveland executive saw when Feller pitched drove all thoughts of Claude Passeau out of his mind.

Baseball law at that time prohibited major league clubs from signing amateur or semipro players. In theory, minor league clubs signed the players and then sold them to major league clubs. In practice, major league clubs signed them, and then assigned the players to minor league clubs in their organizations.

So, Slapnicka assigned Feller to the Fargo-Morehead, North Dakota team of the Northern League and told him to report after he got out of school the next season.

The signing was kept secret, and Feller's performances attracted more and more attention. He averaged 19 strikeouts a game for his Farmers Union team and had a 23-strikeout, one-hitter when he pitched for an Iowa All-Star team in postseason play.

That really brought the scouts around, including a Cleveland scout who had not been told that his organization had already signed Feller. Slapnicka was a man who knew how to keep a secret, all right.

Feller never pitched for Fargo-Morehead, or any minor league team. He developed a sore arm in the spring of '36, and Slapnicka had him report directly to Cleveland, to have his arm checked and taken care of.

Soon, Feller's arm seemed all right again, and Slapnicka arranged for him to pitch for the Cleveland Rosenblums, an amateur league. He won his first game, 3–2, in 12 innings, and then he pitched the previously mentioned exhibition against the Cardinals.

Some strange maneuverings followed. Slapnicka wanted Feller to get more pitching experience, and he had Bob pitch one more game for the Rosenblums. That caused a lot of comment in the amateur league, as you can imagine. Feller lost the game, incidentally, though he struck out 15.

Meanwhile, Slapnicka had transferred Feller's contract to New Orleans, but he didn't send Feller there, either. He decided he wanted Feller to stay in Cleveland, where he would get the best possible handling.

Feller later said it took him three years to learn to pitch in the major leagues, and his deficiencies were obvious that first season. He walked 47 men in 62 innings, for instance; he tipped off his pitches by holding his arms differently when he was throwing a curve; and runners stole bases with ease.

But there was so much natural ability there that it was obvious he was going to be a great pitcher. He had brilliant outings—the 15- and 17-strike-out games mentioned were the best—and he struck out an astounding 76 batters in 62 innings.

Thus, it was a headline story when the news broke that Feller was signed illegally and might be made a free agent.

The story came out when the Des Moines club of the Western Association complained to baseball commissioner Judge Kenesaw Landis that Feller had been signed illegally. Des Moines had offered $7,500 to Feller's father, apparently after Slapnicka had signed Feller.

Landis held a hearing with Feller and his father and Cleveland executives in the winter between the 1936 and '37 seasons. Technically, there was no question Cleveland was in the wrong, and indeed, Landis ruled against Cleveland in the Tommy Henrich case that same winter, in similar circumstances.

But there were extenuating circumstances in Feller's case. Landis, and everybody else, knew that major league clubs were constantly violating the rule. It had obviously been Slapnicka's intention to send Feller to Fargo-Morehead originally, and that plan was changed only because of Feller's sore arm.

The most important point, though, was the fact that if Feller were made a free agent, it would start an unprecedented bidding war among major league clubs. Feller's potential was so awesome that he could certainly have gotten $100,000 as a free agent which, in terms of what the dollar can buy, was comparable to the huge amounts players like Reggie Jackson and Catfish Hunter have since commanded.

Landis didn't want that. He ruled that Cleveland had to pay Des Moines $7,500, but could keep Feller. Both Bob and his father were pleased with the decision. They felt Cleveland had treated him very fairly, and he wanted to stay with the Indians. (If he'd been ruled a free agent, Cleveland could not even have bid for him.) And as it turned out, Feller eventually became a rich man, through the money he made with the Indians and his wisdom in investing it.

The Indians were pleased, too, because they were able to keep a pitcher who became one of the greatest in history. Feller showed steady improvement the next two years, finishing at 9–7 and 17–11, and blossomed into the best in baseball in 1939, when he was 24–9. There is little doubt he ranks with the greatest American League pitchers, Johnson and Grove.

The nearly four full seasons that he lost because of World War II robbed Feller of a chance to compile some incredible career statistics. In the two years immediately before he went into the service and the first full season after he came out, for instance, he averaged 26 wins and nearly 290 strikeouts. Assuming, reasonably enough, that he would have pitched at that pace during the four years he missed, he would have finished his career with 365 wins and a major league record 3,711 strikeouts; his career marks are 266 and 2,581.

As it is, Feller set major league records for strikeouts in a game, 18, against Detroit in 1938, and for a season, 348 in 1946—both of which have since been broken. But his greatness is not measured only by statistics but also by the awe in which he was regarded by his contemporaries. He was in a class by himself.

Some fastball pitchers throw only one pitch. Johnson was like that. Grove learned to throw a curve only after his fastball had lost its steam. Nolan Ryan is essentially a fastball pitcher. Feller was different. He developed his curve early and liked to say it was his most effective pitch. He threw it at nearly the speed of his fastball, and hitters often assumed it was a fastball—until, too late, they saw the ball swerve under their bats.

But it was the fastball that people loved to see. He was a spectacular pitcher and such a draw that he had attendance clauses written into his contract in the postwar years.

Even his one weakness, a lack of control (especially in his early years), was often an asset. Knowing how wild and fast he was, batters were afraid to dig in.

In his first game against the Boston Red Sox, in 1936, for instance, Feller threw his first pitch *behind* Billy Werber!

"When the ball whizzed behind him," recalled Al Schacht, a Boston coach at the time, "Werber went sprawling across the plate. He was white and shaken when he got to his feet . . . I said to myself, 'No wonder this kid gets so many strikeouts.' "

Feller pitched more low-hit games than any pitcher in history. His three no-hit games tied Cy Young's mark (though Sandy Koufax and Nolan Ryan have since pitched four), and he stands alone with eleven one-hit games. No other pitcher has more than five in modern times.

His first no-hitter came on opening day, 1940, and is the answer to a trivia question: In which game did all the hitters on one team have the same batting average at the end of the game as they had at the start? The Chicago White Sox all were hitting .000 at both the start and end of that game.

His third one, in 1951, was the most remarkable because he had lost his great fastball by then and was pitching with guile. But it was his second no-hitter, against the Yankees in 1946, that gave him the most satisfaction— because of the circumstances and because it was against the Yankees, a team he hated.

Feller had come out of the navy in 1945 in time to win five games (losing three) and strike out 59 hitters in 72 innings. After the season, he went on a barnstorming tour to get into prime baseball condition for the next season, and at 27, he was in the age span usually considered to be an athlete's prime.

He pitched a 1-0 win over Chicago on opening day in '46, but then lost his next two starts. Suddenly, there were reports that he had lost his fastball while he was in the service. When he went out to face the Yankees on April 30 in Yankee Stadium, he had a lot to prove.

He quickly silenced his doubters by pitching the first no-hitter against the Yankees since September 10, 1919. There was only one really tough play, and that came on the second Yankee batter of the game, George Stirnweiss, who hit a slow chopper behind the mound. Shortstop Lou Boudreau came in to make a great play and throw, getting Stirnweiss by a split second.

Feller knew he was pitching a no-hitter, but he had another concern: winning the game. Floyd "Bill" Bevens, later to come so close to a no-hitter in the World Series of 1949, was giving up hits—six in the first eight innings—but no runs, and the game was 0-0 through eight.

Finally, Frankie Hayes led off the top of the ninth with a home run and

Bob Feller set a strikeout record in 1946 and was the first pitcher to have his fastball timed — at more than 98 miles an hour. *(Cleveland Indians)*

Feller had a lead for the first time. Then, in the bottom of the ninth, Stirnweiss reached base when his grounder was bobbled by Cleveland first baseman Les Fleming.

The next hitter was Tommy Henrich, consistently the toughest out in the league for Feller. But Yankee manager Joe McCarthy was playing the percentages, going for one run. He had Henrich sacrifice, which he did successfully.

Joe DiMaggio then grounded to Boudreau, with Stirnweiss moving to third. Then, Charley Keller hit a grounder to Cleveland second baseman Ray Mack, who stumbled fielding it. After the game, Feller said he thought the ball would have been a hit if Mack couldn't have made the play; the official scorer said it would have been an error. The decision never had to be made, though, as Mack threw out Keller to save Feller's no-hitter.

Feller went on to have his greatest season, winning 26 games, losing only 15, pitching ten shutouts, notching a 2.18 earned run average, and striking out a record 348 batters. He also completed 36 of the 42 games he started and pitched 371 innings.

He did all of this, too, with a weak ball club. The Indians finished sixth, at 68–86; in the games in which Feller did not figure in the decision, they were only 42–71. With a strong team like the pennant-winning Red Sox, Feller probably would have been the American League's first 30-game winner since Lefty Grove.

That was the year, too, that Feller became the first pitcher whose speed was officially clocked. It happened in Washington. Clark Griffith, the Senators' owner, was seeking to capitalize on the drawing power of Feller, probably the American League's most spectacular player since Babe Ruth, and he borrowed a photoelectric device from the nearby Aberdeen, Maryland, ordnance plant.

Griffith planned to have Feller throw through the device before the game. He advertised that, and probably an additional 20,000 fans came to the game because of it. He didn't tell Feller, though, until just before the game.

Told that he'd have to throw 30 pitches or so through the device, Feller balked. He did, after all, have a game to pitch that night. He finally agreed to do it, for $700, and his fastball was timed at 98.6 mph. Ryan has done better than that since, being timed at slightly more than 100 mph in 1974, though there is some question whether Ryan is actually faster than Feller was or just benefiting from more sophisticated measuring equipment.

Feller always thought he was faster during the 1946 season and in early '47 than ever, and his strikeout statistics support that belief. That great fastball disappeared, though, in a game before the All-Star break in '47.

Pitching against the Athletics in Philadelphia, Feller had what he thought might have been the best fastball of his career, striking out nine of the first 11 batters. He hadn't thrown even one curve.

Then, he threw his first curve of the night to the next hitter, Barney McCoskey. He stepped a little differently for his curve than he did his fastball, and as he stepped, he hit some loose dirt. His leg skidded straight out and he fell hard, injuring his knee and his shoulder. He had to come out of the game, and he missed several starts for the Indians—and the All-Star game, which got him some criticism he didn't deserve.

Feller went on to win 20 games that season, but he was never again the overpowering pitcher he had been. His strikeout statistics tell the story: from 348 in '46 to 164 (though that was still good enough to lead the league) in '48. By 1949, he was down to 108 strikeouts, and his three-year total, 1949–51, was only 338, ten less than in his one great season.

To Feller's credit, he adjusted remarkably well to the loss of his fastball. In fact, he won 118 games in the years after 1947, including a 22–8 season in 1951, when he was the leading winner in the league.

The parallel with Grove is fascinating. Grove, too, lost his fastball, though it was a sore arm and age that caused it, not an injury in a game. In his years with Boston, Lefty never had an outstanding fastball, but he won 105 games and had one 20-win season. Strength of character was obviously a big factor in the success of both Feller and Grove.

The one big disappointment of Feller's career was that he didn't win a World Series game. When he was at his peak, the Indians weren't; when they were champions, he was down.

He did pitch one excellent game, throwing a two-hitter against the Boston Braves in the opener of the 1948 Series. But the Braves won the game, 1–0, when Phil Masi scored the only run of the game in the eighth inning. The loss was particularly galling because Cleveland players thought they had picked Masi off second two batters earlier. Pictures of the play supported that view, but the umpire's decision—and Feller's loss—stood.

The Indians won the next three games, and Boudreau gave Feller another chance in the fifth game, which would have been the last if Cleveland had won.

But Feller was no mystery to the Braves' hitters the second time around. They scored three times off him in the top of the first, added another run in the third and another in the sixth. Still, Boudreau stuck with him, because the Indians were hitting well, too. The score was tied at 5–5 after six innings, and Boudreau hoped Feller could hang on to win.

He couldn't. The Braves knocked Feller out in the seventh with six runs, which held up for an 11–5 win. The Series was extended to a sixth game (which the Indians won, to wrap it up), and that game would be in Boston, making necessary a train trip which Francis Stann of *The Washington Star* called "A Sentimental Journey." Stann and other writers felt that the Indians would have won the game if Feller had been taken out early, and they were probably right, but Boudreau felt that Feller should have had every chance at a win because of what he had done for the Indians over the years, and Lou was right, too.

That was Feller's last chance. The Indians won one more pennant during his career, in 1954, but he was just a spot starter then, though an effective one with a 13–3 record. The New York Giants swept the Series that fall, and Feller never got into a game.

15. Superb Prewar Vintage

Baseball, like wine, has its vintage years, and for connoisseurs of the game, 1941 was a year to savor. Ted Williams did something that year that hasn't been done since, and Joe DiMaggio did something that had never been done before.

Inevitably, the two players were often compared during their careers, which overlapped from 1939 through 1951, because they so dominated the game. That comparison was most apt in 1941, when Williams hit .406 and DiMaggio hit safely in 56 straight games.

Yet, the comparison was invalid. The two were so different as players that picking between them was like trying to decide whether an apple or an orange is better. DiMaggio also had the advantage of playing on Yankee teams which were almost always better than the Red Sox teams on which Williams performed.

DiMaggio was certainly the better all-round player. In American League history, only Tris Speaker and Mickey Mantle rank with DiMaggio in combination of hitting, fielding, and base-running skills.

Truly, DiMaggio could do it all. He hit for average: as high as .381 in a season and .325 lifetime. He hit for power: 46 homers one year. Until crippled by injury, he was the best defensive outfielder in baseball. And he seemed never to make a wrong move running the bases.

Most of all, he made it look easy. Seemingly without effort, he performed the most extraordinary deeds. Baseball writers continually described DiMaggio as smooth, graceful, elegant. He was the aristocrat of baseball players, and he made baseball seem almost more a form of artistic expression than a sport.

His batting swing was flawless; the results, impeccable. One of the most telling statistics in his career is the fact that he never struck out as many as 40 times in a season. He had only 369 career strikeouts. And in his five best seasons, 1937–41, he had more home runs than strikeouts each season.

In the outfield, his greatness was measured not in what he did but in what he didn't have to do. He seldom had to make spectacular catches because he reacted so quickly and smoothly when the ball was hit that he was waiting for drives that went 400 feet. He didn't have to make spectacular throws because base runners so respected his strong and accurate arm that they didn't challenge it.

Playing on a team which consistently sought the big inning, DiMaggio was never asked to steal bases. As a base runner, though, he was probably the most respected in the league. He had the ability to accelerate quickly to top speed, and he was unexcelled at going from first to third on a single. That kind of skill seldom shows in the box score, but it often means the difference between winning and losing a game.

In one area, though, even DiMaggio deferred to Williams: Ted was clearly the better hitter. Williams, in fact, may have been the best hitter in baseball history.

The case for Williams does not rest on absolute statistics; he is clearly inferior to Ruth and Ty Cobb in that department. Cobb hit .367 in his career, Williams .344; Ruth hit 714 home runs, while batting .342, and Williams stopped at 521.

But Cobb and Ruth and Williams all played in different eras. Night baseball, the ever-increasing use of relief pitchers, and improved fielders' gloves have combined to drive down batting averages. It is not fair to measure Williams's marks against those compiled by Ruth and Cobb during epochs in which hitters had more advantages.

In recent years several systems have been invented which attempt to compare players from different eras. These relate a player's career performance to that of his contemporaries. Williams does very well in these comparisons. Let's look at two representative samples.

BaseStats, a system devised by Bob Enderlin, factors in all aspects of offensive play—hitting for average, total bases, run production, and stolen bases—and rates the combined figure against a league average of 100. In that system, Ruth's career comes out at 153, highest in baseball history; Williams is 152; Cobb, 147.

In *Relative Baseball*, Merritt Clifton devised a system which rates hitters against their contemporaries in separate categories: 1) Home runs; 2) Batting average; and 3) Slugging percentage. Williams is the only hitter who ranks in the top 15—indeed, he is in the top three—in every category.

In home runs, Ruth is first, Gavvy Cravath second, Williams third. Cobb is not in the top 15. In batting average, Rod Carew is first, Williams second, Cobb, interestingly, only third. Ruth is not in the top 15. In slugging percentage, Ruth is first, Williams second, DiMaggio third. Again, Cobb does not make the top 15.

Obviously, nobody hits as Williams did without having outstanding physical ability. Williams's special asset was his eyesight. When he was tested in World War II, it was learned that his eyesight was much better than 20/20; American League pitchers and umpires had learned that through empirical testing earlier.

But Ted's biggest asset was probably his determination to become a great hitter. In all baseball history, it's likely only Cobb and Rogers Hornsby ever matched Williams as a student of hitting. Williams was always eager to talk about hitting, and he and Cobb had many conversations on the subject.

Williams's basic theory was this: Never swing at a bad pitch. He would take a pitch an inch off home plate, and umpires never questioned his judgment. Because of this, and because of the caution which pitchers used in working to him, he walked extraordinarily often, leading the league in walks eight times. Twice he walked 162 times in a season, and only Ruth has walked more; Williams's career total of 2,019 walks is also second only to Ruth's.

His critics—and Williams had many—argued that he walked too frequently. They thought that with men on base Williams should have been willing to swing at a close pitch rather than accept a walk. Williams argued that if he started swinging at pitches just off the plate, pitchers would soon have him chasing pitches further and further away. At any rate, Williams knocked in at least 100 runs in every season in which he played at least 140 games.

Williams also was willing to take one strike, and sometimes two, to get his pitch. When he had two strikes, he would swing at anything in the strike zone, but before that, he would not swing at a low strike. He felt the percentages were with him; sometime in the course of his time at bat he would get a pitch at belt or chest level, and he could do a lot more with that pitch than one just above the knees. Usually, he was right.

His swing combined the best features of Ruth's and Cobb's. Even as a skinny kid when he came up, only 170 pounds strung out over a 6'4" frame, he could generate great power with his wrist snap; his first home run in the majors was a 450-foot shot into the right-center bleachers at Fenway. But he didn't overswing, as Ruth often did, so he had relatively few strikeouts, only 709 in his career. Only three times did he strike out more than 50 times in a season, a remarkable figure for a man who ranked third on the all-time home run list when he retired.

Because his power came from his wrists, Williams was able to wait longer on a pitch than most hitters. He could pull even the best fastball, and, unlike many sluggers, he could not be pulled off balance swinging at a change of pace. His ability to hit the change was one of the most remarkable aspects of Williams's hitting, and there was no better example of that than the home run he hit off Rip Sewell's blooper pitch in the 1946 All-Star game.

Because Williams was a pronounced pull hitter, Cleveland manager Lou Boudreau came up with a shift against Williams that pulled all his fielders over to the right side, and put the third baseman in the normal shortstop position.

The shift, of course, left the defense wide open to either a bunt down the third base line or a ball hit to left field, but Boudreau reasoned that he would rather have Williams try that than hit the ball over the right field fence, or against it.

That shift caused an endless debate during the rest of Williams's career. Some (Cobb being in the forefront) argued that Williams should hit to the open spaces in left field and keep hitting there until the defense had to play normally against him. Others argued that Williams was being paid to hit the long ball, not just the automatic singles he would have gotten to the left side.

In fact, Williams did hit more to left field than is popularly assumed today, but most of the time he challenged the defense and hit to the right side. He certainly lost some hits that way, but even the stacked defense could not cope with the line drives he rocketed into the empty spaces or the balls he hit over the fence.

Older than Williams by almost four years, DiMaggio came up before him, too, in 1936. He was billed as the "next Babe Ruth," which he wasn't, quite, but only because the Yankees are *still* looking for the "next Babe Ruth."

DiMaggio was born in Martinez, California, but his family moved to nearby San Francisco, the town with which he has since been identified, when he was only an infant. His father was a fisherman and both parents were Italian immigrants; his birth certificate actually read Guiseppe Paolo, which became Joseph Paul by the time he went to school.

His father thought young Joe lazy because he was unwilling to work mending fishing nets. Joe didn't like school, either. All he wanted to do was play baseball, and he dropped out of Galileo High in his senior year to join a local semipro team.

He was signed for the last week of that season, 1932, by the San Francisco Seals and became a sensation the next year. A shortstop until then, he was switched to the outfield, where he was erratic for the only time in his career, making 17 errors but also leading the league with 32 assists.

But it was his hitting which had everybody talking. He hit .340 and knocked in 169 runs. More important, he hit in 61 straight games, breaking a Pacific Coast League record of 49 which had been set in 1914. And he was only 19. "I was just a kid then," said DiMaggio. "I never felt any pressure in that streak. I was having too much fun."

The Seals were an independent operation, not part of a major league farm system, and they kept DiMaggio for another season, waiting for his value to escalate. As he continued his fine hitting—he hit .341 in 1934—major league clubs were offering as much as $75,000 for him, a tremendous sum.

And then, DiMaggio hurt his knee. Coming home from a dinner at the home of one of his married sisters, DiMaggio had been sitting awkwardly in the back seat of a cab and his left foot had fallen asleep. When he stepped out of the cab on that foot, his leg collapsed and he heard four sharp cracks at the knee. "The pain was terrific," he said, "like a whole set of aching teeth in my knee."

Though it took some time to diagnose what had happened, DiMaggio finally learned he had torn cartilage in his knee. He was through for the season. Most of the major league clubs which had been going after him backed off, so the Yankees were able to get him for $25,000 and five players—with the stipulation that DiMaggio would stay with the Seals for the 1935 season.

His knee sound again, DiMaggio had a great season with the Seals in '35, hitting .398 with 34 homers and 154 RBIs. He was ready. He was more than ready.

Throughout his career, DiMaggio was bothered by a series of injuries which, combined with the loss of three full seasons in his prime to military service, prevented him from amassing even more impressive career statistics. Not surprisingly, then, a fluke injury kept him out of the Yankees' lineup at the start of 1936.

Taking heat treatment for a twisted left foot during spring training, DiMaggio left the lamp on too long and burned his foot. He couldn't play until the 17th game of the regular season, and then he started in left field, not center. Mindful of the great distances that had to be covered in Yankee Stadium's center field, manager Joe McCarthy said, "I wanted him to be comfortable before I put him in center."

Six weeks into the season, the Yankees traded the contentious Ben Chapman and put DiMaggio in center. Except for one game at first base in 1950, he played there the rest of his career.

Once into the lineup, DiMaggio played exactly as everybody had expected him to, hitting .323 for the season, with 206 hits, 44 doubles, 15 triples, and 29 homers. He knocked in 125 runs and scored 132. From the very first game he played, in which he got three hits, he showed that he belonged.

That year, too, the Yankees started their run of four straight pennants. In DiMaggio's 13 years, the Yankees won 10 pennants, and nobody would suggest that was coincidental.

DiMaggio followed his rookie season with a series of exceptional years, but one season, 1941, is the one with which he will always be identified. On bare statistics it was not his best. Five times, for instance, he hit more homers than the 30 he had that season; five times he had more RBIs; six times he scored more runs. Even his .357 batting average was not his best, because he had hit .381 two seasons earlier.

But the day-to-day drama of DiMaggio's hitting streak made 1941 the most memorable of his great seasons. Day after day, the first question of baseball fans everywhere was: Did DiMag get a hit today? And for an unbelievably long time, the answer was always yes.

The streak could not have come at a better time for the Yankees, because they were struggling. So was DiMaggio. On the morning of May 15, DiMaggio was hitting only .306, and the Yankees were in fourth place, 5½ games behind Cleveland, having lost four straight and seven of nine.

DiMaggio singled in the first inning against the White Sox that afternoon, but the Yankees lost another, 13–1. A *New York Journal-American* headline read: "Yank Attack Weakest in Years."

For the next three weeks, DiMaggio's streak went unnoticed because of other events. He had a swollen neck which didn't stop his hitting but bothered his fielding; he had four errors in a double-header against Boston. And on June 2, Lou Gehrig died; McCarthy and Bill Dickey went to his funeral.

By June 6, though, everybody was aware that something special was happening. The Yankees had won eight straight and DiMaggio's streak had reached 24. Newspapermen dug up the first goal: The club hitting mark of 29 games, shared by Roger Peckinpaugh and Earle Combs.

DiMaggio himself still wasn't terribly concerned. Of course, his experience in hitting in 61 straight in the PCL helped him to adjust to the pressure of this streak.

On June 17, he broke the Yankee record with a bad-hop single off the shoulder of Chicago shortstop Luke Appling. That was noteworthy because of its rarity; DiMaggio got very few breaks in his long streak. Only once, in the 43rd game, did he get the benefit of the doubt in a scorer's decision, for instance; the newspapermen who scored the games were determined that

Joe DiMaggio set a record by hitting in 56 straight games in 1941 and he led the Yankees to pennants in 10 of his 13 years. *(New York Yankees)*

only clean hits would keep the streak alive. And not once in 56 games did DiMaggio resort to a bunt to keep the streak alive.

By now, everybody was aware of the streak, teammates and opponents alike, and it brought about some interesting human reactions. In one game, for instance, the Yankees were leading the Browns, 3–1, going into the last half of the eighth, but DiMaggio was hitless against submariner Eldon Auker.

With one out, Red Rolfe walked. Tommy Henrich was the next batter, with DiMaggio to follow. Henrich, realizing that DiMaggio wouldn't get another chance if he hit into a double play, asked permission to bunt Rolfe down. He got permission from McCarthy, and then DiMaggio doubled to left on Auker's first pitch to keep the streak alive.

On June 28, DiMaggio's mark stood at 39, just two away from George Sisler's American League record. Pitching for the Philadelphia A's that day was Johnny Babich, once in the Yankee farm system and a Yankee-killer since; he had beaten the Yankees five times in the 1940 season.

Babich boasted that he would stop DiMaggio's streak, and his strategy apparently was to give DiMaggio nothing to hit. Joe walked the first time up and went to 3–0 in his second appearance. He was given the "hit" sign.

The next pitch was outside, too, but DiMaggio reached across the plate and slashed it through Babich's legs into center field. "After I took my turn at first," said DiMaggio, "I looked at him. His face was white as a sheet."

The next day, the Yankees played a double-header against the Washington Senators at Griffith Stadium. In the sixth inning of the first game, DiMaggio tied Sisler's record with a double off Dutch Leonard.

In between games, a fan jumped onto the field and stole DiMaggio's bat, which Joe had sandpapered down around the handle for the right "feel."

Using a bat borrowed from Henrich, DiMaggio broke Sisler's record with a seventh-inning single and then broadcast an appeal for his bat to be returned. "I need it more than he does." said DiMag.

It was soon learned that the bat had been stolen by a youngster from Newark. Some friends of DiMaggio got the bat back in time for a double-header against the Red Sox at Yankee Stadium.

In the first game, DiMaggio hit a bouncer down the third base line. Red Sox third baseman Jim Tabor hurried his throw trying to get DiMaggio and threw wildly to first. Official scorer Dan Daniel called it a hit, and DiMaggio's streak was at 43.

Only one record remained: Wee Willie Keeler's 44-game mark from 1897. A lot of people thought Keeler's mark shouldn't count because it had been set in an era when home plate was smaller and the rules different. DiMaggio made such discussions irrelevant by singling in the first inning of the second game (fortunate timing, because rain stopped the game after five innings) and then homering the next afternoon off Dick Newsome to extend his mark to 45.

Teammate Lefty Gomez noted that DiMaggio had broken Keeler's record by following Wee Willie's oft-quoted dictum: "You hit 'em where they ain't."

DiMaggio admitted after that game that the pressure had affected his play; he had been swinging at bad pitches to keep the streak going. Now that he had the record, he relaxed. For the next 11 games, he hit .545, with 24 hits in 44 at bats. In between the 48th and 49th game, he played in the All-Star game and, yes, he got a hit in that game, too.

On July 17, the Yankees played the Cleveland Indians in huge Municipal Stadium, and 67,468 fans came out on a Thursday night.

In the first inning, DiMaggio lashed a drive down the third base line. Cleveland third baseman Ken Keltner, who had been playing practically on the outfield grass, made a backhanded stab of the ball on the bounce and threw DiMaggio out from foul territory.

In the fourth, DiMaggio walked. In the seventh, he hit another shot down the third base line, but again, Keltner threw him out.

The Yankees knocked out Cleveland starter Al Smith in the eighth inning, taking a 4–3 lead, and DiMaggio came up again. This time he grounded to shortstop. The ball took a bad bounce, but Lou Boudreau brought it down and started a double play. The streak was over.

During those 56 games, DiMaggio had hit .408, with 91 hits, including 16 doubles, 15 homers, and 4 triples. He had knocked in 55 runs, scored 56. He had struck out only seven times.

The Yankees had prospered, too, winning 41 and losing only 13; there were two rain-halted tie games. Thirty-six games into DiMaggio's streak, they had climbed into first place to stay, and they went on to win in a romp, by 17 games. So much for their weak attack.

Amazingly, DiMaggio started a new streak the next day, and this one went for 16 games, 14 of them Yankee wins, before Johnny Niggeling of St. Louis stopped him. Thus, DiMaggio hit safely in 72 of 73 games, just four less than half the season in those days; had it not been for Keltner's outstanding play on July 17, DiMaggio might have had a hitting streak of 73 games!

There is a footnote to that amazing streak. In recognition of what DiMaggio had done, Yankee general manager Ed Barrow offered him $5,000 less for the 1942 season! There was a war on, you know. "Soldiers are making $21 a month," Barrow pointed out. History does not record whether Barrow cut his own salary.

DiMaggio has always been quiet and introverted, comfortable only with a few friends. Thus, he has been surrounded by an aura of mystery which has intrigued people, and his name is still a famous one, though he has been retired since 1951.

Now and then, he breaks back into the headlines. The biggest story, of course, was his marriage to Marilyn Monroe in 1954. "It has to be better than rooming with Joe Page," cracked one writer. The marriage lasted only nine months, but the two remained friends until Marilyn's death in 1962, and DiMaggio has had flowers placed on her grave regularly since then.

In 1968, Simon and Garfunkel's hit record about the wily Mrs. Robinson asked, "Where have you gone, Joe DiMaggio?" To Oakland, as it happened; he was a coach for Charlie Finley's A's. Predictably, the tie between the bombastic Finley and taciturn DiMaggio could not last, and Joe resigned after that year.

In the '70s, DiMaggio surfaced again, doing a national commercial for a coffee maker. A tea drinker himself, DiMaggio was very convincing in the part, a tribute to the confidence he inspired in people. To most people, DiMaggio symbolized class and dignity.

Williams was an entirely different story. He established a reputation as a brash young man at the start of his career, and he never really shook it. He battled with writers—"The Knights of the Keyboard" in his sarcastic phrase—until the end of his career, and he stubbornly refused to tip his cap to fans after a home run because of early-career run-ins.

Williams was insufferably cocky when he first came to the Red Sox in 1938, as several stories attest. The most famous one involved Bobby Doerr, a teammate of Williams at San Diego in 1937 who had been brought up to the Red Sox late that season. He told Williams, "Wait until you see Jimmie Foxx hit." Williams supposedly replied, "Wait until Foxx sees me hit." (Williams remembers, though, that he was awed by Foxx. "I was just a tall, skinny kid and Foxx had all those muscles.")

Williams was farmed out by the Red Sox in '38 because they had an outfield of Chapman, Joe Vosmik, and Doc Cramer, all of whom had hit better than .300 in 1937 and would do so again in '38. Before he left, Williams told them, "I'll be back, and someday I'll make more money than all three of you combined."

His prediction came true, of course. And whether or not Foxx was impressed, it is a fact that Williams was a better hitter than Foxx, even without Jimmie's muscles.

At Minneapolis in '38, Williams had a great year, hitting .366 with 43 homers, but he nearly drove manager Donie Bush crazy, with his indifferent fielding and base running. In the outfield, he would practice his swing. On the bases, he would daydream.

One day, Williams doubled in the ninth inning of a tie game. Bush yelled at him to be careful taking his lead so he wouldn't be picked off. "Shut up, busher," Williams yelled back. "I got out here by myself and I'll get home without your help." He did, too, scoring the winning run on a single.

Even after he got to the majors, Williams suffered from immaturity. His hearing was as acute as his eyesight, and he could pick out one boo from a chorus of cheers from the fans.

Sometimes, he didn't have to pick out a solitary boo. One time in a game in Philadelphia, the Red Sox starting lineup was introduced. Dom DiMaggio, Doerr, and Johnny Pesky were greeted by cheers. Williams got a chorus of boos. "That," said a teammate on the bench, "is an excellent example of the early worm getting the bird."

Early in his career, Williams became more than normally agitated by fans' booing and announced that he'd rather be a fireman than play baseball in Boston. The Chicago White Sox were in town, and manager Jimmy Dykes dressed in a fireman's uniform and arranged to have a siren blow when Williams came to bat. Williams was embarrassed, but it didn't affect his hitting. Nothing ever did.

Williams's brashness was probably a cover for a lack of confidence, as is often the case. He was the product of a broken home and his mother, a Salvation Army worker, usually left Ted to fend for himself.

What Ted did on his own, generally, was to take hitting practice. He would hit until his hands were blistered, if he could find somebody to pitch to him.

He signed with his hometown team, the Padres, in 1936, when he was only 17, but hit only .271 with no home runs in 42 games that year.

His problem was, ironically, that he was chasing too many bad pitches. The Pacific Coast League at that time had a number of veteran pitchers who didn't have quite enough left to stay in the majors but got by on guile at the Triple-A level. Recognizing that Williams was a great fastball hitter, they never threw him one, tantalizing him into chasing slow curves away from the plate.

But Ted learned to curb his impatience, and his hitting improved. The next year, he hit .291 with 23 homers and 98 RBIs. More important, he impressed two men who knew a lot about hitting: San Francisco manager Lefty O'Doul, who called him the best hitter in the league, and Boston general manager Eddie Collins, who bought Williams, along with Doerr.

It wasn't easy for Collins to persuade Red Sox owner Tom Yawkey. After spending great amounts of money to buy veterans like Foxx and Lefty Grove, Yawkey had finally decided that he had to build a farm system if he were ever going to see a pennant flying over Fenway Park. Accordingly, he vowed that he would not buy any more players. It took a lot of fast talking by Collins to get Yawkey to break his vow for a .291 hitter, but the Red Sox finally purchased Williams for virtually the same price that DiMaggio had commanded—$25,000 and four minor league players. As with DiMaggio, the deal was a bargain.

Like DiMaggio, Williams was a star from the time he first played. He hit .327 with 31 homers and a league-leading 145 RBIs as a rookie, then boosted his average to .344 in his second season.

He had some great moments and seasons. There was 1946, for instance, when he was the league's Most Valuable Player, as he hit .342 with 38 homers and 123 RBIs and the Red Sox won their only pennant during his playing years.

There was 1949, when he hit a career-high 43 homers, had 159 RBIs and a .343 average. The next year might have been even better, but he broke his elbow in the All-Star game, making a catch against the left field wall; in only 89 games, he had 28 homers and 97 RBIs.

In 1952, he went away again to war; when he came back, he hit .407 in 37 games at the tail end of the 1953 season. In 1957, when he was 39, he hit .388, an incredible performance.

But as with DiMaggio, 1941 was Williams's most memorable year. Oddly, it didn't start that way. In spring training, he chipped a bone in his ankle, so he could do nothing more than pinch-hit for the first two weeks of the season. But that may have helped him, because he always had trouble hitting well in the cold weather of the early season.

When he got back into the regular lineup, Williams came out smoking. In June, he was batting .436. His hitting wasn't confined to regular season games, either. In the All-Star game in Detroit on July 8, he came up with two outs in the bottom of the ninth and the American League trailing, 5–4, and hit a three-run homer to win the game.

Harry Heilmann had been the last American Leaguer to hit better than .400, in 1923, and Heilmann was rooting for Williams. Ted's average dipped to .402 in August, and when the Red Sox came to Detroit, Heilmann, then a Tigers' broadcaster, told Ted to forget the short fence in Briggs' Stadium and go for the base hit.

Williams took the advice and, by mid-September, his average had risen to .413. Then, it started to drop again. On the last day of the season, the Red Sox had a double-header scheduled in Philadelphia. Williams's average was at .3995; rounded out, it would have been listed at .400.

Red Sox manager Joe Cronin offered to let Ted sit out those games, but Ted refused; he didn't want to be hanging on to the .400 mark by a fingernail.

When he came to bat for the first time that day, A's catcher Frankie Hayes told him, "Mr. [Connie] Mack told us if we let up on you, he'll run us out of baseball."

It didn't matter. Williams was never better than he was that day. He singled his first time up, homered his second, then hit singles in his next two appearances. His fifth time up, he reached base on an error.

By this time, he was well over .400, but he still wouldn't sit down. In his first two at bats in the second game, he got another single and hit a loud-speaker horn in right center with a drive that would otherwise have been a

Ted Williams was the last player to hit .400 with a .406 year in 1941. *(Boston Red Sox)*

home run but became a double when it bounced back onto the playing field. Not until his third and final at bat in the second game did the A's finally get him out. For the double-header, he was six-for-eight, and his final batting average was .406. That was only two percentage points lower than DiMaggio had batted during his hitting streak.

Which accomplishment was the greater, DiMaggio's or Williams? The baseball writers thought DiMaggio's was, and they voted him the Most Valuable Player. Both, in a sense, were incomparable; no player has approached either mark since. Together, they made 1941 one of the truly memorable years in baseball history.

16. When the Teams Were 4-F

It was fortunate that 1941 was such a good year for the American League, because the next four years were definitely nonvintage, as military service drained more and more good players away.

In 1942, the baseball played in the league could be called major league, though not top quality. In the three years that followed, though, American League baseball could not legitimately be called better than Triple-A ball in a normal year.

The league immediately lost its top pitcher, Bob Feller, and slugger Hank Greenberg, who had so recently challenged Babe Ruth's home run record. Greenberg actually had missed all but 19 games of the 1941 season because he had been drafted. He was discharged on December 5, but when the Japanese attacked Pearl Harbor, he reenlisted. Feller enlisted, too, and neither would return until late in the 1945 season.

Joe DiMaggio and Ted Williams played the 1942 season but were drafted after that. Neither would return until the 1946 season, and DiMaggio would not return to his prewar form until the next season.

World War II meant death and suffering for millions, and the fact that major league baseball suffered and individual stars lost a chance to improve their personal statistics means little alongside that.

Nevertheless, it is true that if the war had not interfered, Feller would certainly have won more than 300 games in his career, and DiMaggio and Greenberg would have ended their careers with more than 500 home runs. Williams, who lost three years to World War II and nearly another two seasons to the Korean War, would have approached and possibly surpassed 700 home runs had he stayed in a baseball uniform.

Most of the league's good players, though not of the stature of Feller, Greenberg, DiMaggio, and Williams, also served in the military: Such players as Joe Gordon, Phil Rizzuto, Dom DiMaggio, Luke Appling, and Mickey Vernon all served at least two years. Only occasionally did a good player escape for physical or other reasons: Lou Boudreau and Rudy York didn't miss a season, and Bobby Doerr missed only one.

In desperation, team owners turned to veterans whose age kept them out of the service. Players such as Pinky Higgins, Doc Cramer, Spud Chandler, Myril Hoag, Al Smith, Joe Kuhel, Jake Powell, Dutch Leonard, and Johnny Niggeling extended their careers, sometimes into their 40s, because of the war.

Marginal players got their chance to star. The best example is probably Nick Etten, who had been in the majors since '38 but with only one good season. In 1944, Etten led the league in homers with 22; in 1945, he led the league in RBIs with 111. But in 1946, Etten played 84 games for the Yankees at first base and pinch-hit in another 24 but hit only .232. He was traded to the Philadelphia Phillies, played 14 games in '47, and was released.

But perhaps the best indication of how desperate team owners were for ballplayers was the fact that the St. Louis Browns in 1945 used one-armed outfielder Pete Gray.

Gray played 77 games for the Browns that year, hitting .218, 61 of them as an outfielder and 16 as a pinch hitter. When he caught a ball in the outfield, he would throw the ball up in the air, throw the glove off his left hand, catch the ball, and throw it back into play.

Two stars were developed during that period, both of them with the Detroit Tigers, outfielder Dick Wakefield and pitcher Hal Newhouser.

Wakefield was the first baseball "bonus baby." He looked a lot like Ted Williams physically, and he had a sweet, left-handed swing, too. For a time, it seemed that he was going to be a big star, but his time at the top was very brief.

He had started to attract attention when he was in high school in Chicago, but his dad, Howard Wakefield, who had played three sessions of American League ball himself, 1905–07, wanted him to go to college. At Michigan State, the offers became more lucrative. Brooklyn, Chicago, Cincinnati, Cleveland, and Detroit all made offers. Wakefield's only criterion was money, so he took the Tigers' offer of $52,000, the highest.

Wakefield stayed with the Tigers for half a season in 1941 but played in only seven games before being sent to Winston-Salem. The next year, he was the Most Valuable Player in the Texas League, playing for Beaumont, and he was brought up in 1943 to stay.

Wakefield had an excellent rookie season, leading the league with 200 hits and 38 doubles and batting .316. The next year, he was even better. After 78 games, one past half a season, he was hitting .355 with 12 homers. He had scored 53 runs and driven in another 53, so he probably would have surpassed 100 in both categories. Then, he was called into the service and missed the next season and a half.

Luke Appling, seen as a White Sox coach in this picture, was a great hitter and shortstop.
(Chicago White Sox)

Dick Wakefield was the first "bonus baby" with the Detroit Tigers, but his effectiveness ended when the stars came back from World War II.
(George Brace)

His success had made Wakefield more than a little cocky. In the service in Hawaii, he met Ted Williams and bet Williams that he would hit more homers, drive in more runs, and hit for a better batting average when they were both back in major league uniforms.

It didn't work out that way, of course. Wakefield, in fact, never hit better than .283 after that, never had more than 12 homers in a season or more than 59 RBIs. By 1950, he was out of the majors. In 1952, he came back briefly, for three games, with the New York Giants, but that was the end, though he was only 31 and should have been in his prime or close to it.

What happened? Wakefield, in a bitter interview years later with Donald Honig, blamed the pressure created by writers because of his bonus money. He also felt he was disliked by baseball owners, largely because of his work in helping establish a pension system, and was blackballed after 1950.

Neither rationale makes much sense. Wakefield hit his best his first two years, when the pressure should have been greatest. And, though he may have been disliked by club owners, there would certainly have been at least one willing to hire him if he had been playing well.

The harsh truth seems to be that Wakefield prospered only because he played in a weakened league during the war. He simply wasn't good enough to hit the better pitching after the war.

Much the same charge is often made against Newhouser, too: that he did well only because of weakened competition. That charge, though, is misleading. Newhouser's postwar problems were the result of a sore shoulder, not better batters.

Like Feller, Newhouser was a child prodigy, coming to the majors for the first time when he was only 18. Indeed, he nearly played on the same team with Feller. Cleveland general manager Cy Slapnicka offered him $15,000, but Newhouser felt an obligation to Detroit scout Wish Egan, who had followed Hal during his high school career in Detroit. Newhouser signed with the Tigers—for $400.

Newhouser had a live, snapping fastball. Unfortunately, he often had little idea where it was going, In his first four seasons, he averaged about six walks per nine innings, and his won-lost record got progressively worse, dipping to a dismal 8–17 in 1943.

Then, it all came together for Newhouser. In 1944, he reduced his walks to three per nine innings (he never had serious control problems again) and had a sensational year, winning 29 games, losing only 9, with an earned run average of 2.22, a league-leading 187 strikeouts and six shutouts.

Hal Newhouser was a great pitcher before an arm injury curtailed his effectiveness. *(Detroit Tigers)*

The next year, as the Tigers won the pennant, Newhouser won 25 games (again losing 9), and in almost every other measurement, he was even better than in 1944.

His ERA was down to 1.81, he struck out 212, he had eight shutouts, he completed 29 games, four more than the year before. He led the league in wins, percentages, ERA, starts (36), complete games, innings pitched (313), strikeouts, and shutouts. He yielded only 239 hits, an average of about seven a game.

In both years, he was the league's Most Valuable Player, the first to win the award back-to-back since Jimmie Foxx in 1932 and '33.

Those who think of Newhouser as strictly a wartime pitcher forget that in 1946, when all the stars were back from the war, he had a year comparable to his two great wartime seasons.

The Tigers finished 12 games back of the pennant-winning Red Sox that year and were never really in the race, but it certainly wasn't Newhouser's fault. He won 26 games, again losing 9, with a 1.94 ERA. He completed 29 games and had six shutouts, and he had a career high of 275 strikeouts—though that figure was a distant second to Feller's 348.

Shoulder miseries kept Newhouser from ever matching those three great years again, but he was a fine pitcher for three more seasons. In 1947, he fell back to .500, at 17–17, but that was at least partly because of a lack of support; he had a good ERA of 2.87 that year and completed 24 games. In 1948, he bounced back to win a league-leading 21 games, and he added another 18 in 1949.

Newhouser was such a good pitcher those three years after the war, that he was often matched against Feller for box office purposes. The last such great matchup, in fact, may have brought about a quicker end to his effectiveness.

In 1948, on the last day of the season, the Tigers were playing the Cleveland Indians, who could have clinched the pennant with a win. Newhouser had won his 20th game just two days before. His shoulder was bothering him quite a bit, but he thought that it would be all right with a winter's rest.

Fred Hutchinson was scheduled to pitch against the Indians that day against Feller, but Hutchinson came down with the flu. Detroit manager Steve O'Neill, not wanting to go with less than his best in such an important game, asked Newhouser if he would pitch. Newhouser didn't want to, but he also didn't want to be put in a position where it would seem that he was backing down from a challenge, so he agreed.

He pitched what he later called his best game of the year. The Tigers knocked out Feller with a five-run first inning and went on to win 7–1, and force a playoff between Cleveland and Boston. But pitching that day further aggravated Newhouser's shoulder problems. Though he pitched into the 1955 season—when he was still only 34—he had only two seasons left as a regular starter, in which he won 18 and 15 games. He never won more than 9 games after 1950, and even in that 15-win season, he was nothing like the pitcher he had been: He had a 4.34 ERA and allowed an average of more than one hit per inning pitched.

Even though his effectiveness was curtailed by his shoulder problems, Newhouser won 207 games. There are pitchers in the Hall of Fame who won fewer. But a cloud has always hung over his reputation because two of his three great years came against the weak teams of the war years.

Though Feller and Greenberg were gone, 1942 seemed a normal year in the American League, which is to say, the Yankees won the pennant, though they lost the World Series, which was certainly not a normal occurrence.

That Yankee team was virtually the same as the year before. Outfielder Tommy Henrich joined the Coast Guard, but not until the last month of the season, when the pennant was already virtually clinched. First baseman Johnny Sturm joined the Air Corps before the season started, but he was no great loss; he had hit only .239 the year before, and that was his only season in the major leagues, as it turned out. His place was taken by Buddy Hassett, a better hitter.

The Yankees seized an early lead and were never really threatened, winning by nine games over Boston. They also had the league's MVP in Joe

Gordon, an award that said more about the animosity of the voting writers toward Ted Williams than it did about Gordon's play. Gordon had a good season, batting .322 with 18 homers and 103 RBIs while playing an excellent second base. But Williams had a great year, winning the Triple Crown with 36 homers, 137 RBIs, and a .356 batting average and also leading the league with 141 runs and a slugging percentage of .648.

The Yankees suffered serious losses before the 1943 season, with DiMaggio, Rizzuto, Hassett, and Red Ruffing joining Henrich in the military, but the rest of the league suffered even more, and the Yankees won easily by 13½ games over Washington. Thirty-five-year-old Spud Chandler won 20 games, lost only four, and had an ERA of 1.64, lowest in the American League in 24 years.

The nadir was probably reached in 1944, when the St. Louis Browns won the only pennant in their 53-year American League history. (The Browns, of course, later became the Baltimore Orioles and achieved great success following their transformation.)

The Browns of that season had a lot of players whose names pop up now only in trivia questions; catcher Red Hayworth and starting outfielders Gene Moore, Milt Byrnes, and Mike Kreevich didn't play an inning after the war, and Hayworth and Byrnes played only in the war years.

Still, it was an exciting race because the reduction of talent had brought the Yankees back to the level of the rest of the league. It was a four-team race until September, with the Browns, Yankees, Tigers, and Red Sox. The Red Sox were the first to fall back, because Bobby Doerr and pitcher Tex Hughson were called into service in the last month. The Yankees were in it until the final week, when they dropped back, eventually finishing third, six games out.

On the last day of the season, St. Louis and Detroit were tied. The Tigers lost to Washington, 4–1, but the Browns beat the Yankees, 5–2, as Chet Laabs hit two two-run homers.

The Browns lost the World Series to their crosstown rivals, the Cardinals, but they scored a moral victory in extending the Series to six games. The Cardinals had suffered very little from losses to the military that year and probably could have won even in a normal year with a lineup that still included Stan Musial, Marty Marion, Whitey Kurowski, Walker Cooper, and pitchers Mort Cooper, Harry Brecheen, and Max Lanier.

Greenberg, the first of the big stars to go into the military, was the first to return, too, on July 1, 1945, and his success was an indication of how weak the league was. Hank had not hit a major league pitch in more than four years, and he was nearing his 35th birthday, but he homered in his first game back and wound up with 13 homers, 60 RBIs, and a .311 average in 78 games, essentially a half season.

The pennant race was again a thriller, and again the Tigers were involved, this time with the Washington Senators. Washington owner Clark Griffith was more than a little surprised at that. Anticipating that his team would be in its normal position—out of the race—in September, he had arranged for Griffith Stadium to be prepared for the Redskins' football team, and the Senators finished their season a week ahead of the Tigers.

So, on September 30, the Tigers were to play a double-header with the Browns in St. Louis and needed to win one of the games to win the pennant; their record was 87–65, the Senators 87–67.

It had been raining for a week in St. Louis, and it seemed that neither of the two games would be played that day. Pitchers Nelson Potter of St. Louis and Dizzy Trout of Detroit had to halt their warm-ups three times because of rain, but finally the rain stopped and the first game started, under very dark skies.

The Browns took a 3–2 lead into the ninth, but in the top of that inning, the Tigers loaded the bases for Greenberg, who drilled a 1–1 pitch into the left field bleachers to make the second game unnecessary. The Tigers' winning percentage of .575 was the lowest in league history.

To call the following World Series between the Tigers and Chicago Cubs undistinguished is giving it better than it deserves. "Neither team can win," wrote Chicago's Warren Brown. "It is the fat men against the tall men at the annual office picnic," added New York's Frank Graham, trying to describe a series of pratfalls and mental and physical errors.

But it was Greenberg's most satisfying of the three Series in which he played, because he hit well (.304 with two homers and seven RBIs), and his team won, in seven games.

And, mercifully, the worst was over. The big boys all came back the next year, and the American League was back to normal. Williams hit .342 and won the Most Valuable Player Award for the first time in his career. Greenberg led the league with 44 homers and 127 RBIs. Feller won 26 games and struck out 348 batters. The lame and the aged limped off to oblivion.

17. Front Office Hustle

To his fellow club owners, Bill Veeck has always been a gadfly, an irritant. He has never had the proper amount of dignity, preferring, for instance, to call himself a hustler, rather than a magnate.

He has had running feuds with some owners and general managers, most notably George Weiss of the Yankees in the early '50s, and it didn't help that Veeck was more often right than not. Led by the Yankees, American League owners forced him out of baseball in 1954, when they agreed that his St. Louis Browns could move to Baltimore only if he sold the club. And, though Veeck has twice since bought his way back into the league, both times with the Chicago White Sox, it was only with the extreme reluctance that club owners let him back in.

Yet, Veeck has been a very influential man, in three separate areas: 1) Economic; 2) Promotional; and 3) Signing black players. Any of the three would guarantee him a secure niche in baseball history. Taken together, they make him probably the most influential club executive in American League history.

Before Veeck bought the Cleveland Indians in 1946, the accepted practice for buying a club was to pay whatever the price was for the club itself. To take advantage of the tax laws, Veeck changed that.

Veeck set up his deal so that $50,000 of the purchase price was for the club's title, and the remainder was for the players, who could then be written off in depreciation for tax purposes for five or ten years.

To see what an advantage that could be, let's take a hypothetical case of a club being sold for $10 million. The new owner could allow $50,000 for the club title and the rest for the players, and then depreciate them over a five-year period. That means that he could make a profit of nearly $2 million in a year before he would have to pay a cent in income tax!

That was a great advantage to a club owner who was making money at the gate. It was of even more value to a man (or woman) who owned another profitable business, because the paper losses from the baseball operation could be applied against the real profits of the other business. Suddenly, a sports franchise was a far sounder investment for a businessman.

Bill Veeck was a great innovator as the owner of the Cleveland Indians and Chicago White Sox. *(Chicago White Sox)*

The tax courts have since cut down the percentage of the sale price which can be attributed to the players, and it is now around 60 percent. Even so, that is a considerable advantage, though not as much as when Veeck pioneered the scheme.

Veeck's idea has had a revolutionary effect on all sports, not just baseball. It brought many businessmen into sports, and it made possible the expansion of sports, not just through existing leagues but through new ones.

Once in baseball, Veeck had another idea: pooling television revenue. His idea was born out of necessity; at the time, he was operating the St. Louis Browns, who had no access to significant television revenue.

Veeck's idea was opposed and beaten back by the Yankees. Operating in the rich New York market, the Yankees had no desire to share the wealth with their poor country cousins. It remained for pro football to demonstrate the practicality of Veeck's idea. But now, baseball has a national television contract, and there is no question that even the Yankees get far more from that contract than they could dealing independently. Score another one for Veeck.

Perhaps the one aspect of baseball management that Veeck is best known for is his promotional genius. That has taken many forms. He pioneered "Cap Day" and "Bat Day" and exploding scoreboards.

At Cleveland, he gave away everything from a year's supply of sardines to 100 gallons of ice cream. He gave away squabs, lobsters, rain capes. He also did something nobody else had dared try: He had promotional nights he didn't advertise. The idea was to get people to come to the park because they thought this might be the night something was given away.

At St. Louis, he used 3′ 7″, 65-pound Eddie Gaedel as a pinch hitter. One night, when Bobo Holloman was pitching, it was so dark and rainy that he announced he would give rain checks to all in attendance. Holloman then went on to pitch a no-hitter!

Veeck's idea was to make it fun to come to the park. He sometimes played practical jokes, as when the "winner" of one promotion got a block of ice delivered to his seat. He had a "Good Old Joe Early Night" at Cleveland for his night watchman, who had complained because only ballplayers who didn't need the gifts got special days and nights.

So much emphasis was put on Veeck's promotion, in fact, that people sometimes got the wrong impression of his philosophy. "I've never suggested the promotions do very much if you're not winning," he told Roger Kahn for *A Season in the Sun* in 1977. "What I do say is that promotions plus a winning team will break attendance records."

It was probably his desire to field a winning team as much as any thought of transforming baseball that led Veeck to be the first American League owner to sign a black player.

Actually, Veeck tried to break the baseball color line before Branch Rickey did. In 1940, when Veeck owned the Milwaukee team of the American Association, he tried to sign a black player. He told Kahn that baseball commissioner, Judge Kenesaw Landis, threatened to throw him out of baseball if he did.

Before the 1944 season, Veeck tried to purchase the Philadelphia Phillies, but was turned down because of a report that he was going to stock them with black players.

Finally, in 1947, with Jackie Robinson playing his first year for the Brooklyn Dodgers, the time was right, and Veeck signed Larry Doby.

Doby was an infielder when he was signed, but he was switched to center field the next season and became a star. A solid defensive outfielder, he also became an outstanding power hitter, twice leading the league in home runs and RBIs.

But it was in 1948 that Veeck made the biggest news when he signed LeRoy "Satchel" Paige, the legendary star pitcher of the Negro leagues. Paige was often called the "Babe Ruth of Negro baseball" because of his dominating pitching feats and his tremendous box office appeal.

There can be no doubt that Paige, in his prime, was one of the greatest pitchers of all time, though his exact ranking cannot be determined because he was denied a chance to pitch in the major leagues then.

According to the curious code of those days, it was permissible for white players to play against blacks in off-season exhibitions, though not during regular season, so Paige had plenty of opportunities to pitch against established major leaguers. He excelled in these games.

Dizzy Dean, never one to suffer from modesty, said after pitching against Paige that Satchel was faster than he. In one game against a major league team with Hack Wilson in the lineup, Paige struck out 22 batters. As late as 1947, when he was definitely past his peak, Paige was able to match Bob Feller in a series of exhibition duels.

Critics accused Veeck of signing Paige only for his publicity value because Satchel was obvious no longer in top form in '48. He had always been coy about his age, and guesses ranged as high as 50. The truth was amazing enough. Sometime later, his birth certificate surfaced: Paige had been born on July 7, 1906. He was 42 when he first pitched for the Indians, the oldest rookie in major league history.

Veeck certainly didn't mind all the publicity he was getting for signing Paige, but he also knew that Satchel could still pitch. So did Cleveland playing manager Lou Boudreau, who had caught Paige and then hit against him in a workout before Paige was signed. Satchel still had that marvelous loose arm. His fastball didn't have the zip it once had, but it was still well above average.

Paige was signed on July 7, a day after his birthday, and pitched for the first time on July 9, throwing two innings of scoreless relief against the St. Louis Browns.

That was the start of a remarkable half season for Paige, who pitched in 21 games that year, 14 of them in relief. In his seven starts, he had three complete games, two of them shutouts. For the season, he was 6–1, with a 2.48 earned run average. There was no more talk about a publicity stunt.

Amazingly, Paige wasn't through. Three years later, Veeck was with the Browns and he signed Satchel, who had been released by the Indians before the 1950 season.

Veeck got the maximum publicity mileage out of Paige in St. Louis, giving Satchel a rocking chair to sit in while he was in the bull pen, but again, Paige was of more than promotional value.

In 1952, at the age of 46, Paige won 12 games and saved another 10 for the Browns; his saves and wins totaled 22, more than a third of the 64 games the Browns won that season. The next year, his won-lost record dipped to 3–9, but he still saved 11 games, and his earned run average of 3.53 and 114 hits in 117 innings indicated that nobody was hitting Satchel at will.

That was thought to be the end of the line for Paige, but he got one last reprise. In 1965, when he was 59, he was brought back for one game by Charlie Finley, owner of the then Kansas City A's. Finley, of course, had brought in Satchel strictly for his publicity value, but Paige still had something left. In three innings, he yielded only one hit and no runs. An amazing man.

As the son of William Veeck, owner of the Chicago Cubs in the '20s, the junior Veeck came naturally to his interest in baseball. He got valuable experience running the Milwaukee club (then a minor league operation) in the early '40s, so when he bought the Cleveland ball club in midseason in 1946, he was ready. For the most part, his operation of the Indians was the model of how a sports franchise should be run.

Veeck operated the Indians for 3½ years, but the unquestioned high point came in 1948, when the Indians won the pennant and set a league attendance record of 2,620,627 which still stands.

Three teams were involved in the race that season. The Yankees, of course; they had won the year before, and they were strong again with Joe DiMaggio having his last great season, hitting .320 with 39 homers and 155 RBIs, both league highs that year.

The Red Sox had coaxed Joe McCarthy out of retirement, and they had a strong hitting team as always, with Ted Williams hitting .369 to lead the attack.

The Indians, though, were a surprise team. They had finished sixth in '46, and a distant fourth in '47, 17 games behind the Yankees. But 1948 was their year.

There were a lot of reasons for the Indians' success that season. Joe Gordon, obtained in a trade with the Yankees before the 1947 season (Allie Reynolds went to the Yankees), hit 32 homers and drove in 124 runs. Third baseman Ken Keltner hit 31 homers and had 119 RBIs. Converted third baseman Bob Lemon won 20 games for the first time.

But two men were really the story for the Indians that season: Boudreau and rookie pitcher Gene Bearden.

Boudreau had been with the Indians since midseason in 1939. In his first full year, 1940, he made the All-Star team for the first of seven seasons and led the league in fielding percentage for the first of eight times.

Though a bad ankle (which also kept him out of military service) limited his range, Boudreau was an excellent shortstop, a master of position. He retired with the best lifetime fielding percentage for a shortstop, .973.

First with Ray Mack and then with Gordon, Boudreau was also part of a strong double play combination, which Cleveland pitchers appreciated. He was also a timely hitter, finishing his career with a .295 average, unusually high for a shortstop. Three times he led the league in doubles and once, in 1944, in percentage, with .327.

He was also the manager of the club, and Veeck wasn't so sure that was a good idea. After the 1941 season, when Roger Peckinpaugh was moved from the bench to the front office, Boudreau went in to talk to club president Alva Bradley and applied for the job. He got it, and at 24 was the youngest manager ever to start a season. (Peckinpaugh, interestingly, had been only 23 when he was first made a manager, late in the 1914 season with the Yankees, but he managed only 17 games and didn't get another chance until he was 37.)

Boudreau was a strong manager, confident in his decisions, and the fans loved him. But after six seasons he was a cumulative 19 games under .500, and Veeck thought he could improve his team by trading Boudreau to the St. Louis Browns in a multiplayer deal.

The deal was leaked to the newspapers (there has always been a suspicion that Veeck was only sending up a trial balloon, anyway, and perhaps trying to light a fire under Boudreau). The fans reacted strongly against the proposed deal—as much as ninety percent against, by some estimates—and the deal was never made.

It was the best deal Veeck never made. Boudreau responded with the finest year of his career, with lifetime highs of 18 home runs, 116 runs, 106 RBIs, and a .355 batting average. None of the marks was good enough to lead the league, but their cumulative result gave Boudreau a well-deserved MVP honor.

But even Boudreau's heroics wouldn't have been enough without the totally unexpected contribution of Bearden, a left-handed knuckleballer who won 20 games and lost only 7.

Bearden was one of those pitchers with one good year, much as Wilcy Moore had been for the 1927 Yankees. He had knocked around the minors for several years, without great success, and a very brief trial at the end of the 1947 season had given no indication of future success with the Indians: In one-third of an inning, he had yielded three runs.

But in 1948, Bearden was magnificent. His ERA of 2.43 led the league,

The great double play combination of Lou Boudreau, left, and Joe Gordon was a key to the 1948 Cleveland pennant. *(Cleveland Indians)*

and he had six shutouts among his 20 wins. His knuckleball danced around the plate and drove hitters crazy.

The race started strangely, with the Red Sox locked in reverse: at Memorial Day, they had a 14–23 record. But then they broke loose and, with the Yankees and Indians, found themselves involved in one of the most exciting pennant races ever.

Not until the next-to-last day of the season were the Yankees eliminated from contention, fittingly enough, by the Red Sox. But the Indians still led by a game and could have wrapped it up on the final day. They couldn't, losing to Detroit and Hal Newhouser as the Red Sox were beating the Yankees again.

So the Indians had to travel to Boston for the first American League playoff, a sudden death, one-game affair, the winner to meet the Boston Braves in the World Series.

The odds favored the Red Sox, who were deadly in their home park, but Boudreau remained confident. "We're just going to Boston a day early," he insisted. "We'll beat the Red Sox and then go on to meet the Braves."

Boudreau selected Bearden to start. It seemed a surprising choice, because Bearden had only had a day of rest, and left-handers were at a disadvantage

Larry Doby, seen as a coach here, was the first black star in the American League as a Cleveland center fielder. *(Cleveland Indians)*

The legendary Satchel Paige was still effective as a Cleveland and St. Louis pitcher, though he was at least 42 as a rookie. *(George Brace)*

Gene Bearden's clutch win in a playoff won the 1948 pennant for Cleveland. *(George Brace)*

at Fenway Park, with its close left field wall. But Bearden had been the Indians' best all season, and Boudreau wanted to stick with him.

Boston manager McCarthy also made a surprising choice, and one for which he was second-guessed for years: veteran right-hander Denny Galehouse, who had won only eight games. But McCarthy didn't have any good choices. His starters were all tired from the efforts of getting the Red Sox into the playoff. Galehouse had pitched well against the Indians in Cleveland a few weeks earlier, and McCarthy hoped he had another good game left.

It probably made no difference. Boudreau was so hyped up for the game, he was ready to win it almost single-handedly. In the first inning, he hit a home run. In the fourth inning, he led off with a single. Gordon also singled and Keltner then hit a three-run homer. In the fifth, Boudreau hit another homer. In the ninth, he singled for a perfect four-for-four day. The Indians won, 8–3. As Lou had said, they were just in Boston a day early.

The World Series, which the Indians won in six games, was anticlimactic. So were the following seasons for both Boudreau and Bearden.

Bearden's demise came because Casey Stengel was made manager of the Yankees in 1949. Stengel had managed Bearden at Oakland of the Pacific Coast League, and he told his hitters to lay off Bearden's knuckleball, because it usually drifted away from the plate. That word quickly spread around the league, and when Bearden had to go to his other pitches, he was shelled. For the remaining five years of his major league career, he was 25–31.

Boudreau played through the 1952 season—ironically, ending up with the Boston club he had knocked out of the pennant in '48—but he played only one more full season, in 1949. He was elected to the Hall of Fame in 1970.

Veeck remained a factor for a much longer time. Forced out of baseball in 1954, he got back in with the Chicago White Sox for the 1959 season—and the White Sox won their first pennant in 40 years. He sold the White Sox in 1961 because of health problems, but then bought them again in December of 1975.

And once again he was the gadfly of baseball. He set up a table in the hotel lobby at the baseball winter meetings, announcing his willingness to make trades; he circulated through the stands at Comiskey Park to talk to fans; he brought back Orestes Minoso so Minoso could be an active player in four decades. He was indeed, as Kahn called him, William the Unconquerable.

18. In the Reign of Casey

The third-place finish in 1948 had embarrassed the New York Yankees' management. After winning seven pennants in eight years, 1936–43, the Yankees had won only one pennant in the five years since. Clearly, something had to be done.

As usual, the something that was decided upon was to change managers. During the 1948 World Series, the Yankees announced that Charles Dillon "Casey" Stengel would be the new manager, replacing Bucky Harris.

The move was not popular with the New York press. Harris had been well liked, and Stengel's reputation was that of a clown, not a serious baseball man.

Stengel had been in baseball since 1910, starting in the Northern Association, a league that folded in midseason of that year. He had come to the majors in 1912, with Brooklyn, and had played through the 1925 season, finishing with a career average of .284 and a reputation as a good defensive outfielder. He had had his moments of high drama, too, notably the 1923 World Series, when he batted .417 for the New York Giants and hit two home runs, the first an inside-the-park job. That was also the first Series homer in Yankee Stadium.

Yet, what most people remembered about Stengel as a player were his comic antics and lines. There was, for example, the time he tipped his hat to booing Brooklyn fans—and a bird came out. There was the time he complained because Giant manager John J. McGraw had a private detective following him and Irish Meusel. "I deserve one of my own," he said.

Stengel's face, as pliable as rubber and resembling nothing so much as a gargoyle, contributed to his reputation as a comic. Even as a hero, he was funny. In a famous bit of sports verse, Damon Runyon described Stengel's inside-the-park home run in the '23 Series humorously, making it seem that Casey had just enough left in his gimpy, bowed legs to make it home. Stengel was married in the off-season that year. When Casey's prospective father-in-law read that bit of verse, he commented to his daughter that she'd be lucky if Casey could make it to the altar.

Stengel's reputation followed him when he turned to managing. In 1925, he was named president and manager of the Worcester club of the Eastern League. (That was also his first contact with George Weiss, who was later to hire him as Yankee manager; Weiss was general manager of the Hartford club in the league.)

The Worcester club was not very good, but Casey soon got an offer to manage Toledo of the American Association. When the Worcester owner refused to let him go, Stengel sat down as club president and released himself as manager. Then he resigned as club president and took the job in Toledo. In 1927, he won a pennant with the Mud Hens.

Stengel made it back to the majors as a manager in 1934 with Brooklyn, leading the Dodgers for the next three seasons. Fired by the Dodgers, he was hired by the Braves and managed the Boston club for six years, 1938–43.

Both teams had very little talent, which Stengel realized. To take the fans' minds off the miserable performances they were seeing, he used various stunts. Once he even polled fans on what lineup to use. His teams never finished higher than fifth.

So, his reputation as a clown persisted; with it went a new reputation as a second division manager. When a cab hit Stengel and sent him to the hospital with a broken leg, Boston sportswriter Dave Egan nominated the cabdriver as "the man who has done the most for baseball in Boston this year."

When Stengel was released by Boston after the 1943 season, his major league career seemed over. He was named manager of the Milwaukee franchise in the American Association in Bill Veeck's absence. When Veeck, then in the military service, got the news, he fired back an angry letter to the club management, insisting that Stengel be fired. Stengel won the pennant that year and then resigned, to get out of a sticky situation. Veeck wrote him a thoughtful letter, apologizing for his error in judgment, and the two later became good friends.

Weiss hired Stengel to manage the Yankees' farm club in Kansas City in 1945, and then Stengel went to Oakland of the Pacific Coast League for the next three seasons, winning the PCL pennant in 1948.

Winning pennants in two Triple-A leagues should have been an indication of Stengel's ability, but his reputation as a clown obscured that. Some writers felt he was being hired because of his friendship with Weiss, though even a casual reading of the Yankees' history would have shown that they did not allow sentiment to cloud their judgment.

That Yankee club was good but not great. Since the arrival of Babe Ruth in 1920, there had been a regular succession of what would later be called superstars, from Ruth through Lou Gehrig to Joe DiMaggio. But at this time, DiMaggio was fading and the next superstar, Mickey Mantle, had not yet arrived.

The best player on the club was probably Yogi Berra, but Berra was just starting to come into his own. Berra was an unlikely looking star, a 5′ 7½″, 185-pound fireplug of a man.

He had a reputation for saying funny things, but most of the comic utterances were actually a product of the fertile imagination of Joe Garagiola, Berra's boyhood friend from St. Louis, who invented wisecracks and attributed them to Yogi.

In reality, Berra was a good-natured but basically humorless fellow who was—as is often true of such men—often made the butt of practical jokes. A typical story was told by Whitey Ford in his coautobiography, *Whitey and Mickey,* written with Joseph Durso.

Berra had a habit at the time of borrowing deodorants and lotions from other players in the clubhouse—without asking first. On a cold day in Detroit, Ford had used a sticky substance so he could get a better grip on the ball, and he had put that substance in a jar of roll-on deodorant.

Mantle took the jar and put it on the shelf in Ford's locker, where Berra could see it easily. As Mickey had anticipated, Berra grabbed it and used it. Soon, he was yelling—because his arms were stuck to his sides! The trainer had to apply alcohol and then cut the hair under Berra's arms to free them.

When Berra first came up to the Yankees, he had some defensive problems, particularly against the Dodgers in the 1947 World Series. To keep his bat in the lineup, he was often used in the outfield, playing 50 games there in 1948.

But by 1949, he was strictly a catcher and a good one, and there was never any question about his prowess at the plate. He hit everything, literally; he was one of the best bad-ball hitters ever. Pitches that should have been ball four he frequently slammed for base hits, and sometimes home runs.

Starting in 1949, he had ten straight seasons in which he hit at least 20 home runs, and in five of those seasons, he had more than 100 RBIs. Three times in his career he batted over .300, and he averaged .285 in his career, an excellent mark for a catcher. And statistics alone don't demonstrate his true value, because he was an especially dangerous hitter in the clutch. From the seventh inning on, he was the Yankee hitter opposing pitchers feared most.

The Yankees had other solid players. Tommy Henrich, "Old Reliable," was still around. Phil Rizzuto was a superlative shortstop, and Jerry Cole-

Yogi Berra hit everything from his shoe tops to the bill of his cap as a Yankee star of the late '40s and '50s. *(George Brace)*

man a sound second baseman; together, they formed a double play combination that was the bulwark of a sound defense.

But mostly, the Yankees had outstanding pitching. Vic Raschi won 21 games in each of the first three seasons Stengel managed the club. Ed Lopat, a junk-balling left-hander, was in double figures in wins in each of Stengel's first five seasons, with a high of 21 in 1951.

Allie Reynolds, though he won 20 games only once in that stretch, was probably the most feared pitcher on the staff. Reynolds had an overpowering fastball and an equally overpowering manner on the mound. In 1951 he threw two no-hitters.

Those first three years, especially, Stengel had an enormous advantage because he could throw Reynolds, Raschi, and Lopat at his closest challengers; nobody else had three starters of that quality.

Joe Page was a great reliever for the Yankees in the pennant years of 1947 and '49. (George Brace)

Relief pitchers? Joe Page was outstanding in 1949, winning 13 games and saving another 27. Page faded quickly, doing little after that season, but Stengel got good relief after that from Bob Kuzava and, later in his career, Reynolds. When Allie came in from the bull pen in the ninth inning, he was very effective; pitching mostly in relief in '53, he won 13 games and saved another 13.

The Yankees had pitching depth, too. Tommy Byrne, for instance, won 15 games in both '49 and '50 as Stengel's fourth starter. And whenever a pitcher started to falter, the Yankees had somebody else ready to take up the slack: Johnny Sain, Bob Turley, Whitey Ford.

Ford deserves special mention, because he was the best of the many fine pitchers Stengel commanded in his Yankee managerial career.

Whitey came up to the Yankees in midseason in 1950, when he was only 21, and played an important role in the pennant drive, winning nine and losing only one, with an ERA of 2.81.

His next two years were spent in an army uniform, but he was never in any danger from enemy bullets, since his military career was spent at Fort Monmouth, New Jersey, only 60 miles from New York. He picked up in 1953 with what was to become a typical season for him, winning 18 games and losing only 6.

Even as a rookie, Ford was a polished pitcher, not just a thrower. He had a good, live fastball and a sharp-breaking curve, but what made him effective was his control, his ability to move the ball around and keep hitters off-balance. He could strike out hitters if that was needed—he had as many as 209 strikeouts in the 1961 season—but he usually preferred to let batters hit the ball and make his defense work.

Whitey was also willing to use trick pitches, particularly in his later career when his fastball was fading. He had a special ring made which looked like a wedding band, but which had a rasp hidden in it which he used to rough up the ball to make it move in unpredictable fashion. He seldom used the spitball, though, for a practical reason: He couldn't control it consistently.

The hallmark of Ford's career was his reliability. Not until 1961 did he win as many as 20 games, but he was in double figures for each of his first 13 full seasons.

Conversely, he lost more than nine games only twice in his career, and when he retired after the 1967 season his .690 winning percentage was highest in baseball history among pitchers who had won at least 200 games.

Only four seasons in his career did Ford yield an average of more than three earned runs a game. His high was only 3.24, and his career average was a brilliant 2.75. Not once in the 14 seasons in which he pitched more

Clever left-hander Whitey Ford was the clutch pitcher for the Yankees in the '50's and early '60's. *(George Brace)*

than 100 innings did he yield as many hits as innings pitched, a valid measure of a moundsman's ability.

His most spectacular year was 1961, when he won 25 games and lost only 4, and he came close to matching that two years later when he had a 24–7 record. It was a foregone conclusion that he would be named to the Hall of Fame, and he made it in 1974, seven years after his retirement.

So, Stengel had the players, which is always necessary; no manager wins without good ones. But he also knew what to do with them, which not every manager does. Especially in his first two years, he had to do a lot of scrambling to win, but he always had what it took.

Casey had learned a lot while bouncing around in the majors and minors, as a player and as a manager. He had the ability to think ahead, to realize

Casey Stengel was regarded as a clown until he managed the Yankees to 10 pennants in 12 years. *(New York Yankees)*

that a move he made in the seventh would have an influence on what would happen in the ninth.

He always regarded himself as a teacher. One of his methods was to ask questions of a player: Why did he do this? What would happen if he did that? The result was that the player would think about what he was doing and, if he applied himself, improve as a player.

He became very popular with writers and fans, but he was certainly not loved by his players. He and DiMaggio had what might be called a "correct" relationship, but hardly a warm one. DiMaggio was particularly upset because in one game in 1951, Stengel sent out a defensive replacement—Cliff Mapes—during an inning. DiMaggio waved Mapes back in and took himself out at the end of the inning.

Other players could not act as imperiously as DiMaggio toward the manager, and they often seethed with resentment because of Stengel's public criticism. Casey had played and managed in an era when athletes expected such criticism, and he would not change. As with everything else he did, his criticism was made with a purpose: He expected players to listen to it and improve themselves. He only criticized players he thought were capable of doing better, and thus, he was much more critical of the good players on the Yankees than of the bad ones on his previous teams—and the inept New York Mets team he managed in the '60s.

Stengel developed a circuitous manner of speech which became known as "Stengelese" that he used when he wished to confuse listeners—the classic example is his testimony at a 1958 Senate hearing—but he could be quite direct when that suited him. Certainly, his players knew what he meant when he talked to them.

But mostly, his genius lay in his ability to get the most out of his players by using them in situations where they could do their best. Often, this meant platooning players, depending on the opposing pitcher.

So much has been made of Stengel's platooning (he was by no means the first manager to platoon but was probably the first to do it so extensively and be successful) that some misconceptions have arisen about his policy.

First, it should be noted that he did not platoon everybody. The solid players—like Berra and Rizzuto, for instance—always played, unless they were hurt.

Second, Stengel did not platoon on a rigid schedule, left-hand hitters against right-handed pitching, and right-handed hitters against left-handers. The pitcher's other characteristics were as important as what arm he threw with.

For instance, it has been an assumption that Stengel platooned the left-handed hitting Gene Woodling and the right-handed hitting Hank Bauer in right field. Yet, the statistics of that period show that Woodling and Bauer usually each played more than 100 games and batted more than 400 times. Obviously, they couldn't do that and share the same position.

Against some pitchers, both Bauer and Woodling would be in the lineup. But when the Yankees faced an especially good right-hander, Bauer would not play. When they faced a tough left-hander, Woodling sat on the bench. Neither man liked that, but in the long run, it probably helped their careers. Certainly, it helped the Yankees win.

And Stengel would go against the percentages when he felt there was a good reason for it. In the World Series of 1951 and '52, for instance, he used the left-handed Bob Kuzava in relief against two teams whose hitting was predominantly right-handed—the New York Giants and Brooklyn Dodgers —because Kuzava's pitches tended to run in on right-handed hitters. So, Kuzava saved the final game wins in both Series.

Stengel needed all his juggling ability in his first year with the Yankees, 1949, because the club had a staggering total of 71 injuries during the season. Some were minor, but others were not: Berra had a broken thumb, Johnny Mize had a torn shoulder, Henrich broke a bone in his back.

The most serious injury, though, was DiMaggio's bad heel. Joe had had an off-season operation to remove a calcium deposit in his right heel, and he recovered very slowly from it, missing the first 65 games of the season. His return from that injury was the most dramatic moment of his career since his 56-game hitting streak in 1941.

The Yankees had a three-game series, starting June 28, with the Red Sox at Fenway Park. As they had the year before, the Red Sox had started slowly that season but were gaining ground, standing 5½ games behind the league-leading Yankees as the series began.

In his first at bat of the season, DiMaggio singled off young Boston left-hander, Mickey McDermott, considered by some the fastest pitcher in the league. His next time up, in the third inning, with Rizzuto on base, he hit a drive into the screen atop left field. The Yankees won the game.

The next night, the Yankees were trailing, 7–1, when DiMaggio came up in the fifth with two men on. He homered to close the gap to 7–4, and Woodling tied it up in the seventh with a bases-loaded double. DiMaggio then hit another home run in the eighth inning, and the Yankees won again.

The next afternoon, a plane pulling the banner, "THE GREAT DI MAG-GIO" flew over Fenway Park. In the seventh inning, the Yankees were ahead, 3–2, when Snuffy Stirnweiss and Henrich hit singles back-to-back off Mel Parnell, who was to win 25 games for the Red Sox that season. Up came DiMaggio and on a 3–2 count, he hit still another home run, and the Yankees won again. In the three-game series, he had hit four home runs, knocked in nine runs and scored five. The next week, he was on the cover of *Life* magazine.

That put the Yankees ahead of the Red Sox by 8½ games, but the race was far from over. In fact, the Red Sox came with a rush down the stretch and swept the Yankees in a three-game series in Boston on the next-to-last weekend of the season, moving into first place.

The Red Sox still had a one-game lead when they came into Yankee Stadium for the final two games of the season. A split would have won the pennant for them, but the Yankees pulled out both games, 5–4 and 5–3, beating Parnell and 23-game winner Ellis Kinder on successive days.

DiMaggio hit .346 in half a season in '49, and he came back with 32 homers and 122 RBIs, on a .301 average, the next year. But it was obvious that injuries and age had caught up to him, and the next season was an embarrassment, even though the Yankees won their third straight pennant: a .263 average, and only 12 homers and 71 RBIs. DiMag was hurting.

A scouting report had been prepared for the Dodgers by Andy High; when the Giants beat out the Dodgers that year, it was given to the Giants. After the Series, it was printed by *Life,* and High's assessment of DiMaggio was brutal:

"Fielding—He can't stop quickly and throw hard. You can take the extra base on him if he is in motion away from the line of throw. He won't throw on questionable plays. . . .

"Speed—he can't run and he won't bunt.

"Hitting vs. righthanded pitcher—his reflexes are very slow and he can't pull a good fastball at all. . . ."

None of that came as a surprise to DiMaggio, of course, and he retired after that season. The Yankees offered him another $100,000 contract (he had become baseball's first $100,000 player in 1949), but he valued his pride more than that.

Fortunately for the Yankees, Mantle was there to take DiMaggio's place, though it would be a couple of seasons yet before Mantle fully realized his potential.

That potential was enormous. Probably no player has ever come to the majors with the combination of speed and power that Mantle possessed. The Pirates' Branch Rickey called him the best prospect he had ever seen and offered the Yankees home run champion Ralph Kiner and $500,000 for Mantle before Mickey had played an inning of a regular season game. The Yankees, laughing, turned it down.

Mantle could get down to first from home plate in an incredible 3.1 seconds. He could hit the ball 600 feet—and from both sides of the plate. No switch-hitter had ever had his kind of power. He seemed to explode at the ball, and his big cut led to a record number of strikeouts, but he also made contact consistently enough to hit for a good average.

Starting his professional career as a shortsop, Mantle was also a wretched fielder, making 47 errors in just 89 games in his first minor league season. He wasn't much better in his second season, committing 55 errors for Joplin of the Western Association. But he also hit .383 for Joplin, with 26 homers.

Obviously, a spot would be made for that kind of hitter. Stengel decided to switch Mantle to the outfield, and Mickey became outstanding there. New Yorkers liked to argue whether Mantle or Willie Mays (Duke Snider's prowess was sometimes dropped into the argument, too) was a better out-fielder, and the question was never resolved to everybody's satisfaction. Clearly, though, Mantle was a great one.

His rookie year was not terribly good. Facing far better pitchers than he had ever seen before, Mantle became uncertain at the plate and even had to be sent back to the minors for a time at midseason. He hit only .267 for the year and had an unsettling end to his debut when he stepped into a drain-pipe in right field in the fifth inning of the second game of the World Series and tore knee cartilage, necessitating off-season surgery.

The next year, though, he was shifted from right field to center and hit .311 with 23 home runs. The succession was assured.

It is one measure of Mantle's ability that when he retired after the 1968 season, with a .298 career average and 536 home runs in 18 seasons, some thought of his career as a disappointment. Some disappointment. His marks were good enough to get him into the Hall of Fame in 1974 with his good friend and teammate, Ford.

Yet, there is reason to think of Mantle's career as a disappointment. His last really good season was in 1964, when he was not quite 33. He should have had some strong years left, and he could have done better than he did in some earlier seasons.

But his problems were not of his own making. The muscular body which was capable of such great feats had built-in frailties. Mantle had a bone disease, osteomyelitis, resulting from a leg injury suffered while playing high school football; that kept him out of the Korean War but also hampered

Mickey Mantle was an unparalleled combination of power and speed for the Yankees before injuries ended his career prematurely. *(New York Yankees)*

him during his baseball career. In addition, he suffered many other injuries during his career and often played in great pain.

Playing injured, Mantle was very good. When he was healthy, he was awesome. He hit as high as .365 in 1957, and he belted as many as 54 home runs, in 1961. But it was in 1956 that he had his best season, hitting 52 homers, knocking in 130 runs and batting .353. In all of baseball history, only three other men have ever hit 50 homers and batted .350 or better in the same season: Hack Wilson, who did it in the freak year of 1930; Jimmie Foxx, in 1932; and, of course, Babe Ruth, who did it three times.

It was an oddity of Stengel's managerial career with the Yankees that in only one season did his team win more than 100 games—and that was the only season in his first ten years with the Yankees that they did not win the pennant!

That happened in 1954, at a time when Stengel's Yankees had won an unprecedented five straight pennants *and* World Series. Not even McCarthy's Yankees of the late '30s had done that. The Yankees would have one more stretch, 1960–64, when they won five straight pennants, but they won the World Series only twice in that period. Stengel's record of five straight World Championships will probably stand forever. Contrary to popular belief, the best team does not always win the World Series. There are too many variables in that short span, too many chances for fluke plays or lucky ones. But Stengel's Yanks simply ignored the imponderables and kept winning. They were, in fact, extended to seven games only once, in 1952.

By 1954, though, the Yankees were in what amounted to a down cycle for them in Stengel's years. Don't be misled by the 103 wins; those victories were achieved primarily because it was also a bad year for the league as a whole. The Yankees were hurting, mostly because of a pitching staff which had suddenly grown old. Raschi was gone, and Reynolds and Lopat were slipping. Ford had his customary good year, winning 16 games, but only the fact that rookie Bob Grim won 20 games saved the club from slipping further.

It was strictly a two-team race that year between the Yankees and Cleveland Indians; Chicago, in third place, was 17 games out, and Boston, in fourth, 42!

The Indians were a team with serious deficiencies. They had, no speed— only 30 stolen bases all year. They were no more than average defensively. They had the league's leading hitter, second baseman Bobby Avila at .341, the leading power hitter in Larry Doby (32 homers, 126 RBI), and another strong hitter in third baseman Al Rosen, who hit .300 with 24 homers and 102 RBIs, despite a broken finger. But they hit only .262 as a team and had three regulars under .240 (catcher Jim Hegan, .234; outfielder Dave Philley, .226; and shortstop George Strickland, .213).

But the Indians had magnificent pitching, with Bob Lemon (23–7), Early Wynn (23–11), Mike Garcia (19–8), Art Houtteman (15–7), and Bob Feller (13–3), backed up by relievers Don Mossi and Ray Narleski, who had 20 saves between them.

That pitching, and a weakened league, was enough to enable the Indians to win an American League record 111 games. Then, they lost the World Series in four straight to the New York Giants. It is ironic that the two most successful teams in history—the Indians and the 1906 Chicago Cubs, who set

Early Wynn was a 20-game winner on the 1954 Cleveland team which broke the Yankees' string of pennants, and he eventually won 300 games, the last to do it. *(George Brace)*

Bob Lemon, another 20-game winner for Cleveland in 1954, later managed the Yankees to a pennant. *(Cleveland Indians)* the National and major league mark with 116 wins—both lost in the World Series.

For the 1955 season, the Yankees redid their pitching staff, getting Bob Turley and Don Larsen from the St. Louis Browns in a multiplayer deal. They resumed their accustomed position in first place and started another string, this time of four straight pennants. Those Yankee teams, though, weren't as overpowering in the World Series, as they ended up splitting them.

The string was broken in 1959 by the Chicago White Sox, and another baseball irony surfaced. The White Sox manager was Al Lopez, who had also managed Cleveland in 1954. As a player, Lopez had played for Stengel in both Brooklyn and Boston—and had been traded both times. Revenge, though, was not Lopez's motive in either '54 or '59. He was too nice a guy to harbor a grudge, and, besides, he liked Casey.

Stengel had one more winning year left, 1960, when his team romped to an eight-game win over Baltimore, before losing one of the weirdest World Series ever; the Yankees won games by 16–3, 12–0, and 10–0 and outscored Pittsburgh, 55–27, but the Pirates won the Series in seven games, taking the final game, 10–9. "If this had been medal play," cracked a golf fan, "the Yankees would have won in four."

The Yankees fired both Stengel and the man who had hired him, George Weiss, after that season. Both men were old—Stengel was 70 and Weiss 66—and in Stengel's case, they had planned to replace him eventually with Ralph Houk, a coach on his staff, and suddenly feared that Houk would be hired by somebody else if they didn't make a move.

The Yankees wanted to make it seem that Stengel had retired, but he was too honest for that. He told newsmen that he had been given no choice. As if to confirm that, he returned in 1962 to manage the New York Mets, a collection of misfits that were even worse than the Brooklyn teams with which he had started his major league managerial career. He had come full circle.

But nothing he did before or after can dim the luster of his accomplishments with the Yankees. In just 12 years, he had tied John McGraw's major league record of ten pennants (it took McGraw 33 years) and broken Connie Mack's American League record of nine (in 50 years). His seven World Championships stand alone. Not bad for a clown.

19. The Night Rider Is Perfect

In most respects, the 1956 World Series was totally unremarkable. It matched the Yankees against the Brooklyn Dodgers, for the sixth time in a decade and the seventh time since 1941, and the Yankees won, as they had in all but one of those matchups.

Neither of those facts is important now. What everybody remembers is that the 1956 Series was the one in which Don Larsen pitched a perfect game.

To say that Larsen's perfect game was unexpected is to underline the obvious. There had never been a no-hitter in Series play, and there had not been a perfect game in regular season play since 1922.

And if such a game were to be pitched, it would be more reasonable to expect it from somebody like Yankee ace Whitey Ford or the Dodgers' Don Newcombe, who had won 27 games that season—anybody, in fact, but Larsen. Among the starting pitchers in that Series, seven had won more regular season games than Larsen.

It was not that Larsen lacked ability. A *Sports Illustrated* "scouting report" before the Series noted that Larsen had a good fastball and slider, could throw a knuckler occasionally, and had worked successfully on a change of pace that season. Many pitchers have been successful with less.

Larsen, in fact, was a fine all-round athlete. As a youth in San Diego, he was an excellent hitter and sometimes played the outfield, though he preferred to pitch. When he hit .284 as a major league rookie, there was talk of shifting him to the outfield.

But the same scouting report that detailed Larsen's strengths also referred to him as erratic and noted that he was easily rattled in tight games. There are many athletes like that, blessed with physical ability but lacking the emotional strength to be standouts.

Larsen was an easygoing man who liked the nightlife, to the point that he was nicknamed "Night Rider." His second manager, Jimmy Dykes, cracked that, "The only thing Larsen fears is sleep."

And thus, for most of his career, his story was one of unrealized potential. He pitched 14 years in the majors, largely on the strength of his potential

Don Larsen, an erratic right-hander, pitched the first perfect game in a World Series in 1956. *(George Brace)*

and one great game, but managed only five winning seasons, ending his career with but 81 wins against 91 losses.

Even in the minors, he was an indifferent pitcher, with one 17–11 season the only good one in four years. That was good enough to get him to the majors in 1953 only because he belonged to the St. Louis Browns, who had been as high as sixth place in the American League only once since the end of World War II.

Larsen pitched decently as a rookie, finishing 7–12 with the last-place Browns, but the next year he led the league in defeats with 21, winning only 3.

But good baseball men were always seeing the potential for an outstanding pitcher in Larsen, always certain that next year would be the big right-hander's year. And so, after the 1954 season the Yankees concluded a 16-player deal with the Baltimore Orioles (the Browns had moved and changed names before the season), sending outfielder Gene Woodling, pitchers Harry Byrd and Jim McDonald, catchers Gus Triandos and Hal Smith, and shortstop Willie Miranda to Baltimore in exchange for pitchers Larsen and Bob Turley and shortstop Billy Hunter.

Turley, a hard-throwing right-hander who had won 14 games and led the league with 185 strikeouts in 1954, was the key to the deal, but the Yankees were also eager to get Larsen.

"When we got Turley and Larsen," said Yankee general manager George Weiss, "we plugged the major weakness of the Yankee club. They are two of the finest and fastest young right-handers in the game. Both of them figure to get better and they are young. Turley is only 24 and Larsen 25."

Turley had his moments for the Yankees, winning 17 games in '55 and going 21–7 in 1958, but his overall record in New York—82 wins in eight seasons—was unimpressive, considering the fact that he was with a team that won seven pennants in that stretch.

Larsen did even less, winning only 45 games in five years before the Yankees finally realized he would never be a big winner for them and traded him to Kansas City.

In his first year with the Yankees, Larsen was so erratic in early season that he was sent down to the minors. He pitched well there and finished strong when he was brought up in midseason. With the Yankees, he was 9–2; with Denver of the American Association, he was 9–1, so he had a combined 18–3 mark for the year. Perhaps, he was finally on his way.

But Larsen hadn't changed. In spring training the next year, his car went off the road at 5:30 A.M., running into a telephone pole and demolishing a mailbox. Incredibly, he was not hurt. The club curfew was midnight. What was he doing out at that hour? "He was mailing a letter," said Yankee manager Casey Stengel.

Though Stengel had his rules, he was not one of those managers who felt that being in bed at midnight was the most important thing a player could do. Casey had broken a few curfews in his time, so perhaps he sympathized with his high-living players. If a player performed on the field, Stengel would overlook some things.

So, in this case, after a long talk with Larsen, Casey announced he would not fine his pitcher. Larsen was made to understand, though, that a repeat performance would mean either a stiff fine or a trade. Larsen got the message.

The chastened Larsen was not an improved Larsen, however. He was in-and-out for most of the season, winning seven and losing five in his first twelve decisions. Stengel used him both as a starter and in relief, but he was erratic in both roles.

Then, in September, Larsen seemed to find himself, winning his last four games impressively, a three-hitter and three four-hitters. He had been experimenting with a no-windup delivery (the kind pitchers generally use with runners on base), and that seemed to have helped him, psychologically if in no other way.

Stengel had Ford ready for the World Series opener, of course, but Ford didn't have it this time and was knocked out in the fourth inning as the Dodgers went on to win, 6–3, before their home fans at Ebbets Field.

Casey had used Johnny Kucks, an 18-game winner as a starter that season, in relief of Ford, so he couldn't come back with Kucks in the second game. He had 16-game winner Tom Sturdivant available, but Casey believed in going with a hot hand. Larsen had been a strong pitcher down the stretch, so he played a hunch and started Don in the second game.

Larsen was a disaster. Staked to a six-run lead in the second inning, he couldn't hold it and was knocked out in the bottom of that frame. The Dodgers tied the score in that inning and went on to win, 13–8.

At that point, the Dodgers had a 2–0 Series lead. The year before, they had lost the first two games but bounced back to win their first Series. It seemed they might finally have gotten the hang of it, but the Yankees soon disabused them of that notion, winning the next two games to tie the Series.

The next game, in Yankee Stadium, was critical for the boys from the Bronx. They could not reasonably expect to lose that one and then win two straight in Ebbets Field. So, writers were astounded when Stengel nominated Larsen to pitch the game.

"He was just pushing the ball up to the plate in Brooklyn," explained Stengel. "Maybe he was scared of the fences. He can pitch better."

But even Stengel did not know how much better. The first to realize how sharp Larsen was that day was veteran umpire Babe Pinelli, behind the plate in the next-to-last game of his career. (Pinelli had told the National League office that he was retiring after the Series but had not made an official announcement.)

When Larsen caught leadoff Dodger hitter Jim "Junior" Gilliam looking at a curve for strike three, Pinelli made a mental note. "He was a master of control that day," remembered Pinelli years later. "His change of pace, particularly to the right-handed hitters, was great, because it kept curving away from them, but the biggest thing is the way he was pinpointing his pitches. He wasn't an overpowering pitcher that day, but he was making them hit his pitch."

Pinelli was right. Indeed, Larsen seldom went to a three-ball count on a batter and threw only 97 pitches.

Larsen was so sharp that there were few plays that were even close to being hits. The first challenge occurred in the second inning, when a smash by Jackie Robinson caromed off the glove of third baseman Andy Carey to shortstop Gil McDougald, who threw Robinson out by an eyelash.

Larsen's opponent—first-game winner Sal Maglie—was equally sharp through the first three innings, pitching hitless ball, too. Pinelli, who had worked four no-hit games before, recognized what was happening. "The atmosphere carries you right along," he said. "You can tell by the way the players act and the noises from the fans when you've got a no-hitter going."

Mickey Mantle ruined Maglie's no-hitter in the fourth when, with two outs, he lined a drive into the right field seats to put the Yankees on the scoreboard.

Then, in the fifth inning, Mantle made the best fielding play of the day. With one out, Gil Hodges hit a long drive that seemed to be going into the alley in left center, but Mantle reached down at the last moment and made a backhanded stab for the out.

Larsen had one more shaky moment in that inning, his worst. Sandy Amoros lashed a drive into the right field seats—but it curved foul by a few feet. Larsen then got Amoros to ground out to end the inning.

In the sixth, Carey opened with a single to center and Larsen sacrificed him to second. Hank Bauer followed with a single to left to score the Yankees' second and last run of the day. It was more than enough for Larsen.

By the ninth inning, everybody knew what was happening, and the pressure was enormous on Larsen. He knew that another Yankee pitcher, Bill Bevens, had lost a no-hitter and the game in the ninth inning in the 1949 Series against these same Dodgers.

"I'm not what you call a real praying man," he said later, "but once out there, in the eighth or ninth, I said to myself, 'Help me out somebody.' "

Catcher Yogi Berra could not mention the no-hitter to Larsen, for fear of breaking baseball tradition. Anyway, Yogi had another concern. "They're still in the game," he told Larsen as they came out for the ninth. "Let's get the first guy. That's the important thing."

The first guy was Brooklyn right fielder Carl Furillo, always a dangerous hitter. Furillo fouled off the first two pitches, the crowd sighing each time he swung, and then took a ball. The next two pitches were also fouled off, before Furillo finally flied out to Bauer in right field, a few feet in front of the fence.

The next batter was the Dodger's powerhouse catcher, Roy Campanella, nearing the end of his career but still dangerous; he had hit 20 home runs that season. Campanella pulled one pitch down the left field line, but foul, before grounding out to Yankee second baseman Billy Martin. Larsen was just one out away.

That one out was a tough one: pinch hitter Dale Mitchell, a lifetime .312 hitter who almost always made contact; he had struck out only 119 times in an 11-year major league career.

Larsen threw a ball, then two strikes to Mitchell. By now, the crowd was roaring with each pitch. The fourth pitch was fouled back to the screen by Mitchell.

The next pitch was a fastball, low and outside. Mitchell started to swing, then held up, but Pinelli threw up his right arm. It was a strike and the game was over, the first perfect game in World Series history!

Mitchell complained a little about the call, and others questioned it later, but Pinelli had made up his mind that Larsen would get the benefit of the doubt on a close one.

Berra ran to the mound and leaped into Larsen's arms, and Larsen had to carry his staggering burden for a few steps before all the Yankee players surrounded him.

Larsen's celebrity status lasted only for the six months of the off-season, after which he lapsed once again into the familiar pattern of win-a-few, lose-a-few.

But for one rousing day, there was never anybody better, and his record will never be broken. How do you beat perfect?

THE EXPANSION ERA

20. Who's in Seattle, and Milwaukee, and . . . ?

For the first 53 years of its existence, the American League was a tight little group, the same eight teams in the same eight cities, year after year.

This couldn't last, because there were too many reasons to change. For one thing, the league had become terribly imbalanced, with a huge gulf separating the haves and the have-nots.

At one end, the Yankees almost always won, and the well-financed Red Sox, Tigers, and Indians were usually contenders. At the other end, the White Sox hadn't won a pennant since 1919, the Senators since 1924, and the A's since 1931, and the Browns' only pennant had come in the abnormal 1944 season.

It was becoming obvious that only the nation's two largest cities, New York and Chicago, could support two teams; the National League Braves had already moved out of Boston.

Because of the growth of the country there were now more cities with enough population to support major league baseball, and television was creating an appetite for major league ball among people—particularly in the western half of the notion—who had been content to watch minor league baseball before. The airplane would soon replace the train as the mode of travel for baseball clubs, which would make it possible to put teams west of the Mississippi.

So, change was inevitable, but nobody could have predicted how many changes would be made—14 in the 24 seasons starting with 1954. The American League would never be the same.

Some of the changes were smart and well considered. Many were not. Too often, owners acted hastily, preferring to move franchises or create new ones other than to try to solve the existing problems. Franchises were moved into cities which were not prepared for them, and then moved out—less than a week before the start of the season in one case. As a result, the league faced the embarrassment of being sued by a city.

The first move was a logical one, taking the Browns out of St. Louis and moving them to Baltimore. There they took the name of Orioles, which was rich in tradition; the Orioles had been a great team in the National League of the 1890s before moving to New York as the Highlanders and then the Yankees.

The Browns' problems in St. Louis were insoluble. Early in the century, the Browns had been on a relatively equal footing with the National League Cardinals—indeed, they had outdrawn the Cardinals in the very early years of the century—but that situation had changed when Branch Rickey moved from the Browns to the Cardinals. Rickey had nurtured a farm system which had won nine pennants for the Cardinals in the 1926–46 period. It was obvious St. Louis could not support two teams well, and it was equally obvious that the Cardinals were the team which would be supported. The Browns had to move.

Bill Veeck had wanted to move the Browns to Milwaukee where he had operated a minor league team in the '40s, but the Braves moved there before he could. At any rate, Veeck wasn't going anywhere, even if his team did. American League owners made it plain that the franchise would not be moved until Veeck sold it. Veeck knew he couldn't last much longer in that situation, so he sold the club, and it was transferred to Baltimore before the '54 season.

The new Orioles looked much like the old Browns that first season, losing 100 games and finishing seventh, but they soon started rebuilding under Paul Richards who took over as manager and general manager after that first season. By 1957 the Orioles were at .500, and they have been one of the most successful teams in baseball ever since.

In 1966 the Orioles traded pitcher Milt Pappas to the Cincinnati Reds for outfielder Frank Robinson, one of the most lopsided trades in baseball history. Robinson, a natural leader (he later became baseball's first major league black manager, with the Cleveland Indians), had a tremendous season, winning the Triple Crown as he hit 49 homers, drove in 122 runs, and hit .316. He also led the league in runs scored with 122 and won the Most Valuable Player award. The Orioles won the pennant and then shocked the Los Angeles Dodgers by sweeping the World Series; the young Oriole pitchers, Jim Palmer, Wally Bunker, and Dave McNally, shut out the Dodgers in the last three games.

Jim Palmer of Baltimore
was the American League's
top pitcher in the '70s,
notching eight 20-win
seasons in the decade.
(Baltimore Orioles)

Earl Weaver, often con-
sidered the finest manager
in baseball, had his
Baltimore team back on
top in 1979 despite free
agent losses.
(Baltimore Orioles)

Since then, the Orioles have been a consistent contender, and sometimes champion. They won three straight pennants, 1969–71, though taking the World Series only in 1970. In 1973 and '74, they won divisional championships, losing to the Oakland A's in the league playoff series each time. They took the pennant again in 1979, only to blow a three games to one lead in the World Series to the Pittsburgh Pirates.

The year after the Browns' move, the A's were purchased from the Mack family by Arnold Johnson and shipped to Kansas City. This, however, did not turn out as well as the St. Louis to Baltimore move.

Like the Browns, the Philadelphia Athletics were fighting a National League rival in the same city. Not that the Phillies were unconquerable rivals; their two pennants had come 35 years apart, 1915 and 1950, and there was certainly an opportunity for a better team to capture the imaginations of Philadelphia fans.

The A's were not that team. In the 20 years ending with the 1954 season they had finished last eleven times and in the first division only three. Only seven times in the 20 years had they won as many as forty percent of their games. Philadelphia was not awash with tears when they left.

Different ownership and a different location didn't help the A's. In fact, when the American League expanded, the chief effect in Kansas City was to give the A's a chance to finish even lower, in tenth place; in Philadelphia, they could go no lower than eighth. In 13 seasons in Kansas City the A's finished last five times and never higher than sixth.

A minor league farm club for the Yankees for many years, Kansas City seemed cast in the same role when it finally got (marginal) major league baseball.

The construction company owned by Yankee co-owner Del Webb got the contract to enlarge the Kansas City stadium. The new A's general manager was Parke Carroll, who had been the general manager for the Yankee farm club in Kansas City. In his dealings with Yankee general manager George Weiss, who had hired him for his first baseball job, Carroll acted as if Weiss were still his boss.

Did the Yankees need a player? Kansas City sent off such as Roger Maris, Clete Boyer, Ryne Duren, and Art Ditmar. Was a Yankee player going downhill? Kansas City had room for the likes of Bob Cerv and Bill Renna. One time, the Yankees sent Enos "Country" Slaughter to Kansas City for a season and a half and then, deciding that Slaughter could still help, "recalled" him. It was a travesty.

In 1961, the American League made three changes. First, the Senators moved from Washington to the Minneapolis-St. Paul area, and were re-named the Twins. Then, an expansion team was put into Washington, inher-iting the name of Senators, and another expansion team was put into Los Angeles, and named the Angels.

The Twins, nee Senators, had been identified with the Griffith family since 1911 when Clark had bought into the club. Clark's nephew (and adopted son) Calvin took over for him. Traditionally the club had been run on a limited budget, and it was becoming harder and harder for Calvin to compete. It was hoped that a switch to an area which had never known major league baseball would help.

It did, especially at the gate; in their first ten years, the Twins drew well over a million each season.

On the field they had their moments, too, winning the pennant in .1965 before losing to the Dodgers in the World Series, and winning divisional championships in 1969 and '70, losing each time to Baltimore in the league playoff.

And Twins' star Rod Carew, a throwback to Ty Cobb as a hitter, flirted with the .400 mark all season in 1977 before finishing at .388, the highest since Ted Williams's identical batting average 20 years earlier.

But by the second decade in Minnesota, Griffith—the last of the pure baseball owners—was having problems. Attendance had dropped below a million, and he had been forced to trade Carew to the Angels because Carew was threatening to play out his option.

The Angels were a happier story, though often accidentally, from the time they were created.

Legendary movie cowboy Gene Autry was the owner of the Golden West Broadcasting Corporation, and the firm's flagship station in Los Angeles, KMPX, had just lost the rights to the Dodgers' broadcasts. Autry went to the American League meetings to try to sign up the new franchise. Learning that the league was having trouble even selling the new franchise, Autry decided on the spot to buy it.

The Angels were the Los Angeles Angels then, because they were playing in Los Angeles—at Wrigley Field in 1961 and in Dodger Stadium the next four seasons. In 1966 they moved into a brand-new stadium in Anaheim and became known as the California Angels.

By any name, the Angels have been a colorful lot. In their second season, they finished a surprising third, and a fast-talking left-hander named Bo Belinsky became famous for pitching a no-hitter and dating movie actresses, not necessarily in that order. Belinsky was a fluke but Dean Chance, Cy

Mike Marshall, whose career had seemed ended by back trouble two years earlier, bounced back in 1979 to notch a league-leading 32 saves with the Twins. *(Minnesota Twins)*

Rod Carew won seven batting titles in 12 years in Minnesota, including a .388 mark in 1977, then forced a trade to the California Angels in 1979. *(California Angels)*

Young Award winner in 1964, and Nolan Ryan, who has pitched four no-hitters and struck out a record 383 batters in one season, 1973, were certainly not.

Addition of the two expansion teams forced the league into an unwieldy ten-team alignment, which was a serious mistake because it increased the number of teams which were out of the race. It took league owners eight years, though, to decide what to do about that problem.

By 1968, the league lineup was changed again. Charlie Finley had taken over the A's in 1961, after the death of Arnold Johnson, and he had feuded constantly with writers, fans, and civic officials. He had acquired some good young players who would form the nucleus of a championship team in the '70s, but they were not yet playing to that standard, and the A's were the second division team they had always been.

Finley was shopping his team around, eyeing Seattle, Louisville, and Oakland. He got a marketing report that told him Seattle was the best choice, but he was determined to move to Oakland and got league permission before the '68 season. Kansas City fans were decidedly ambivalent. They didn't want to see the team go, but they were delighted to get rid of Finley. Missouri Senator Stuart Symington called Oakland "the luckiest city since Hiroshima."

Kansas City was out of baseball for only one season; the American League expanded again in 1969 and put teams into Seattle and Kansas City.

This move solved two problems and created another. It enabled the league to split into two six-team divisions, which created at least the illusion of more competition, and it stilled a threat by Senator Symington to introduce legislation which would end baseball's antitrust exemption.

The new Royals quickly became competitive, finishing second in 1971,

George Brett was the key to Kansas City's success in the late '70s and, some thought, the best all-around hitter in the league. *(Kansas City Royals)*

'73, and '75 and winning division titles, 1976–78. Meanwhile, an impressive new stadium was opened in 1973, and the Royals' attendance zoomed to 2,255,493 by 1978.

The picture in Seattle was not so bright. The new Pilots had to play in an antiquated minor league stadium, and their only claim to fame was as background for Jim Bouton's book *Ball Four*. Fans were painfully aware that they were paying major league prices for what was essentially a minor league operation, and attendance was only 677,944.

The league's solution to that problem was to move the franchise to Milwaukee, where it became known as the Brewers. Seattle civic officials sued.

Meanwhile, the situation in Washington, D.C. was also reaching a crisis point.

The new Senators had been altogether too much like the old ones, finishing as high as sixth place only once in their first eight years of existence. Then, Bob Short bought the team.

Short, a Minneapolis trucking executive who had once owned the (then) Minneapolis Lakers of the National Basketball Association, tried a lot of things to stir up interest in Washington. His first big move was his best: hiring Ted Williams to manage.

In Williams's first year, 1969, he brought the Senators in fourth in their division but over .500 for the first time, for which he was named Manager of the Year. Williams helped several of his players with their hitting, as he had always maintained he could. The Senators' best hitter, though, was massive Frank Howard, who hit 48 home runs.

Short's other moves, though, backfired. He brought in Curt Flood, who was suing baseball over the reserve clause, but Flood had nothing left after sitting out a year; he was seven-for-thirty-five in early-season 1971 and then left the club.

Giving up the left side of his infield, shortstop Eddie Brinkman and third baseman Aurelio Rodriguez, Short brought in Denny McLain, the last 30-game winner. But McLain had lost his fastball. He also lost 22 games, the league high, in 1971, winning only 10, as the Senators sank to fifth place.

Williams left after that season. So did the Senators, moving to Arlington, Texas (near Dallas) for the '72 season, amid a series of charges and countercharges between Short and Washington civic officials. Once again, the nation's capital was without the national pastime.

If all these changes make you dizzy, it's understandable, but there was more to come.

In 1977, the American League decided to expand again, moving back into

Seattle and into the thriving Canadian city, Toronto. Both moves were smart, for different reasons.

The move into Seattle brought about the dropping of the city's suit against the league. This time, the city was better prepared, too. For openers, it had a stadium which was major league and then some—the domed Kingdome, which seats 59,438 in comfort and became the scene of the 1979 All-Star game.

The Mariners were a typical expansion team—the owners of established teams are never generous in supplying players for expansion teams—and finished sixth, a half game ahead of Oakland in 1977, slipping into the cellar in 1978.

The first year, helped by the presence of the new stadium as well as the new team, attendance was a good 1,338,511. The next year, it slipped to 877,440. Still, there was reason to think that a good team would draw well in Seattle.

The outlook for the Toronto Blue Jays was brighter, though the Blue Jays had played even more poorly than the Mariners, finishing seventh in their division each year and winning only 113 games in two years, compared to 120 for the Mariners.

The Seattle Mariners became the first American League club to play in a domed stadium, the Kingdome. *(Kingdome)*

Toronto's Rico Carty was one of the older hitters who benefitted from the designated hitter rule. *(Toronto Blue Jays)*

A progressive bustling city, Toronto had been eyed by major league baseball for some time. In 1976, in fact, it seemed that the city would get the National League Giants. A conditional deal had been made to move the Giants from San Francisco, but it was canceled when Bob Lurie and Bud Herseth bought the club from Horace Stoneham.

The following year the American League moved into Toronto with an expansion franchise, and the city was ready. A new 43,000-seat stadium was finished in time for the season opener on April 7. A crowd of 44,649 attended (temporary seats enlarged the capacity for that day). For the season, the Blue Jays drew 1,701,052; the next season, they pulled 1,562,585. Baseball seemed on a sound footing in Toronto.

The same could not be said of the league as a whole. The Minnesota franchise seemed to be shaky. In Oakland, attendance was incredibly low, around 3,000 a game, and there were constant rumors that the A's would be moved. For the American League, the expansion era had been a mine field.

21. Roger Earns an Asterisk

The year 1961 should have been the highlight of Roger Maris's career because it was the year he broke the most famous record in baseball: Babe Ruth's mark of 60 home runs.

Instead, the season became a nightmare for Maris, who was reviled and ridiculed by writers, fans, and even baseball personalities. Rogers Hornsby said early in the chase: "It would be a shame if Ruth's record is broken by a .270 hitter," proving once again that Hornsby's mouth should have been taped shut at birth. The commissioner of baseball made a special ruling which took the luster off Maris's feat. The unending pressure made Roger so nervous that his hair fell out, and he nearly had a nervous breakdown by the end of the season. It wasn't easy chasing a ghost.

And that was really the crux of the problem: that Maris was chasing a ghost. Jimmie Foxx had hit 58 homers only five years after Ruth had set his mark, and Babe was still playing at the time. Hank Greenberg had hit 58 only eleven years after Ruth's record season, and Babe was still in baseball for part of that season, as a coach for the Brooklyn Dodgers.

But by the time Maris came along, Ruth was dead. As Mark Twain commented, nothing improves a person's reputation like dying, and that was certainly true of Ruth, who had become a myth. Babe wouldn't have recognized himself from the mental picture in fans' minds.

Ruth's record had seemed to be one that would stand forever, but all of a sudden, it was being threatened by a player who was a relative unknown, though Maris had been the American League's Most Valuable Player the year before.

Worse, Roger was an outsider, in only his second year with the Yankees, and he was desecrating the temple. Yankee Stadium, after all, was The House That Ruth Built.

Fans saw the whole thing as a fluke, a man who was not even a .300 hitter (Maris finished at .269 that year and never had a season of .300 or better) but was lucky enough to be playing in an expansion year, when the talent was diluted. For reasons we'll get into later, that was terribly unfair to Maris, but who ever said fans have to be fair?

Who exactly was Roger Maris? Well, he was a young man who had been born in Fargo, North Dakota, which was a key to his personality. Maris was basically a small-town boy, shy and brusque with strangers (who included sportswriters). He was never comfortable with the pace of life in the nation's largest city.

He was a solid ballplayer, a fact which tended to be obscured by the attention which surrounded his home run feat. He was an excellent outfielder with a good arm, perfectly suited to playing right field. He was a good base runner who used better than average speed to take the extra base. He hustled, which impressed both teammates and opponents.

Maris started his major league career with Cleveland in 1957, hitting 14 home runs in 116 games and batting only .235. Fifty-one games into the next season, he was traded to Kansas City in a deal involving first baseman Vic Power, and he bettered his statistics to 28 home runs and a .240 batting average in 150 games for the Indians and A's.

The next season, Maris improved to a .273 average but hit only 16 home runs in 122 games, which certainly gave no indication that he would be a premier power hitter.

But Yankee general manager George Weiss thought that Maris's hitting style—he was a left-handed hitter who pulled everything down the right field line—would be ideally suited to Yankee Stadium, with its short right field wall. So, Weiss got Maris from Kansas City, along with a couple of other players who have been forgotten. In return he gave perfect game pitcher Don Larsen, first baseman Marv Throneberry, and outfielders Hank Bauer and Norm Siebern. It was a typical Yankee-A's deal; only Siebern did much for the A's.

Maris's first season in New York, 1960, fulfilled all of Weiss's hopes. Roger played a strong right field for the Yankees and had a solid, all-round season, hitting 39 homers, scoring 98 runs, leading the league with 112 RBIs, and notching his best average, .283. He beat out teammate Mickey Mantle for the MVP award as the Yankees returned to the A.L.'s winner's circle after a year's interruption. It seemed Roger would be a solid power hitter who might even be able to hit for a .300 average, if he kept improving.

But 1961 changed all that.

That season was both the best and the worst thing that happened to Maris. It made him famous, of course, and no doubt earned him a lot of extra money. But it also seemed to stop his progress as a player. Though he was only 27 in 1961 and in his prime, his post-1961 career was an anticlimax.

Forget 1961, that incredible year. Maris never even had another season as good as 1960, and he should have had one or two better ones.

Because it was an expansion year, which automatically added 20 pitchers who would not otherwise have been there, 1961 was a hitter's year. The Yankees set a team home run record with 240. Norm Cash of Detroit hit a league-leading .361, 90 points over his lifetime average, and hit 41 homers, also a career high. Jim Gentile of Baltimore hit 46 homers, more than one-fourth of his career total.

How much was Maris helped by the lowered quality of pitching? Probably not as much as some have assumed. Only two of the pitchers off whom he hit home runs—Jim Archer and Norm Bass, both of Kansas City—had not been in the league the year before, and he hit only 13 homers off expansion team pitchers, a hair below his average against the other seven clubs. And his batting average was 14 percentage points lower than the season before.

Whatever, players do not set the level of their competition, and it is unfair to criticize them for the failings of others. Hack Wilson would not have hit 56 homers or Bill Terry batted .401 if the baseball had not been hopped up in 1930. For that matter, Ty Cobb wouldn't have hit .420 in 1911 if the ball hadn't been juiced up.

The only thing that can be properly expected of a player is that he do his best, whatever the circumstances. Other batters were hitting the same ball and against the same pitchers in 1961, but only Roger Maris hit 61 home runs.

Oddly enough, Maris got off to a slow start that season, going without a home run in his first ten games; he got his first at Detroit on April 26 against Paul Foytack.

In Ruth's record year, he, too, had gotten off fairly slowly, but he started hitting home runs at a good clip earlier than Maris, and Roger remained behind Ruth's pace for the first third of the season. Then, he began hitting them in bunches, as home run hitters usually do, and he passed Ruth by hitting his 25th homer in game Number 63; Ruth hit his 25th in the Yankees' 70th game, and Babe's 66th.

From that point, Maris was ahead of Ruth's pace until home run 59, which Ruth hit in the Yankees' 153rd game and Maris got in the 155th game.

At one point, Maris was far ahead: He hit his 40th homer in game 96, compared to game 120 for Ruth. But Babe had that tremendous September in 1927, crashing 17 homers, which has always made comparison of his pace with others misleading—and which has also put tremendous pressure on a challenger coming down the stretch.

For most of the season, Mantle was just behind Maris in home runs and also had a legitimate shot at Ruth's record. When Maris had 40, Mantle had 39; when Maris had 48, Mantle had 45; when Maris had 53, Mantle had 50.

But the big pressure was always on Maris because he was the leader. And Mantle had been in many pressure situations over the years, which Maris had not.

There was another important factor: Mantle was an established star, and writers had relatively little interest in him. Maris was the new star, and writers were eager to know every little detail about him.

The questions got very personal at times. One writer asked Maris, "Do you play around on the road?"

The dumfounded Maris responded, "Do you?"

"Sure," said the writer.

"Well, I don't," said Maris.

But the worst thing about the questions was that they were the same ones, over and over. More and more writers started following the Yankees as Maris closed in on Ruth's record, and the new ones asked the same questions the old ones had asked. That's not surprising. There are only so many questions which can be asked.

Nothing in Maris's background had prepared him for this kind of attention. He was not a glib man; if a one-word answer was enough, he gave it. His teammates had known him as a friendly man before he got so much national attention, but he turned surly under the constant, repetitious questioning. Most likely that was a defense mechanism, the only one he had.

One day he came into manager Ralph Houk's office and started crying. "I can't handle this," he said. "They keep asking the same questions. It never lets up."

Houk tried to reassure Maris, but he had no words to cope with the situation. If it had been one writer, or even a half dozen, he could have talked it over, but dozens were involved. Trying to turn off the publicity at that time would have been like trying to spit into a typhoon.

"Look at this," said Maris, pulling out some hair. "My goddam hair is coming out. Did your hair ever fall out from playing baseball?"

To Maris's credit, the pressure didn't stop him. He just kept hitting home runs, and soon the pressure increased because he was alone at the top. The injury-prone Mantle had gotten an infection from an injection, and he missed several games, taking him out of the chase; he finished with 54.

Mantle could joke about it now. "I got my guy," he said, referring to the fact that he had hit more than the 47 homers Lou Gehrig had hit as the Number 2 man in the Yankees' power tandem of 1927. "Now, it's up to Roger to get his (Ruth)."

In fact, Maris and Mantle had already set a record for most homers by two teammates, passing the Ruth-Gehrig mark of 107. But that was only a sideshow to Maris's chase of Ruth's mark.

To make it worse, Commissioner Ford Frick had ruled that Maris would have to break the record inside of 154 games, instead of in the 162 games the league had gone to with expansion. If Roger took more than 154 games, his record would go into the book with an asterisk beside it to denote the longer season.

The decision enraged Maris, with reason, because it made no sense. A season is a season. Because Maris had not hit a homer in his first ten games, his home runs would all come well within a 154-game span.

Frick's decision carried the implication that it is possible to equalize circumstances but, of course, it is not. Sometimes, because of tie games, players get extra games; the American League record for triples in a season, for instance, is shared by Sam Crawford, who played in 157 games, and Joe Jackson, who played in 152. Some hitters get more at bats than others, which gives them additional opportunities; should there be an asterisk for that, too?

It was a strangely decisive action for Frick who usually evaded decisions with the comment, "That's a league matter." Why did he move on this? Some theorized that it was because Babe Ruth's widow, Claire, was still living in New York and often in attendance at Yankees' games. Others suspected it was because Frick resented the way the Yankees operated, openly flaunting the fact that they didn't worry about what the commissioner thought; the most obvious example was their flagrant shuttle to Kansas City, to which Frick had never openly objected though it was clearly not in the best interests of the sport.

The Yankees themselves did not protest Frick's ruling, though they could probably have forced him to change it. They thought the controversy was good for the gate. As usual, Maris was caught in the middle, and not liking it.

Six times that season, Maris hit two homers in a game (Ruth had done it eight times in '27). The last time came on September 2, in Detroit, in the Yankees' 135th game and Maris's 134th, as he got Number 52 off Frank Lary and Number 53 off Hank Aguirre.

He went four games without another, then hit three in four games, tagging Tom Cheney in Washington and Dick Stigman and Jim "Mudcat" Grant in Cleveland.

But the pace was telling on Maris. He went another eight games before hitting Number 57; only once before, since he had hit his first homer, had he gone that long between home runs. The next day, he got Number 58, off Terry Fox of Detroit.

And now, because of Frick's strange ruling, another question arose: What constituted the 154th game of the season? Maris had sat out one game. So, was the 154th game, for record purposes, to be the one the Yankees played or Maris's 154th the next day?

As it happened, it didn't matter. Maris couldn't reach Ruth's record under either interpretation. Through the Yankees' first 154 games, he stood at 58 homers. The next night—in Baltimore, Ruth's birthplace—he hit Number 59 off Milt Pappas in the third inning, but in three more at bats that night, he struck out, flied to center, and grounded to the pitcher.

The Yankees, nevertheless, celebrated that night. In the midst of all the home run excitement, there was a pennant race of sorts, and the Yankees had clinched the pennant that night. Maris celebrated with everybody else, showing no disappointment that he hadn't hit Number 60.

Maris was not carried away with the excitement of his 59th home run. The fan who caught the ball reportedly told Maris he could have it for two sets of tickets to the World Series and an expense-paid trip to New York, all of which would have cost Maris between $500 and $600. Maris decided he didn't want the ball that badly.

The Yankees were home for the final week of the season and, on Tuesday night, in game Number 159 (the Yankees actually played 163 that season with one tie game), Maris slammed Number 60 into the upper right field seats off Jack Fisher of Baltimore.

Maris took the next night off, returning for the final series of the season, starting Friday night against the Red Sox. He was blanked that night by Bill Monbouquette. Two games left.

The television cameras had been following Maris for the last few games, but the fans were surprisingly blasé in New York. Only about 19,000 were there on Saturday, as Maris was held to a single by Don Schwall. And on Sunday, only 23,154 were there (in a park which then seated more than 60,000) to watch Maris give it one more shot.

His first time up, Maris flied weakly to right field off young, hard-throwing Boston right-hander Tracy Stallard. But in the fourth inning, he got

Roger Maris set a home run record with 61 in 1961 and found it was no picnic chasing a ghost.
(New York Yankees)

everything behind a Stallard fastball and rocketed it into the right field stands for his historic 61st home run.

This time he didn't even have to worry about paying for the ball. A restaurant owner in Sacramento, California, Sam Gordon, had announced he would pay $5,000 to whomever caught it and then turn it over to Maris. Sal Durante, a 19-year-old truck mechanic, was the one who caught it.

For Maris, the hunt was over. "I'm happy," he said. "It's a good feeling."

It wasn't a bad feeling even for Stallard, who gained a piece of fame as the pitcher who served up the historic home run. He gained some more before a radio interview by Howard Cosell. Unaware that the microphone was on, Stallard said, "What'll it be tonight, Howard? Do you bullshit me or do I bullshit you?"

Anyone familiar with Cosell's career can answer that one.

Maris played five more seasons with the Yankees, his production going steadily downhill. When he hit .233 in 1966, it was obvious his usefulness to the Yankees was gone, though he was still only 32. He was traded to the St. Louis Cardinals.

He played well for the Cardinals the next two seasons, a key man in the two pennants they won in that period, and he seemed happier than he had been in the pressure years with the Yankees. One indication of that in later years was the fact that he more often wore the two Worlds Series rings he got playing for the Cardinals than the five he got playing for the Yankees.

St. Louis owner Gussie Busch, whose fortune had come from the Budweiser beer operation, liked the way Maris had played for the Cardinals. When Roger retired, Busch made it possible for him to get a beer distributorship in Florida.

With retirement, Maris virtually disappeared from the public eye. The Yankees would invite him to Old-Timers games, but he always refused. Then, new Yankee owner George Steinbrenner made a change for the 1978 season, inviting Maris and Mantle to the opening day ceremonies. This time, Maris accepted.

It was an emotional ceremony. Mantle and Maris were introduced by old-time Yankee announcer Mel Allen, and then taken on a cart out to center field. Opera star Robert Merrill sang the national anthem as the American flag and World Series banner were raised on the flagpole.

But there was still something missing. The Yankees had retired the uniforms worn by Mantle, Ruth, Gehrig, Whitey Ford, Yogi Berra, Bill Dickey, and Casey Stengel—but Maris's Number 9 was being worn by Graig Nettles.

Off the field, there was a "memorial park" with monuments to Ruth, Gehrig, and Miller Huggins. Plaques honored Jake Ruppert, Ed Barrow, Joe DiMaggio, Joe McCarthy, Stengel, Mantle—and Pope Paul VI, who had celebrated a Mass in 1965 at the stadium. But there was nothing there honoring Maris.

Roger Maris was still the outsider.

22. The Impossible Dream

A strange, almost unbelievable thing happened to the American League in the mid-1960s: The New York Yankees collapsed.

The demise of the empire began in 1964, but it went unnoticed at the time because the Yankees won their fifth straight pennant and fourteenth in 16 years. A hot September and the pride and confidence that comes from winning so frequently saw them through, but it was the last gasp of a once-great team.

Manager Ralph Houk had been elevated to general manager before the start of the season, and the popular Yogi Berra had been named manager. But Berra was neither the firm leader that Houk had been nor the imaginative one that Casey Stengel had been, and he had a hard time gaining the respect of his players, most of whom had known him as a player before. An incident on the team bus after a loss in mid-August, was typical of the club's internal problems. Berra got into an argument with reserve infielder Phil Linz because Linz was playing a harmonica.

At that time, the Yankees were only third, behind Baltimore and Chicago, but they soon made their move. Mel Stottlemyre was brought up from the minors and won nine games in two months. Pedro Ramos was bought from Cleveland to strengthen the bull pen. Mickey Mantle recovered from a leg injury, and the Yankees went 22–6 in September, clinching the pennant on the next-to-last day.

That was not enough to save Berra; Houk had decided to replace Yogi even before the Yankees lost to the St. Louis Cardinals in the World Series. He replaced Berra with Johnny Keane, who had been the Cardinals' manager. (That was part of a bizarre story. St. Louis owner Gussie Busch had planned to replace Keane with Leo Durocher before the Cardinals had rallied to win the pennant. Busch then tried to rehire Keane, but the proud Keane walked out.)

Houk soon learned that although Yogi might have been part of the team's problem, he wasn't the major part. The Yankees fell to sixth in 1965 and didn't secure higher than fifth place for the rest of the decade. Not until

1976 would they win another pennant, by far their longest dry spell since Babe Ruth had arrived.

What happened? As in most such cases, there were a number of reasons.

One was that the farm system had dried up. For decades, Ed Barrow and then George Weiss had run an organization which had a continual stream of good young players coming up. Some players stayed; some were used to trade for veterans the major league club needed. By 1965 there was no supply of good youngsters, and it didn't help when the major leagues adopted a player draft in June of that year. No longer would the Yankees have a monopoly on signing high school players.

Meanwhile, key players were getting old. Roger Maris had gone steadily down since hitting 61 homers in 1961. Whitey Ford won 16 games in 1965 but only 2 in each of the next two seasons; he retired after the 1967 season.

Most damaging of all, Mantle's string of injuries had curtailed his effectiveness and would soon bring an early end to his career. His 1964 season, in which he hit 35 homers, drove in 111 runs, and hit .303, was his last good one. In his last four years before retirement, Mantle never hit more than 23 homers, drove in more than 56 runs, or hit .300; his last two averages were sickly, .245 and .237, and brought his career average below .300.

One reason the Yankees had no replacements for Mantle and Ford was their reluctance to go after black players. As a league, the American League trailed the National in signing black players, which resulted in the National League gaining a superiority for perhaps the first time, and the Yankees trailed even other American League clubs.

Officially, the Yankees explained this by saying they wanted their first black player to fit the "Yankee image." Certainly, that player—catcher Elston Howard—did. Howard was a fine player and a gentleman, and his bearing was that of an ambassador.

Howard came up in 1955. Before that, the Yankees had traded away Vic Power, a fine-fielding first baseman and good hitter who went on to have a good 12-year major league career. Power did not fit the "Yankee image."

Not many blacks did. The word in baseball was that Yankee scouts had been told not to look too hard for black players. Certainly, they didn't find many. By 1964, 17 years after Jackie Robinson's debut in the National League, 16 years after Larry Doby and Hank Thompson had played in the American, the Yankees had only one black starter, Howard, and one black pitcher, Al Downing.

In contrast, the Cardinal team that beat the Yankees that fall had three blacks (Lou Brock, Curt Flood, and Bill White) and one Latin (Julian Javier) in the starting lineup. And the Cards' best pitcher was another black, Bob Gibson.

The Yankees had, in effect, ignored a whole new market of players, and they paid for it. But what was bad news in New York was great news around the rest of the league because there was suddenly real competition for the pennant.

There is no better example of that than 1967, when four teams went down to the final week of the season in what was certainly one of the most dramatic and exciting pennant races in history.

The most dramatic story of all was the Boston Red Sox, whose pennant became known as "The Impossible Dream," and for good reason. Anybody predicting a Red Sox pennant before that season started would have been locked up immediately, before he could endanger himself or others.

The Red Sox have always been a colorful, unpredictable team, mainly because of the park in which they play. Fenway Park is certainly the most enjoyable in the league in which to watch a game because it is small and everybody is close to the action, and its high left field wall, only slightly more than 300 feet from home plate, makes big innings and high-scoring games the rule rather than the exception.

That wall, known as "The Green Monster," has a great influence on the Red Sox. The team management has always gone after strong right-handed hitters who could pop the ball over that wall, and the Red Sox have always been very tough at home because of that.

But on the road, the hitters who found it so easy to hit the ball out at Fenway find the same hits becoming nothing but easy flies, and the Red Sox have traditionally been a poor road team. In 1949, for instance, they won 61 games of 77 at home but were only 35–42 on the road and lost the pennant; the two losses which cost them the pennant, of course, were in Yankee Stadium.

The Red Sox also have a history of pitchers who have one or two good seasons and then go bad, and the pressure of pitching in Fenway is certainly a big factor. That pressure is especially tough for a left-hander; since the advent of the lively ball, Mel Parnell is the only left-hander to win 20 games for the Red Sox.

The situation was also complicated by the Red Sox owner, Tom Yawkey, who had bought the club in 1933. Yawkey was a millionaire several times over, and he spent a lot of money trying to get a winner at Fenway. He bought players like Jimmie Foxx and Lefty Grove, and he made offers for others that were rejected, notably $1 million for Herb Score.

Yawkey was equally generous with his salaries; too generous, some said. The atmosphere in the Red Sox clubhouse was likened to a country club. The team's many critics said the players were spoiled by huge salaries and unwilling to play hard enough to win; a more objective view would have been that they lacked the balance of the Yankee pennant-winners.

The Red Sox had long had a natural rivalry with the Yankees because the cities were so close, but the rivalry had been terribly lopsided; from 1949 through 1966, the Yankees had finished ahead of the Red Sox every year. In 1966, the Red Sox finally beat out the Yankees—by finishing in ninth place, half a game ahead of the tenth-place Yanks. That wasn't quite what Boston fans had in mind.

All that changed in 1967, and the change began with the hiring of Dick Williams, who changed the whole approach.

"There was too much talent on that team to finish ninth," Williams recalled, years later. "The problem was that they weren't playing fundamentally sound baseball. I had to virtually go back to the beginning with them, almost to the point of explaining what a baseball was."

He also was much stricter. "I was a real tyrant," he said. "I was strict about curfew, about hair length—of course, that was a different era. I don't think there were many players on that club who liked me, but I didn't hear of any who turned back their World Series checks because of that."

Williams was, and is, a fine manager, a man who insists that his players do the little things that win games: taking the extra base, knowing when to steal, executing the hit-and-run properly, throwing to the right base. As he would do later with another champion, the Oakland A's, Williams insisted that his players always be prepared, that they always know what the situation was.

It was a different looking Red Sox team that took the field that spring, playing alertly and intelligently. And nowhere was the difference more obvious than in left field, where Carl Yastrzemski played.

Yastrzemski had been signed for a $100,000 bonus by the Red Sox in 1958, when he was at Notre Dame. His first year of professional ball, with Raleigh of the Carolina League, he had hit .377. His second year, at Minneapolis of the American Association, he had hit .339. That year, Ted Williams retired, and when Yaz came up the next year, he was heralded as the "next Ted Williams."

He hit only .266 that first year, though, and spent most of his first six seasons with the Red Sox struggling to match his potential. He had his moments—his .321 led the league in batting in 1963—but not enough of them. He hit .300 only twice in his first six seasons, never hit more than 20 home runs, and didn't have a season of 100 RBIs.

The trouble, most thought, was that Yastrzemski didn't have the right mental approach. Chicago White Sox manager Eddie Stanky, who had made the most of very limited ability as a player, called Yastrzemski "a great player from the neck down."

But in 1967, Yastrzemski came of age, mentally and physically. He started a string of seasons which will no doubt put him in the Hall of Fame eventually, and the first one was his best: His .326 batting average and 121 RBIs led the league, and his 44 homers tied Harmon Killebrew—and were also one more than Williams's best season.

But the statistics don't begin to tell the story. It wasn't just what he did but when he did it. That year, Yaz always seemed to be there when the Red Sox needed a big play. Whether it was a home run or a single, a great catch or a perfect throw, Yastrzemski always seemed to make it. Never has a player been a more obvious choice as Most Valuable.

Dick Williams had played on the great Brooklyn Dodger teams of the '50s that had Jackie Robinson, Roy Campanella, Duke Snider, Gil Hodges, and Pee Wee Reese, but he said after the 1967 season that he had never seen a player have the kind of year Yastrzemski had had.

There was a portent of things to come in the first game of the season, at Fenway, when Jim Lonborg beat Chicago, 5–4, as Rico Petrocelli hit a three-run homer into the screen. Lonborg was a young right-hander with impressive size (6′ 5″, 200 pounds) and the pitches to be a big winner, but he had been only 9–17 and 10–10 in his first two seasons. He wasn't mean enough, some said, but on opening day, when a Red Sox hitter was dusted off, he went to Williams and said, "Who do you want me to get?" Batters soon stopped digging in on Lonborg, and he went 22–9 that season.

Only a few days into the season, 21-year-old Billy Rohr held the Yankees hitless for 8⅔ innings before Elston Howard's single broke the spell; the Red Sox won, 3–0.

In Chicago, the Red Sox won a double-header and Yaz went six-for-nine, including a home run. As he circled the bases after his homer, he tipped his hat to Stanky, who had insulted him.

Even unhappy players were contributing. Third baseman Joe Foy said, after an argument with Williams, that he should be playing in New York, his hometown; he then hit a grand-slam at Yankee Stadium as the Red Sox won, 7–1. Tony Conigliaro, also unhappy with Williams, nonetheless homered in the bottom of the 11th at Fenway to give the Red Soxs a 1–0 win, again over the Yankees.

Not until July, just before the All-Star game, did the Red Sox slump, losing two to the Angels and three to Detroit, all on the road. But Lonborg and Yastrzemski combined to break the slump, Lonborg pitching well and Yaz homering to beat the Tigers in the last game before the break.

After the All-Star break, the Red Sox ran up ten straight. Until then, it had been a five-team race, but in August, the Angels slumped and fell out of the race. That left the White Sox, Twins, and Tigers battling with the Red Sox, and it would remain that way nearly to the end.

On August 18, tragedy struck the Red Sox as young slugger Conigliaro was hit by a pitch by Jack Hamilton of the Angels. Conigliaro said later that the pitch seemed to follow him in. He had pulled away from the plate so fast that his helmet had flipped off, and the pitch fractured his left cheekbone.

Conigliaro had seemed on his way to becoming one of the top home run hitters of all time. He had hit 24 homers in his rookie season, a league-leading 32 in his second season, 28 in his third. He was leading the league with 20 after 95 games in 1967—and he was still only 22. His 104 homers dwarfed what Ted Williams (54), Jimmie Foxx (49), and Lou Gehrig (22) had had at the same age. (Ruth had only nine but was still a pitcher, which makes a comparison irrelevant.)

The injury kept Conigliaro from ever reaching the heights expected of him. He was sidelined until the 1969 season and then put together two good seasons, hitting 20 and 36 homers, respectively. But he was plagued again by double vision and, after being traded to California before the 1971 season, retired halfway through the season, having hit only 4 homers. He unretired briefly in '75, again with the Red Sox, but made it permanent after getting only seven hits, two of them homers, in 57 at bats.

The human tragedy aside, the Red Sox needed somebody to at least partially replace Conigliaro, which wasn't easy. First, they picked up veteran outfielder Jim Landis, who had been released by Detroit, but Landis wasn't the answer; he was released five days after he'd been signed.

In the meantime, though, a power-hitting right-handed outfielder had become available through the most bizarre of circumstances. Kansas City A's owner Charlie Finley had become embroiled in a dispute with his players as a result of a plane ride during which some players had apparently insulted the stewardesses.

Finley fired his manager, Alvin Dark, because he felt Dark had lost control. Several players backed up Dark, and the most vocal was Ken "Hawk" Harrelson, who made public statements that Finley deemed insulting.

The enraged Finley then "fired" Harrelson, making him a free agent. The workings of Finley's mind are mysterious indeed, and never more so than in that case. His intent was to punish Harrelson, but his action made it possible for Harrelson to reap a big financial benefit.

In the past, there had been many cases of players getting big bonuses out of high school, but once a player signed with a club, he could negotiate only with that club. This time, Finley had made it possible for Harrelson to negotiate in what was an outstanding seller's market.

The White Sox immediately offered Harrelson $50,000. He just laughed. Shortly after, the Red Sox offered him double that, and he accepted.

Harrelson did not have a great season that year; the next season, when he hit 35 homers with the help of the friendly Green Monster in left, was his best. He had just three home runs and 14 RBIs in 23 games down the stretch for the Red Sox in '67. But considering how close the race was, it is safe to say the Red Sox could not have won without Harrelson's contribution.

But it was still Yaz's contribution that was the biggest, without question. A homer in the eighth inning on August 30 brought a 2–1 win over New York; two homers against Washington on September 5 ended a three-game Boston losing streak.

And the tighter the race got, the looser Yaz got. For the final two weeks of the season he hit an incredible .522; included among his 23 hits in that span were five homers and four doubles, and he knocked in 16 runs.

With a week to go, only a game and a half separated the top four teams: Boston and Minnesota, 90–68; Chicago, 89–69; and Detroit, 88–69.

The White Sox folded shortly after that, losing a double-header to Kansas City and then five straight to Washington, dropping out of the race. But the other three were still in it.

The Red Sox lost two straight to Cleveland on Tuesday and Wednesday of that last week and then had two days off; next were single games against Minnesota on Saturday and Sunday in Boston.

The Tigers, meanwhile, were scheduled for four games against California in Detroit, but it rained both Thursday and Friday, which meant they'd have to play double-headers both days. The standings at that point: Minnesota, 91–69; Detroit, 89–69; Boston, 90–70. The Red Sox not only had to win both games against Minnesota but had to hope that Detroit would lose at least one game to the Angels.

The Red Sox won that first game, 6–2, as Yaz knocked in the go-ahead run (at 2–1) with a single and hit a three-run homer in the seventh. The Tigers split, so at the end of the day, the Red Sox and Twins were tied for the lead at 91–70 and the Tigers were a half game back, at 90–70.

Baseball doesn't get any more exciting than the final day of that season. In Boston, the two best pitchers in the league were matched—Lonborg against the Twins' Dean Chance, a 20-game winner that year and a past winner of the Cy Young Award. In Detroit, the Tigers won the first game of their double-header while the Red Sox and Twins were still playing and thus climbed momentarily into first place.

The Twins scored first, with Tony Oliva's double driving in a run in the first and an uncharacteristic error by Yastrzemski allowing the second run in the third.

In the sixth, Lonborg startled everybody by beating out a bunt as the leadoff hitter; he had noticed that third baseman Cesar Tovar was playing deep and that Chance's motion threw him off the mound, in no position to field a bunt.

Jerry Adair and Dalton Jones singled to load the bases, and guess who came up next? Yastrzemski singled in the tying runs. Harrelson followed with a grounder to shortstop, and when Zoilo Versalles threw home, Jones was safe and Yaz moved to second. Al Worthington came in to relieve for the Twins and threw two wild pitches, Yaz scoring on the second one. Harrelson scored the fifth run of the inning on an error by Killebrew before the Twins finally got the side out.

Yastrzemski had one great play left. In the eighth, the Twins had Tony Oliva on first and Killebrew on second with two outs. Bob Allison lined a shot into the left field corner. Killebrew scored easily, and Oliva rounded third.

Yastrzemski realized he had little chance to get Oliva, so he put his right foot against the wall in left field and threw a bullet to second base. Allison was nailed there, and the inning was over. The Red Sox were only three outs away from at least a tie for the pennant.

Ted Uhlaender opened the top of the ninth with a single, but Rod Carew hit into a double play and pinch hitter Rich Rollins popped out. Boston had won, knocking Minnesota out of the race.

But there was still that unfinished business in Detroit, and the Red Sox players could only fidget in the clubhouse, listening to the radio and rooting for California.

The Tigers were ahead when the Red Sox came into the clubhouse, but then the Angels tied it and went ahead. Finally, the game ended with Dick

McAuliffe hitting into a double play, and the Red Sox had won the pennant and clinched "The Impossible Dream."

The World Series was an anticlimax after that, especially since the Red Sox were given little chance against an obviously superior St. Louis Cardinal team which had won 101 games and breezed to the National League pennant by 10½ games. Nevertheless, with Yaz batting .400, the Red Sox extended the Cards to seven games. Lonborg finally ran out of gas in the final game, pitching with only two days rest, and the Cards won the game, 7–2, and the Series.

That didn't really matter. To baseball fans everywhere—and most particularly in Boston—1967 belongs to the Red Sox.

23. A Bad Boy Wins 31

Isaac Newton would have loved the years 1930 and 1968. Newton postulated that for every action, there is an equal and opposite reaction, and those years certainly proved his point. The hitters went wild in 1930; the pitchers got their revenge in 1968.

Statistics tell the story graphically. In 1930, Lefty Grove was the only pitcher to allow fewer than three earned runs a game; in 1968, there were five starters who allowed less than *two* earned runs a game. In 1930, only one team had a staff ERA of under four runs a game; in '68, seven teams had a staff ERA of under three.

In the entire league only two hitters had truly outstanding seasons. Frank Howard, a 6'7", 255-pound bruiser who seemed as big as a two-story house at the plate, had his best year, hitting 44 home runs (Howard also hit 48 and 44 in the next two seasons before tailing off). Ken Harrelson hit 35 home runs and led the league with 109 RBIs while playing his first full season in Fenway Park, a park which was ideally suited to his batting style.

But Carl Yastrzemski won the batting title at .301, lowest in the league's history, and only a hot last week got Yaz to that figure and saved the league from the embarrassment of having a batting champion hitting under .300.

Some fine hitters had bad years. Frank Robinson, who had hit 49 home runs and batted .316 just two seasons earlier, had only 15 homers and a .268 batting average; it was the only season in Robinson's first five in the American League that he batted under .300.

Tony Oliva, a three-time league batting champion with a lifetime average of .306, batted .289. Rod Carew, who would bat as high as .388 in 1977, could manage only .273 in '68. Norm Cash, a .363 hitter in 1961, was exactly 100 points under that in 1968. Mickey Mantle hit .237. Detroit shortstop Ray Oyler, Boston first baseman George Scott, New York shortstop Tom Tresh, Oakland catcher Dave Duncan, Minnesota shortstop Jackie Hernandez, California catcher Bob Rodgers, Washington shortstop Ron Hansen, and Washington catcher Paul Casanova all hit under .200 as regulars!

There were 150 shutouts (in 810 games) and individual exploits were common. Luis Tiant won 20 games for the first time in his career and had a

1.60 ERA. Tiant allowed only 152 hits in 258⅔ innings, an average of about 5⅓ hits per 9 innings, and had nine shutouts.

Sam McDowell had a 1.81 ERA and struck out 283 batters in only 269 innings. Ray Culp, an in-and-out pitcher who had 22 shutouts in a 12-year career, got 4 of them in succession at one point in the '68 season. Jim "Catfish" Hunter, a young pitcher who would later play a critical role in baseball history, pitched a perfect game.

But all of these accomplishments paled alongside that of Denny McLain, a brash, baby-faced, 24-year-old right-hander for Detroit who won 31 games, the first time an American League pitcher had gone over 30 since Grove's 31 in 1931 and the first time in the major leagues since Dizzy Dean's 30–7 season in 1934 for the St. Louis Cardinals of the National League.

Unlike Grove, who had gotten four of his wins in relief (so had Dean, incidentally), McLain was strictly a starter, and his statistics were very impressive: 41 starts, 28 complete games, 336 innings pitched (all league-leading marks), only 241 hits, 280 strikeouts, 6 shutouts, and an earned run average of 1.96.

McLain was not exactly an unknown before that year—he had already won 59 major league games—but his personality tended to overshadow his pitching abilities, and he'd had trouble convincing teams that he was as good as he said he was.

Denny had been signed by the White Sox in 1962 after winning 38 games and losing only 7 for Chicago's Mt. Carmel High, but the White Sox didn't protect him after his first professional year, and Detroit picked him up for $8,000 on first-year waivers.

He pitched in the minors for most of the next season, 1963, and then was brought up at the end of that campaign long enough to pitch in three games. The next year, he pitched in 19 contests but was only 4–5. In 1965, however, he made his breakthrough, winning 16 (losing only 6) and setting a major league record by striking out the first seven batters he faced in relief in a June 16 game.

The next year, he won 20 games and seemed to have a very bright future, though he dipped to a 17–16 record in 1967. But the Tigers were not impressed. They tried to trade McLain to Baltimore after the 1967 season, seeking shortstop and leadoff hitter Luis Aparicio from the Orioles in what would have been a multiplayer trade.

Instead, the Orioles traded Aparicio to the White Sox, apparently because they feared that Aparicio would be what the Tigers needed to win the pennant. If so, that is ironic indeed, because the Tigers did win the pennant with

Luis Aparicio was a star shortstop and stolen base champion for the Chicago White Sox.
(Chicago White Sox)

McLain that year, and they certainly would not have if he'd been traded. McLain didn't win his first game until his third start, but from that point he was the very definition of a stopper, winning virtually every time out—23 of his first 26 decisions. Since he was pitching every fourth game, the Tigers had no worry about long losing streaks.

Winning didn't change McLain's style much, if at all. He was as cocky as ever, saying the first thing that came to his mind, even if it meant he had to apologize for it later.

Early in the season, for instance, he indulged himself in a long diatribe against the Detroit fans, accusing them of being front-runners. After all the writers but one had left the dressing room, he told the remaining writer that he had been referring to one percent of the fans. But that, of course, is not the way it appeared in the papers the next day, and McLain was roundly booed on his next appearance.

For the first few games, McLain appeared with dyed red hair, but he got so much kidding about it that he let it grow back to its natural brown and then denied that he had dyed it. "It was Mother Nature," he explained ingenuously.

In June, he claimed that a smoke bomb had been put under the hood of his car, where it was detected by a service station attendant. In July he claimed that the Tigers' success (they were 7½ games in front at the time) was due to the fact that the Detroit newspapers were on strike. "The big thing is the writers are not around demoralizing the players," he said.

In July, too, after throwing a shutout against Washington, he said he hated Tiger Stadium. "It's been a long time since I threw a shutout in this park," he said.

In August, he told UPI's Milt Richman in New York that he had been pitching with a torn shoulder muscle, though he was 25–4 then. Pressed on that, Denny amended his statement to say the muscle was stretched.

And in September, after he had caught a Boog Powell line drive and turned it into the start of a triple play, he told reporters that he had caught the ball at forehead level, and if he hadn't, it would have hit him in the head. Newspaper pictures showed him catching the ball at belt level.

But that was Denny McLain. Immature? Certainly. Impetuous? Indeed. But he didn't let any of that bother him when he was on the mound, and in 1968, he was a great pitcher.

McLain won his first five games before losing. He notched his 12th win (against 2 losses) on June 20, and he had a no-hitter until George Scott singled to left with two outs in the seventh.

On July 3, with the season less than half over, McLain won his 15th game, and writers were beginning to track his progress as they had followed Roger Maris in his home run chase in 1961. McLain, though, was better equipped to handle the crush of reporters than Maris because he always had something to say. Sometimes what he said even made sense, but that was not a requirement for McLain, who would often contradict himself in successive sentences.

After his 15th win, for instance, he told reporters that he didn't consider himself the best pitcher in the league; he put that endorsement on Sam McDowell. But then he said, "I consider myself the best pitcher in the league on nights when I go out to pitch."

On July 7, McLain won his 16th in the first game of a double-header against Oakland and then played "Satin Doll" on the stadium organ. Playing the organ and flying were two of McLain's off-field passions, and he indulged himself in the latter on July 10, before and after the All-Star game in Houston. He flew in from Las Vegas in a borrowed Lear jet and pitched two scoreless innings, and then flew back after the game.

On July 27, McLain won his 20th, the first since Grove to reach the 20-game mark in July, with a three-hit shutout over Baltimore. On July 31, he won his 21st, against Washington, and told the press that he had been given an organ by Hammond and that he would be performing in Las Vegas after the season.

McLain's 23rd win came on August 8 against Cleveland, after which he told writers that he was cutting a record and making clothing endorsements. "If I win 30 games and don't get $200,000, I might not be here next year," he said. He did win 30, he didn't get half $200,000, but he was there next year.

After his 24th win, McLain revealed that Ed Sullivan and Joey Bishop were after him for TV appearances and that he was going on the "Today Show." Later, there were interviews with *Time* and *Life*. The attention didn't seem to be bothering McLain.

His great pitching was bringing McLain in touch with some show business personalities. In Anaheim, he spent a day conferring with the Smothers brothers and came away raving about Tommy Smother's house. "It's worth $350,000 to $400,000," he said. "I want one like it someday." After his 29th win, he left the clubhouse with singer Glen Campbell and told him, "I always wanted to be in show business."

On September 14, against the Oakland A's in Detroit, McLain went for Number 30. It was a moment of high drama, relieved somewhat by A's catcher Jim Pagliaroni who walked around before the game with a sign on his back: DOBSON GOING FOR NO. 10 TODAY.

Dizzy Dean was in town to watch McLain's try, but Dizzy was thrown out of the press box by Watson Spoelstra, who said Dean wasn't a baseball writer.

It was not one of McLain's classic games. Reggie Jackson homered twice off him and the A's were ahead, 4–3, going into the bottom of the ninth. A pitcher other than McLain would probably have been out of the game by then.

In the bottom of the ninth, Al Kaline pinch-hit for McLain to lead off the inning and walked. Dick McAuliffe then fouled out, but Mickey Stanley singled to center and Kaline raced to third.

The A's infield played halfway to cut off the run, and Jim Northrup bounced to first baseman Danny Cater. Kaline broke for the plate and might have been out, but Cater's throw was high, sailing over catcher Dave Duncan's head as Kaline scored. Stanley moved to third on the play.

That forced the A's to play their outfield shallow because a deep fly would have scored Stanley easily. Then, Willie Horton laced a long drive that sailed far over the head of left fielder Jim Gosger and Stanley came in with the winning run. McLain had Number 30.

McLain ran out of the dugout with the other Tigers to embrace Horton and then stayed out to wave at the fans. The fans, the same ones who had booed him early in the season, let loose a mighty collective roar. "Those people," says Denny. "It's fantastic! They're the best fans in the world."

The writers gathered around his locker later kept McLain a long time, answering questions of all descriptions. Finally, one asked what McLain would do to celebrate.

"I'm going home and have a couple of cool ones," said Denny. "Then my wife and I will think of something."

The next day, Detroit manager Mayo Smith, who had tried to trade McLain before the season, talked to Mike Rathet of the Associated Press about McLain:

"This is a 24-year-old boy reaching for Utopia. You accept what he is and work with that. But this is what makes him a great pitcher. He's brash enough. You can't take that brashness away from him, and you wouldn't want to. I like him for what he is.

"Last year he couldn't throw a slider. But in spring training, the second day in camp, all of a sudden he got it. As for concentration, I couldn't do that for him. [Pitching coach] John Sain couldn't do that for him. He did that himself.

"That's why I say Denny has grown up a lot since last year. He has learned to keep his emotions better under control. There have been times he could have blown his top in a tough situation. But he hasn't."

McLain won his 31st in his next start, beating the Yankees despite Mickey Mantle's 535th (and last) career home run. Still, there were many who questioned his ability, much as they had Maris's in 1961, because he hadn't had a long record of success, and because his great accomplishment came in a weak year for the league.

Those doubts became greater when McLain lost his first two starts in the World Series against the Cardinals, both against Bob Gibson, who had had a fantastic year (22–9, 1.12 ERA) himself. McLain partially redeemed him-

Denny McLain won 31 games for the 1968 Tigers, the first American Leaguer to win more than 30 in 37 years. *(Detroit Tigers)*

self with a sixth-game win, but it was three-game winner Mickey Lolich who was the pitching hero as the Tigers won the Series in seven games.

Despite his Series setbacks, McLain had a great off-season, reaping the benefits of his incredible season. He was unanimously named the league's Most Valuable Player. He got a lucrative new contract, though short of the $200,000 he had announced as his goal. And he played the organ and sang at the Riviera Hotel in Las Vegas.

"A Frank Sinatra I'm not," he admitted, after singing an off-color version of "Bye, Bye Blackbird."

The Las Vegas appearance also gave McLain another opportunity to put his foot firmly in his mouth, a technique that he had mastered. The first night he walked on the stage he said, "I wouldn't trade a dozen Mickey Loliches for one Bob Gibson." Realizing later that he hadn't meant to say that, he went out the second night—and said the same thing! Finally, on the third night he told his audience, "I wouldn't trade a dozen Bob Gibsons for one Mickey Lolich. That's what I meant to say."

Because McLain's stay on center stage turned out to be very short, there is a tendency to think that he had just one fluky year, and only because of a dead ball. But that overlooks the fact that he came back in '69 with an excellent year.

Considering everything, in fact, it was certainly comparable to his 31-win season. The rules-makers, shuddering at the thought of a repeat of the 1968 season, had lowered the pitching mound for '69 and juiced up the ball, and the hitters were back in command. But McLain led the league in wins with 24 (losing only nine), had a 2.80 ERA and a league-leading nine shutouts. He was no fluke.

Incredibly, though, 1969 was his last effective season. The next year, he was suspended for half a season by commissioner Bowie Kuhn when it was learned he had been betting on games, and when he came back in midseason, he had lost his fastball. He was only 3–5, with a miserable 4.65 ERA.

Was it just one of those seasons that happen to even the best? Washington owner Bob Short thought so. He traded for McLain in the off-season, and then learned to his dismay that McLain was only a shadow of the pitcher he had been. He was still a league leader, but this time in the loss column—22, against only 10 wins.

McLain hung on for one more major league season, split between Oakland and the Atlanta Braves of the National League, and went 4–7. That was it. The hero of 1968 was all washed up just four seasons later. He was 28 years old.

24. The Angry A's

By the 1960s, the American League had settled into a definite pattern of the haves and have-nots, and in the latter group, there was no sadder example than the once-proud A's.

Since Connie Mack had broken up his last championship team in the early '30s, the A's had spent most of the time in the second division. Incredibly, in the 35 years following their third-place finish in 1933, the A's had only two first-division finishes, fourth place in both 1948 and 1952. Meanwhile, they had finished last a staggering 16 times.

The franchise was moved to Kansas City in 1955, but that meant nothing; the A's finished sixth that first year and never again got that high in their 13-year stay in Missouri.

Then, Kansas City owner Arnold Johnson died and Charles O. Finley bought the club, buying 52 percent in 1960 and then, before the start of the next season, buying the remaining 48 percent from those who had been minority owners with Johnson. The A's—and baseball—would never again be the same.

Before Finley was allowed to buy the club, American League owners had commissioned a detective agency to supply them with a report on Finley. In essence, the report said: Don't let this guy into the lodge. Nevertheless, the owners did—and they have spent considerable time regretting their rashness ever since.

Finley is an incredible man, bombastic, energetic, vulgar, inventive . . . the list of adjectives could go on and on. He careens through life like a bowling ball, and woe be it to anyone who gets in his way. *Los Angeles Times* sports columnist Jim Murray put it best: Finley is a self-made man who worships his creator.

When he chooses, he can be the most charming of men. He is a super-salesman, and it was his selling of a group insurance policy to the American College of Surgeons in 1952—which earned him $441,563 in commissions—that started him on his way to a fortune.

His charm is such that even those he has fired and insulted forgive him. Hank Bauer and Alvin Dark served two separate terms as managers under

Charlie Finley, yelling advice to his Oakland A's, was an influential baseball figure in the '70s. *(Jonathan Perry)*

Finley, for instance. Frank Lane was fired by Finley and went to court to collect his back salary—he eventually settled out of court for $113,000—but he and Finley became friends again later.

"Maybe I'm as crazy as he is," said Lane, "but it's hard to hate Charlie. He's quite a salesman. He can sell himself to his own worst enemy. He can talk himself out of any tangle."

Those weren't just words. One time at a Baltimore-A's game in Oakland, I watched in amazement as Lane, then a superscout for the Orioles, relayed the game, pitch by pitch, over the telephone in the press box to Finley in his Chicago office.

Finley can also be a generous man. He often helped players with stock market tips, for instance, and even told them he would make up losses out of his own pocket.

But under that charming facade is a mean-spirited, vindictive man. In divorce proceedings, his wife testified that he beat her. In Kansas City, he gave sportswriter Ernest Mehl the "Poison Pen Award." He has called baseball commissioner Bowie Kuhn "the village idiot." He has had fourteen managers and only one—Dick Williams—lasted more than two seasons. Once, he even fired a player, Ken Harrelson. And in 1979, he was sued for

$1 million by the management of the Oakland Coliseum, the home of the A's, for failing to promote the team.

His love of publicity is legendary. It has even caused him to do things which seem contrary to his own best interests. The Vida Blue and Reggie Jackson stories are the best examples of that.

In 1969 Jackson, in his second full season in the majors, started off at a home run pace that matched Roger Maris and Babe Ruth in their record years. The pressure got to him in late season and he tailed off, finishing with 47 homers, but he was the hottest draw in the league. On the field and at the box office, he was just what the young A's team needed.

Yet, the next year, Finley had a protracted contract struggle with Jackson that left Reggie emotionally exhausted. And when the season began, Finley started telling manager John McNamara when to play and when to bench Jackson. The dispirited Jackson had an off season and never again was a big gate attraction for the A's.

The Blue case was even more dramatic. Vida had an electrifying year in 1971, winning 24 games with a 1.82 earned run average and striking out 301 batters.

Coupled with the fact that he had thrown a no-hitter when he had been brought up in the last month of the '70 season, that made Blue the hottest attraction in the league. Approximately one-twelfth of the people who paid to see American League games in 1971 did so when Vida Blue was pitching.

Yet, the next spring, Finley again got into a prolonged contract struggle with Blue. Only Kuhn's intervention finally got the two together, after the season had already started. The disheartened Blue was only 6–10 that year and, though he came back to have good years for the A's, he was never again that kind of box office attraction.

There is only one explanation for Finley's behavior with his two young stars: Charlie resented the publicity Jackson and Blue were getting. Finley has always wanted to be the center of attention with the A's, and he could not allow Jackson and Blue to snatch the spotlight away.

Even those who thought they knew him well marvelled at things Finley did. Typical was an incident Dick Williams remembers from the time he was managing the A's.

"We had just won a game," remembers Williams, "and I had just gotten into the clubhouse when the phone rang. It was Charlie, of course. 'I'm having a heart attack, Dick,' he said, 'but I wanted to call you and congratulate you on your win before I go to the hospital. I'll call you in a couple of days.'

"The next day, sure enough, it was in all the papers that Charlie had had a heart attack. I called back to Chicago and talked to his secretary, and she assured me he wouldn't be talking to anybody for at least ten days. But, sure enough, two days later, he was on the phone to me again!"

Almost to a man, other baseball owners dislike Finley, but in many ways, he has had a positive effect on the game. Like Bill Veeck, he is not bound to tradition, and he has constantly pushed for change. Some of the changes have been made, some have not. Here are some of Finley's pet projects:

1) Night games for the World Series. Finley argued that the backbone of baseball's support comes from people who work nine to five shifts and were thus prevented from watching day games. The ratings for the televised night World Series games in recent years—much higher than day games—bear out his contention that playing the games at night would make them available to many more people.

2) Colored uniforms. When Finley first brought out the garish gold and green A's uniforms, they were greeted with derision. The most frequent comparison was with softball uniforms. Yet, since then, many teams have gone to more colorful uniforms, though none as bold as the A's.

3) Orange baseballs. Finley contended that orange baseballs were easier to follow than white, but tradition was too much against the change. Finley did use the orange balls in some exhibition games but never got permission to use them in regular season. In one exhibition, A's outfielder George Hendricks hit home runs over the left, center and right field fence. Asked if he liked the orange ball, Hendricks said, "No. I couldn't pick up the spin."

4) A three-ball walk, two-strike strikeout. Finley's thought was that this would increase the action. When it was tried in spring training, it increased the number of walks and created longer games, which nobody wanted.

5) Designated hitter. Finley pushed this idea until it was adopted by the American League.

6) Designated runner. This one failed because there was no logical spot for the runner. Finley then tried variations of his own. First, he used Allen Lewis, whom he dubbed "The Panamanian Express," as a frequent pinch runner. Unfortunately, Lewis was a poor base runner despite his speed and was frequently thrown out trying to steal. Sportswriter Herb Michelson redubbed him, "The Panamanian Local," because, said Michelson, he always stopped at second.

In 1974, Finley hired world-class sprinter Herb Washington as a pinch runner, but that experiment was also a failure. Washington had not played baseball since high school, and he lacked baseball sense. He stole 29 bases but was thrown out 18 times. He also hurt the A's because he was often picked off base, and he sometimes hesitated before advancing on a ball to the outfield, delaying too long to see if the ball would drop in. He was released after one season.

Finley's years in Kansas City were unhappy ones, for him and the fans. He tried several offbeat stunts, the most notorious being a mechanical rabbit which popped up to give the plate umpire a new baseball, but that couldn't make up for bad teams.

Three times in Finley's seven years in Kansas Ctiy, the team finished last. Its highest finish was seventh. When news surfaced that Finley was trying to move the team, Kansas City fans were ambivalent in their reaction. When Finley got permission to move his team to Oakland, Kansas City cars sported bumper stickers reading "Chuck Farley O."

But in those years in Kansas City, Finley was building a strong team. He had signed players like Jackson, Sal Bando, Rick Monday, and Catfish Hunter for large bonuses. They matured in Oakland.

In the A's first season in Oakland, they finished sixth in the last year of the ten-team league (the next year the league was split into divisions), but their 82 wins (against 80 losses) was the most for an A's team since 1948.

The next two seasons, the A's finished second in their division to the Minnesota Twins. Then, Finley hired Williams, who became the A's fourth manager since they had moved to Oakland.

Only four years before, Williams had managed the "Impossible Dream" Red Sox to a pennant, but he had fallen into disfavor with Boston owner Tom Yawkey since and was fired before the end of the 1969 season. In 1970, he was a coach for the Montreal Expos, so he was ready when Finley beckoned—even though he knew Finley's reputation.

Williams was the perfect manager for the young A's. He taught sound, fundamental baseball—and he chewed out anybody who didn't play that way. He made it so uncomfortable for players who made mistakes that they soon learned not to make them. As with the Red Sox, he was not popular with the players, but he made the team a champion.

The A's weren't quite there in '71. With Blue having a magnificent year, the A's swept to 101 wins—the only time in the championship years when they won more than 100 games. But in the American League playoffs, they fell to Baltimore, which won its third straight American League pennant.

The next year, Finley traded for pitcher Ken Holtzman and the A's came of age. This time they won the American League playoff, beating Detroit in a five-game series that was certainly the best of the league playoffs to that point.

But the victory came at a high cost: Jackson broke his leg sliding into home plate and was out of the World Series. The Cincinnati Reds, the fabled "Big Red Machine," had won the National League pennant, and the Reds fully expected to demolish the A's in the World Series. In the words of Oakland sportswriter Ron Bergman, the Reds thought they would win it in three.

The Series, though, turned out much differently than the Reds—or anybody else—had anticipated, and the main reason was a catcher named Gene Tenace, who was hardly known outside his immediate family before then.

Tenace was one of Finley's favorites at the time—Charlie had a habit of adopting certain players as his favorites, until they did something unreasonable, such as ask for more money than he wanted to pay them—but he had not even been a regular most of the season.

A good hitter but only average catcher, Tenace had played some in the outfield and some at first base. He had caught only 49 games; Dave Duncan, a weak hitter but a better defensive catcher, had caught 113 that season.

Gene Tenace was an unexpected hitting star in the 1972 World Series.
(Jonathan Perry)

And in the playoff series with Detroit, Tenace had gone just one-for-seventeen.

He quickly made up for that. His first time at bat in the first game, after George Hendrick had walked, Tenace hit a home run to give the A's a 2–0 lead. His next time up, in the fifth inning, the score was tied at 2–2, and he hit another home run, again off Gary Nolan, and that was the winning margin for the A's in the 3–2 game, won by Holtzman.

The next game was won by the A's, 2–1, as Catfish Hunter pitched and Joe Rudi made a sensational catch, leaping against the wall in the ninth inning to grab a drive by Denis Menke. The Series shifted to Oakland with the A's ahead, 2–0, and the Cincinnati fans in shock.

The Reds got back in it in the third game, as Jack Billingham blanked the A's, 1–0, but the A's came back to win the fourth game, 3–2. Tenace got another home run, and his single kept alive a two-run rally in the ninth that won the game.

Tenace wasn't through. In the next game, he hit his fourth homer, tying him in the Series record book with Lou Gehrig, Babe Ruth, Duke Snider, and Hank Bauer. But the Reds hung on to win that game, 5–4, and in the sixth game, back in Cincinnati, they blew out the A's, 8–1.

Joe Rudi was a clutch hitter and outstanding outfielder for the championship A's teams of the 1970s. *(Jonathan Perry)*

At that point, everybody figured the party was over for the A's, especially since the seventh game would be played at Riverfront Stadium in Cincinnati. But somebody forgot to tell the A's.

In the first inning, Tenace came up with two outs and a runner on third, and he hit a grounder that bounced off a seam in the artificial turf and went over the head of third baseman Menke.

In the sixth, the score was tied at 1–1. Again, there were two outs and a runner, Bert Campaneris, on third. Again, Tenace came through, and this time it was no fluke, as he doubled in Campaneris. Bando followed with another double, and the A's made that third run stand up for a 3–2 win.

For the Series, Tenace had eight hits in 23 at bats, for a .348 average, with four homers, one double, nine RBIs, and an incredible .913 slugging average. He was, of course, the Most Valuable Player of the Series.

"I was feeling great, seeing the ball good, had my timing just right, and was confident," Tenace told Donald Honig for *The October Heroes,* adding that, "It didn't seem to matter what they were throwing—fastballs, curves, sliders, changes of speeds. I felt I was going to hit it hard somewhere."

And after it was all over, Finley and his wife danced on the top of the dugout with Williams and his wife. A year later, Finley's wife sued him for divorce, and Williams quit as manager. Nothing is forever.

The A's win was a popular one, outside Cincinnati and environs. They were an appealing bunch that team, in many ways a throwback to the earlier, looser days of baseball. They said what they thought, without worrying about the consequences; they fought with each other in the clubhouse; they railed at Finley, publicly and privately.

Early in the season, Finley had had one of his offbeat promotions, this one giving prizes to the most imaginative moustaches and beards. As part of it, he had offered bonuses to players (and manager Williams) if they grew moustaches or beards.

Like most of Finley's promotions, this one did little to stimulate the gate, but it left its mark on the players, most of whom kept their moustaches. They became known as the "Moustache Gang," and they formed quite a contrast to the Reds, who were not even allowed the luxury of long sideburns under manager Sparky Anderson.

Perhaps it was the moustaches; perhaps it was the fact that the Reds considered themselves members of a stronger league; perhaps it was the fact that the A's had not been in the World Series in so long. Whatever, the Reds seriously underestimated the A's. When it was over, the Reds couldn't believe they had lost. Probably, they still can't.

The Reds weren't alone in underestimating the A's; a lot of people who should have known better did the same in those days. The A's weren't a spectacular team, like the 1927 Yankees. They seldom destroyed their opponents, as the 1936–39 Yankees did. They won with an economy of effort, scoring just enough to win. Personal statistics didn't seem to mean a lot to them. Winning did.

Like the A's dynasty teams of 1910–14 and 1929–31, they had great balance. It started with the pitching. Catfish Hunter seemed on his way to becoming the next 300-game winner as he steadily and efficiently won game after game, 105 of them in a five-year period for the A's, 1970–74. Holtzman, the intellectual left-hander who liked to say he was in baseball only for the money but who showed up at the park three hours or more before every game, won 77 games in four years after coming from Chicago. Blue won 20 or more in three of the championship years, and added 17 in another.

And in the bull pen, the A's had Rollie Fingers, quite possibly the best relief pitcher in American League history. Certainly, no A.L. reliever has ever strung together the years that Fingers had for the A's in the '70s. In the five championship years, he made 326 appearances with a composite ERA of considerably less than three runs a game, and had 48 wins and 102 saves— an average of 30 wins/saves a year.

A lot of us who watched the A's regularly in those days thought Fingers was the club's most valuable player. The A's themselves divided games into two segments: the first eight innings and "Hold 'em, Rollie Fingers time."

Oddly, Fingers had been a failure as a starter because he was too nervous; he could never sleep the night before a start. But when he came in with the winning run on base in the ninth inning it was the batter who was nervous, and with cause.

Defensively, the A's were sound in both the infield and the outfield. To Williams, the key man was second baseman Dick Green, who got little publicity because he was not a strong hitter. "He was the glue for the infield," says Williams. "He made Campaneris a good shortstop."

The A's offensive figures were not overwhelming. Rudi's .305 in 1972 was the only .300 performance by an A's hitter in the five-year championship reign. Jackson hit 36 homers once and 32 twice, but no other player hit as many as 30 in a season.

But the statistics were misleading because the A's knew how to hit with men on base. Jackson, Rudi, Bando, and, yes, Tenace were superb clutch hitters. It mattered little if they got just one hit in a game, because that hit was likely to come with a runner on.

The A's also had good base runners. Campaneris, though his best years were behind him, had three years with 34 steals and another with 52. Bill North, traded to the A's in '73 by the Chicago Cubs, stole 53 and 54 bases in his first two years. Even Jackson was a base-stealing threat, with consecutive years of 22, 25, and 17 steals.

It seemed almost a matter of will with the A's. If they needed a home run to win, they usually got it. If they needed a sacrifice fly with a runner on third, they got that. If it took a walk, stolen base, and a single up the middle, they could do that, too.

The best of the A's teams in that stretch was probably the 1973 squad. North's presence in center field strengthened the defense. The starting pitchers were never better; Hunter and Holtzman each won 21 and Blue 20. Jackson had his finest all-round season, leading the league with 32 homers, 117 RBIs, 99 runs, and a .531 slugging percentage (as well as with 111 strikeouts), and also hitting .293. Bando backed him up with 29 homers, Tenace—installed at first base—hit 24 and designated hitter Deron Johnson added 19.

Campy Campaneris, shown sliding into third with another stolen base, was a key figure at shortstop in the A's success. *(Jonathan Perry)*

It took the A's five games to subdue the Orioles in the American League playoff and seven to beat the New York Mets in the World Series, but the most important action was taking place away from the field, as manager Williams smarted under Finley's orders.

"I wish I'd had the foresight to buy Bell stock before I took the job," sighs Williams today. Finley called him all the time to tell him who to play and when. Williams did not want anybody to know how many times he was ordered to do something by Finley, but some things were obvious. Bothered by Green's weak bat, Finley had adopted a system of pinch-hitting early for Green and rotating second basemen; that almost cost the '72 playoff when Tenace ended up at second in the late innings and made a crucial error.

In 1973, Williams had his appendix removed just before the All-Star break and had planned to recuperate during that time. Finley decided he wanted his manager managing the American League All-Stars, as was traditional for the previous year's pennant winner. Williams managed the team.

Finally, in the '73 World Series, Finley "suspended" infielder Mike Andrews after Andrews's critical errors had cost the A's a game. The A's owner tried to get a medical report saying Andrews was incapable of playing, which would have allowed a substitute on the A's roster, but that subterfuge was so obvious it was soon discarded.

That was the final straw for Williams. He called Jackson and Bando, the team leaders, to his hotel room and told them he was quitting after the Series.

Williams wanted to manage the New York Yankees, who wanted him, too, but he had signed a contract in midseason in '73, and Finley held him to it. The Yankee job went to Bill Virdon. Finley signed Alvin Dark to replace Williams, and Williams sat out most of the 1974 season. When the California Angels job became open, due to the firing of Bobby Winkles, Finley released Williams from his contract so he could manage the Angels. The Angels were a weak team, and Finley was doing Williams no favor.

Under Dark, the A's won their third straight pennant and third straight World Series in 1974. This one, in fact, was the easiest of the bunch; it took them only five games to subdue the Los Angeles Dodgers. Like the Reds in '72, the Dodgers were convinced the A's had done it with mirrors, because every game in the Series was decided by one run. But that was the A's style. Roger Angell captured it best in *Five Seasons*: ". . . rarely has any of these October seminars offered so many plain lessons in winning baseball, or such an instructive moral drama about the uses of baseball luck and the precision with which experienced, opportunistic veterans can pry open a tough, gnarled, closed-up game and extract from it the stuff of victory."

There was also vindication in the Series win for Dark, who had suffered silently under criticism from press and players all season, as well as having to deal with Finley.

Dark had undergone a complete metamorphosis from his earlier times as manager of the San Francisco Giants, Kansas City A's, and Cleveland Indians. His arrogance had been replaced by an overwhelming piety, and he was soft-spoken to the point of invisibility. He was kind to everyone, even the press. "The Lord taught me to love everybody," he said, "but the last ones I learned to love were the sportswriters."

Early in the season, Dark had had problems because he didn't know the league, having been away from it since 1971. He made no secret of the fact

Sal Bando played out his option in Oakland to sign a big contract with the Milwaukee Brewers.
(Milwaukee Brewers)

that Finley was running the show. That did not go over with his players. Blue accused him of "worshipping the wrong God—C.O.F." After a tough loss in extra innings in which Dark had made some critical errors in judgment, Bando stormed into the dressing room and, as I watched from a few feet away, threw his glove against the wall and shouted, "He couldn't manage a fucking meat market!"

By the end of the season, though, the players had come to respect Dark for his judgment and to understand his attitude toward Finley; they were, after all, thorough pros.

It would have been nice if the team could have stayed together for a longer period. Possibly, the A's could have matched the Yankees' records of five straight pennants or four straight World Series championships.

Sadly, they never got the chance. Hunter discovered a loophole in his contract and became a free agent the next year, eventually signing with the Yankees. His loss was enough to keep the A's from winning a fourth straight pennant, though they did win the American League West title.

The next years, with the free agent market officially open, Finley traded away Jackson and Holtzman and lost Rudi, Fingers, Bando, Tenace, and Campaneris as they played out their options. By the end of the decade, the A's had disintegrated as thoroughly as Connie Mack's old champions and they were the worst team in the majors. But that can't obscure the brilliance of those three straight World Series wins. Only the Yankees have ever done better.

25. No More Good-Hitting Pitchers

Before the 1973 season, American League owners passed a resolution establishing the designated hitter rule, destined to be the most controversial rule of at least the decade. It read:

A hitter may be designated to bat for the starting pitcher and all subsequent pitchers in any game without otherwise affecting the status of the pitcher(s) in the game. A Designated Hitter for the pitcher must be selected prior to the game and must be included in the lineup card presented to the umpire-in-chief.

It is not mandatory that a club designate a hitter for the pitcher, but failure to do so prior to the game precludes the use of a Designated Hitter for that game.

Pinch hitters for a Designated Hitter may be used. Any substitute hitter for a Designated Hitter himself becomes a Designated Hitter. A replaced Designated Hitter shall not re-enter the game in any capacity.

The Designated Hitter may be used defensively, continuing to bat in the same position in the batting order, but the pitcher must then bat in the place of the substituted defensive player, unless more than one substitution is made, and the manager then must designate their spots in the batting order.

A runner may be substituted for the Designated Hitter and the runner assumes the role of Designated Hitter.

A Designated Hitter is "locked" into the batting order. No multiple substitutions may be made that will alter the batting rotation of the Designated Hitter.

Once the game pitcher is switched from the mound to a defensive position, this move shall terminate the Designated Hitter role for the remainder of the game.

Once a pinch-hitter bats for any player in the batting order and then enters the game to pitch, this move shall terminate the Designated Hitter role for the remainder of the game.

Once the game pitcher bats for the Designated Hitter this move shall terminate the Designated Hitter role for the remainder of the game.

Once a Designated Hitter assumes a defensive position, this move shall terminate the Designated Hitter role for the remainder of the game.

Once again, the American League had demonstrated its independence, adopting the rule though National League owners refused even to seriously consider it. By the end of the decade, the National League still showed no signs of adopting it, though colleges and minor leagues were using it, as well as the American League.

As with all changes that have been made in baseball to get more offense into the game, the motive behind the rule was to get more fans into league stadiums.

The American League had become known as a pitcher's league, quite a change for the league which had been known for such great sluggers as Babe Ruth, Lou Gehrig, Hank Greenberg, Jimmie Foxx, Ted Williams, Joe Di-Maggio, Roger Maris, and Mickey Mantle.

As owners had known for a long time, far more people pay to see hitting than pitching. American League owners felt the new rule would create more hits and runs and thus increase attendance, and as a side effect, it would prolong the careers of top hitters who could no longer do the job in the field.

National League owners professed to fear the change the DH rule would make in the game. They thought it might open the way to more specialization. Baseball had always prided itself on being a game which required athletes to play both offense and defense, unlike football, but it would be easy enough to change that to have offensive and defensive platoons. The DH rule, argued N.L. owners, also took some strategy out of the game, specifically the decision a manager has to make when a pitcher is scheduled to bat with runners on base.

And, of course, the National League had most of the power hitters in baseball and attendance was higher on the average than in the American League, so N.L. owners had no incentive to change.

Neither the hopes nor the fears of owners were fully realized. The DH rule did increase hitting and scoring, but only marginally. Cause and effect cannot be directly measured in this case, but it seems unlikely that the rule has greatly increased attendance around the American League.

At the same time, it did not open the way for further specialization. There has been no pressure on baseball owners to go to a platooning system, and no significant support has arisen for the designated runner idea proposed by Charlie Finley.

Unwittingly, American League owners took away much of the impact of the rule by not insisting that the designated hitter be forced to bat ninth, in the pitcher's spot.

When a pinch hitter is brought into the game, it is usually a moment of high drama because everybody is aware that it is a new hitter facing the pitcher, and usually in a situation that has a run-producing potential.

But the designated hitter is allowed to bat anywhere in the order, so he becomes just another hitter. There is nothing particularly noteworthy about a DH hitting sixth, for instance. If he were to bat ninth, there would be, because he would be replacing the pitcher, usually a notoriously weak hitter. It is quite possible for a fan who is not keeping a scorecard to be unaware even of the identity of a designated hitter in a game.

The individual reactions of hitters cast in the DH role have been interesting, though. Some hitters have enjoyed it, but many have hated it.

It has caused players to adopt a different approach to the game because, for the first time, they are in the game offensively but not defensively.

Some players have stayed on the bench. Others have adopted the opposite approach, even to the extent of going into the clubhouse and listening to the game on the radio, swinging a bat to keep warm between appearances.

For some hitters, the mental problem has been just too much. Billy Williams was like that, when he came over to the Oakland A's in 1974 after a brilliant career in the National League. Williams had slowed down in the field, but his bat seemed almost as quick as ever, and the DH role seemed ideal for him. But he complained that he could not stay mentally alert for three or four plate appearances a game, and he hit only .244 and .211 in two seasons with the A's before retiring.

Jim Rice, the Boston strongboy, was frequently used as a DH, and he was the best in the league in 1977 when he hit .316 in 116 games and hit 31 of his 39 homers and got 87 of his 114 RBIs as a DH.

But even Rice preferred to play every day, feeling that he was more effective when he played the whole game. In his great 1978 season his statistics supported his point. He played nearly one-third of his season (205 of 677 at bats) as a DH but hit only .273 (compared to his seasonal average of .315) and had only 10 of his 46 homers and 31 of his 139 RBIs in that role. By 1979, Boston manager Don Zimmer was using Rice most of the time as an outfielder.

The rule also complicated voting on a Most Valuable Player: How much consideration should a player get if he did nothing but hit?

Still, there were some real advantages to the rule. A team with a surplus of good hitters naturally benefitted the most. The Boston Red Sox could get Rice, Carl Yastrzemski, and first basemen George Scott or Bob Watson in the lineup at the same time; without the DH, one would have had to be benched.

Certainly, it has extended the careers of some older players, such as Rico Carty, Willie Horton, and Orlando Cepeda. Al Kaline was able to play long enough to get 3,000 hits because he could be used as a DH late in his career. Yastrzemski found that an occasional turn as a DH kept him fresher.

Younger players with defensive deficiencies—such as Glenn Adams of Minnesota and Don Baylor of California—were more valuable in the DH role.

Probably nobody liked the rule better than Rusty Staub, who was an indifferent fielder in his youth and did not improve with age. Staub had no trouble adjusting to the DH role. In 1978 he was the best in the league, leading all designated hitters with 175 hits, 279 total bases, 76 walks, and 11 sacrifice flies. He was second with 75 runs and 30 doubles and third in home runs among DHs with 24. Most impressive of all, his 121 RBIs were second only to Rice among all major league hitters and represented a career high.

Unfortunately for Staub, a contract dispute led to his trade back to the Montreal Expos of the National League in '79.

The most important aspect of the DH rule, though, has been one that nobody foresaw: The chief beneficiaries have been the pitchers.

Because managers no longer have to pinch-hit for their pitchers in close games, starters are left in the game longer and get more decisions. More decisions inevitably means more wins for good pitchers. It was no coincidence that a record 12 pitchers won 20 or more games in '73, the first year of the DH rule. The extreme was Wilbur Wood of Chicago, a knuckleballer who won 24 games and lost 20.

"Frankly, I can't see how any pitcher can't like it," says Montreal manager Dick Williams, who managed the A's the first year the rule was in effect. "It keeps the starters in longer."

Jackie Brown, who pitched four years in the American League before going to Montreal, said he became a better pitcher because of the DH rule.

"Our job is to pitch, to get hitters out, not to hit," he says. "I love to hit and swing the bat; I think all players do. But it tires you out to run the bases. In the late innings, if I'm pitching a good game, I don't want to hit and have to run."

Hal McRae won an Outstanding Designated Hitter award with the Kansas City Royals. *(Kansas City Royals)*

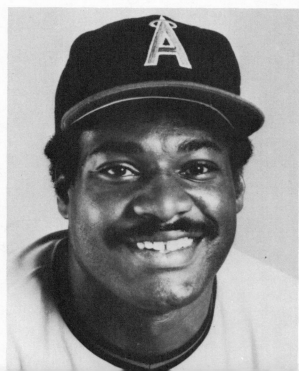

Don Baylor's hitting led the California Angels to their first divisional championship in 1979. *(California Angels)*

Most pitchers feel the same way, though Baltimore's Jim Palmer is an exception. "I don't like the DH rule," he says, "because I consider myself a complete athlete. I feel I can help myself hitting, especially bunting and hitting behind the runner."

Few pitchers are as adept with the bat as Palmer, though, and in most cases, it's doing them—and the fans—a favor not to make them hit.

26. What's the Price of Catfish?

In 1974, as the Oakland A's administered a baseball lesson to the Los Angeles Dodgers in the World Series, more important things were happening off the field. Catfish Hunter and Charlie Finley were locked in a contractual battle that was to result in Hunter being named a free agent, and that, in turn, was to start a train of events that drastically restructured major league baseball.

Hunter had been an early find of one of Finley's scouts, signing for a $75,000 bonus out of high school in 1964 (and, incidentally, being nicknamed by the A's owner; Hunter had before that been known by his first name, Jim).

He never pitched an inning of minor league ball, partly because of his polish, unusual for such a young pitcher, and partly because the A's were so bad in that stretch that it was easy to break in. Catfish was 8-8, 9-11, and 13-17 in his first three years, but his 2.81 ERA in his third year showed that he was becoming a good pitcher, needing only decent support from his teammates.

Hunter improved to a 13-13 mark in 1968 and pitched a perfect game against the Minnesota Twins, first in the American League regular season since 1922. The next year he slipped to 12-15 but in 1970 had his first year over .500, at 18-14.

Hunter had been one of Finley's favorites, too, benefiting from Finley's no-risk stock market tips, whereby Charlie guaranteed to cover any losses. And before the 1970 season, Finley loaned Hunter $150,000 to buy a 400-acre farm in North Carolina. Then, mysteriously, Finley's attitude toward Hunter changed, though there seemed no reason for it. Unlike teammates Reggie Jackson and Vida Blue, Hunter never bucked Finley—until the dramatic moment in '74.

Years later, Catfish said Finley had constantly called him in the final three months of the 1970 season, reminding him about the debt. The calls often came on the days that Hunter was scheduled to pitch. Finley claimed that was a coincidence, but, Hunter said, "Who knows more about this club than Finley?"

Bothered by the calls, Hunter fell short of 20 wins. He paid Finley what he owed at the end of the year, selling off 300 acres to do it. Four years later, that became academic, because Catfish could afford anything he wanted.

At about the same time, Finley started squeezing Hunter on contract negotiations, and Catfish had no choice but to endure it, because the reserve clause bound him to the A's.

Arbitration started in 1974, and Finley predictably had more players go to arbitration than any other owner in the majors. But Hunter didn't seem to realize the importance of the new procedure. He settled for a two-year contract at $100,000 a year and then burned as he watched what others got. Jackson got $135,000; Ken Holtzman, after one 20-win season (Catfish had had three) got $93,000.

But there was a stipulation in Hunter's contract that Finley was supposed to pay half of it to an insurance company, and by World Series time, Finley had not complied with that.

So, Hunter took his case to an arbitration panel and Peter M. Seitz cast the deciding vote on the three-man panel in his favor, and Catfish was a free agent.

In retrospect, it seems that Hunter really had no intention of leaving the A's. Though he was angry with Finley, he had enjoyed pitching for the team because of its great success. He only wanted to get what was coming to him.

But Finley was enraged because Hunter was crossing him. In the arbitration hearings, he fumed and blustered and denigrated Hunter, and Catfish vowed he would not return. His agent, Jerry Kapstein, put him on the open market.

The results were unprecedented, though predictable. If Catfish had been worth $75,000 as an untried high school pitcher, what was he worth ten years later as the best starting pitcher in baseball? Millions, decided 22 of the 24 major league clubs.

This is what they were looking at: Hunter was 28, in his pitching prime. He had won 106 games in the previous five years, and his last season had been his best, 25–12 with a 2.49 earned run average and 23 complete games. He had pitched 318 innings. His combined hits (268) and walks (46) were fewer than innings pitched. He was a great money pitcher, 4–0 in the World Series.

Only the A's in the American League and San Francisco Giants in the National refused to get into the big-bucks bidding for Hunter. Eventually, it was narrowed down to the San Diego Padres and New York Yankees, and Hunter chose the Yankees, as much because they had a chance to win a championship (which the Padres did not have) as the money.

With the A's, Catfish Hunter was a smiling young man. After becoming a free agent and signing a big contract with the Yankees, Hunter had his problems. *(Jonathan Perry)*

But the money was incredible. It was called a $3.7 million deal, though the actual cash outlay was far less. Reportedly, it called for a $1 million bonus, a five-year contract at $200,000 a year, a ten-year retirement plan at $50,000 a year, a $1 million life insurance policy for Hunter, a $25,000 policy for each of his two children, and $200,000 in attorneys' fees.

"I never thought I would make this kind of money," said Hunter, who felt that he had to add that it was not the happiest moment in his life. "The happiest was when I was in the World Series."

Hunter's signing was a big story, and its effect on major league baseball was even greater. Salaries went up on virtually every team because the top limit had been raised so greatly. More important, Catfish's contract made other star players wish they could be in a position to command that money, and his actions showed the way to do it.

The restriction on baseball players' freedom had always been the reserve clause, which supposedly bound a player to the team that signed him for life.

Curt Flood had unsuccessfully challenged the reserve clause in court at the start of the decade but had ruined his career in so doing. No player was anxious to sacrifice himself that way, but going to arbitration, as Hunter had done, was a quick and painless way to attack the same problem. And so,

National League pitchers Andy Messersmith and Dave McNally took their contracts to arbitration after the '75 season, claiming the reserve clause was actually only a one-year option clause. Casting the deciding vote on a three-man panel, Seitz ruled in their favor.

That created a bonanza for the players, many of whom have since gotten incredibly lucrative contracts on the free agent market. At least three—Jackson, Pete Rose, and Rod Carew—have signed contracts far surpassing Hunter's.

Predictably, the A's were severely hurt by the events, both because of Hunter's immediate departure and the fact that so many eventually left the club.

Although it was hardly apparent on the field, the A's were already headed downhill even before Hunter left, because Finley had begun to abandon the methods that had made his team a success. Over the years he had gotten rid of all but one of his scouts and had stripped his minor league organization bare. Trading for immediate success, he had also traded off some good prospects such as outfielder Dan Ford, who went on to star for the Minnesota Twins.

Hunter's departure accelerated the decline. Trying to compensate for that loss, Finley traded away another strong youngster, Chet Lemon, for veteran pitcher Stan Bahnsen. He failed to sign catcher Jim Sundborg after drafting him, and Sundborg went on to become the best defensive catcher in the league.

The A's won their fifth straight divisional title that year but lost in three straight to the Boston Red Sox in the American League playoff, and nobody thought the superior team had lost. Their spectacular reign was clearly nearing its end, but nobody could have guessed how rapid and steep the A's decline would be.

The next year, the A's went to camp with eight stars unsigned—Jackson, Ken Holtzman, Campy Campaneris, Sal Bando, Joe Rudi, Rollie Fingers, Gene Tenace, and Vida Blue. If they were unsigned by the end of the year, they would all be free agents.

Finley had always paid his stars less than players of comparable ability on other teams, which had understandably rankled his players. They were determined that now they were going to get what they thought they were worth. But in the spring there was little serious talk among them about playing out their options and going elsewhere. They wanted to stay together and prove that they could get back in the World Series, and they were waiting for Finley to open serious negotiations.

He never did. Instead, he coped with the problem in two ways. In the first, he traded off Jackson and Holtzman to Baltimore for pitchers Mike Torrez and Paul Mitchell and outfielder Don Baylor. But that defiant gesture failed because Torrez and Baylor were asking as much as Jackson and Holtzman had, and Finley couldn't sign them, either.

Then, just hours before the June 15 trading deadline, Finley shocked the baseball world by selling Blue to the Yankees for $1.5 million and Rudi and Fingers to the Red Sox for $1 million each. Blue was the only one signed to an A's contract; according to Vida, he had signed when he was promised by Finley that he would stay in Oakland. Finley, of course, had signed him only because the Yankees had insisted on that as part of the deal.

Finley claimed he was going to use the money from those deals to buy young players. He never got a chance to prove that, though, because baseball commissioner Bowie Kuhn negated all three sales. It would, Kuhn said, destroy competitive balance in the league. Certainly, it would destroy the A's. The fact that it was Finley who made the sales seemed to many people to have had a bearing on Kuhn's decision, because the two, to all appearances, hated each other.

(Finley made one other attempt to sell Blue, for a reported $1.75 million and a player, first baseman Dave Revering, to the Cincinnati Reds the next season. Kuhn ruled that sale void, too, and Finley eventually traded Blue to the San Francisco Giants for seven players and $400,000.)

Whatever his motives, Kuhn effectively punctured Finley's balloon. Charlie was stuck. He couldn't unload his stars and, even if he had wanted to at that point, he couldn't sign them. They were openly talking of leaving, and at season's end, Rudi, Fingers, Campaneris, Bando, Tenace, and Baylor all did. Torrez, who had one year left on his contract, was unloaded by Finley early in the '77 season.

Even with the turmoil in '76, the A's finished only two games behind Kansas City in their division, but after that, the club disintegrated as quickly and thoroughly as the old Connie Mack champions. By 1979, they were the worst team in baseball.

Finley made a deal before the 1978 season to sell the club to oilman Marvin Davis, who planned to move it to Denver, but the Oakland Coliseum management had an ironclad contract with Finley through the 1987 season and would not let the A's go.

By 1979, Finley was running a caretaker operation, keeping his overhead to an absolute minimum and trying to outwait the Coliseum management, hoping he could get a release from that contract. Meanwhile, he got enough cash in player deals to make a profit, even though attendance averaged under 5,000 a game. His operation was giving the city of Oakland and the American League a black eye, and it was costing other clubs money because their traveling expenses exceeded the gate receipts they got in Oakland. It's not likely that any of that bothered Charlie a great deal.

One other club, Minnesota, also suffered great losses because of the free agent market. Lyman Bostock (killed in an off-field incident in 1978) and Larry Hisle both played out their options and left, and Twins' owner Calvin Griffith was forced to trade Rod Carew because he knew Carew would do likewise when his contract was up after the 1979 season.

Griffith, the nephew and adopted son of Clark Griffith, was operating on a limited budget, just as Clark had done, and with the Twins' attendance running below the league average, he couldn't pay the kind of money offered by richer clubs. It didn't help his cause when he made remarks at a luncheon that he thought of as jokes but which Carew interpreted as racial slurs.

And who benefitted from the new rules? The Yankees, obviously, signing free agents Hunter, Jackson, Torrez, Don Gullett, Rich Gossage, Tommy John, and Luis Tiant. That earned them the nickname, "The Best Team Money Can Buy."

Larry Hisle took advantage of the new free agent rule, playing out his option in Minnesota to sign a fat contract with Milwaukee. *(Milwaukee Brewers)*

But that obscured the fact that the Yankees were a solid team before they signed any free agents, largely because of a good minor league system and some astute trades made by Gabe Paul.

Catcher Thurman Munson, who died tragically in a small plane crash during the '79 season, was a 1968 draft selection. Outfielder Roy White was signed in 1962 as a minor league free agent. First baseman Chris Chambliss, second baseman Willie Randolph, shortstop Bucky Dent, third baseman Graig Nettles, and pitchers Ed Figueroa and Sparky Lyle were all obtained in trades. Perhaps most important was a trade that wasn't made. When owner George Steinbrenner wanted to trade a minor league reliever named Ron Guidry who had failed in two tries with the Yankees, Paul persuaded Steinbrenner to give Guidry another chance.

The Boston Red Sox, the Yankees' main competition in the A.L. East in the mid-'70s, got pitching help in the reentry draft, in Torrez, Bill Campbell, and Dick Drago.

The California Angels, with owner Gene Autry's big pocketbook behind them, made a big splash in the free agent market, signing Rudi, Baylor, Bobby Grich, and Jim Barr, and getting Carew in a forced trade. Those moves made the Angels a solid team by the end of the decade and boosted attendance sharply.

Meanwhile, Baltimore and Kansas City were proving that free agents aren't the only way to success. Kansas City had relied strictly on its own farm system and trades to shoot to the top of the A.L. West, but it was Baltimore which was the most amazing story. The Orioles seemed to be hit hard by the free agent rules, as Jackson and Holtzman moved on after one season, and Grich, an outstanding second baseman, played out his option and left. But the Orioles' farm system continued to come up with excellent, though largely unknown, players, and the Orioles were back on top in '79, ahead of the well-bankrolled Yankees and Red Sox.

And Minnesota, despite the star players it had lost, was in the thick of the A.L. West battle.

Thus, when emotion and hysteria were separated from the facts, it could be seen that the free agent reentry draft had, if anything, increased competition in the American League, not destroyed it, as many had feared would happen.

Of the fourteen league clubs, there were only three who were badly outclassed—Oakland, a special case, and the expansion teams in Seattle and Toronto, which could reasonably be expected to improve. The A.L. East was probably baseball's strongest division in 1979, with Baltimore, Boston, Milwaukee, and New York; the A.L. West, though not as strong, was extremely well balanced, except for Oakland and Seattle.

Sadly, the man who had started it all—Hunter—had not fared so well. After his first year with the Yankees, in which he won 23 games, Catfish seemed well on his way to being a career 300-game winner.

He had won 129 games in six years, 184 in his major league career, and he did not celebrate his 30th birthday until the first month of the 1976 season. Nor did he appear to be the kind of pitcher who would lose his ability quickly, because he had never been a strikeout pitcher. He mixed up his pitches well, had great control, and never threw a lot of pitches in a game. He gave up a lot of home run balls but seldom at a time when they could hurt him. He threw so easily, it seemed he could go on forever.

But nothing went right in New York for Catfish. Even in that first season, he had problems, although he rallied to win 23. Emotionally, he was not equipped to handle the kind of pressure that goes with the territory in New York; he's basically an unassuming, friendly, quiet country boy. Physically, it seemed he had one problem after another.

His main problem, though, may have been the fact that he didn't bring Rollie Fingers with him. In Oakland, more often than not, Fingers had saved Hunter. In '74, Catfish had completed 23 of 41 starts, but that was the only year he ever completed as many as half of his starts. Here are his other figures in the '70s: 1970, 40 starts, 9 complete games; 1971, 37 starts, 16 complete games; 1972, 38 starts, 16 complete games; 1973, 36 starts, 11 complete games. In five years, he had started 192 games, completed only 85.

But in New York, he had to do it all. The Yankees had a good reliever in Sparky Lyle, but Lyle was used in relief of other pitchers, not Catfish.

In Hunter's first year with the Yankees, he pitched 328 innings, most in the league and most in his career. He started 39 games and completed 30, again high in the league and high for his career.

The next year he slipped to 17–15 but pitched 299 innings. He completed 21 of 36 starts. In three years, including his last one in Oakland, he had pitched 945 innings and had completed 75 games.

He had pitched himself out. By 1979, in the fifth year of his celebrated contract, he had nothing left, and it was painful to watch him struggle to get out batters who would have been lucky to hit a three-bouncer to the short-stop off him in his prime. His case was another reminder of how ephemeral baseball success can be.

27. The Best Season Ever?

Baseball may never have known a better season than the American League had in 1978. Jim Rice and Ron Guidry each had individual seasons comparable to the best in history, and their performances came against the backdrop of an unprecedented pennant race.

In previous years, the great comebacks had all been in the National League: the 1914 Boston Braves, the 1942 St. Louis Cardinals, the 1951 New York Giants.

But in '78, the New York Yankees came from 14 games back in July to win the pennant, and they did it despite incredible turmoil within the club, including a managerial switch in midseason. To say that no club ever had a year like the 1978 Yankees is understating the obvious.

Their success would not have been remotely possible without Guidry, a Horatio Alger story come to life.

Guidry had bounced around the minors for five years before he even got a shot with the parent club, an unusually long term in the bush leagues these days, and he did little when he was brought up.

At one point he was so discouraged he wanted to quit. At another, Yankee owner George Steinbrenner was ready to trade him. Fortunately for the Yankees, neither happened.

Guidry's ability was obvious from the day the Yankees signed him in 1971 off the campus of the University of Southwestern Louisiana, but his inconsistency seemed to doom him to a minor league career.

Frail-looking with only 160 pounds on his 5'11" frame, Guidry nonetheless has a whipping fastball which has been timed at 95 miles an hour, and a slider which travels just as fast; at his best, he is as close to unhittable as any pitcher has ever been. In six minor league seasons, he allowed only 284 hits in 393 innings—and struck out 424 batters.

But, like a lot of young pitchers, Guidry also had considerable control problems, and he walked 250 batters in that same span, which projects to about six batters each nine innings. The Yankees wanted him to be a relief pitcher, but he was in-and-out, good one time, bad the next. He seemed to be an all too familiar type: a pitcher who would never realize his potential.

He was finally brought up at the end of the 1975 season. In 16 innings he gave up 15 hits, struck out 15, walked 9 and allowed 6 earned runs, an ERA of 3.38. That was enough to earn him a shot at the start of the '76 season, but he was his consistently inconsistent self: In seven games and 16 innings he allowed 20 hits and 10 earned runs. The Yankees sent him back to Syracuse of the International League.

By this time, Guidry was nearly 26, and he wondered about his future. Instead of heading north to Syracuse, when he got in his car, he started driving south to his home in Louisiana. He was quitting.

His wife, Bonnie, was in the car with him. "Ron," she said, "do you really want to quit? You know you won't be happy not playing ball. Don't do something you'll regret the rest of your life."

Guidry saw the point and turned his car north, and he pitched exceptionally well for Syracuse in relief the rest of the year: In 40 innings, he yielded only 16 hits, struck out 50, and walked just 13. He was 5–1 with a 0.68 ERA.

And yet in spring training the next year, he was erratic again. The Yankees had hoped to use him in relief, but he had a lackluster spring. Steinbrenner was willing to throw him into a deal he had working with the Chicago White Sox for shortstop Bucky Dent. (Eventually, it became Dent for outfielder Oscar Gamble, pitchers Bob Polinsky and Dewey Hoyt, and $200,000.) White Sox manager Bob Lemon, who had been the Yankee pitching coach in 1976, knew Guidry's potential and wanted him. But Gabe Paul refused to include him in the deal. Lemon would later be thankful that Guidry stayed with the Yankees.

In May, Guidry was finally used as a starter, when manager Billy Martin decided he needed a left-hander for that role. Actually, Martin had a good one—Ken Holtzman, who had been one of the aces on the A's pitching staff in the World Series years. But for reasons which have never been satisfactorily explained, Martin didn't like Holtzman and wouldn't use him. So, Guidry got his chance, and he made the most of it. In what remained of the season, he was 16–7, and the Yankees' best starter.

As it happened, he was merely warming up for 1978, when he had a season which ranked with the most shining years of Lefty Grove, Bob Feller, Hal Newhouser, and Denny McLain as the best in the lively ball era of American League history.

Guidry won his first 13 games, ironically topping the Yankee record of 12 which had been set by Atley Donald, who as a scout, signed Guidry to his first contract.

He won 25 and lost only 3, and his .893 percentage was the best in history for a pitcher winning 20 or more games. Counting his wins in the American League playoff and World Series, he was 27–3 for the season. Counting all that, plus his 1977 wins in the playoffs and World Series and the last part of the '77 season, he was 37–4 between August 10, 1977 and the end of the '78 Series!

He set a Yankee season record with 248 strikeouts and an American League record for a left-hander when he struck out 18 California Angels on June 17.

He had nine shutouts, which led the league and tied the A.L. record for left-handers. He had an earned run average of 1.74, and he held hitters to a collective .191 average.

And for all that, he was paid $38,500—though the Yankees signed him to a three-year contract worth $600,000 starting in 1979.

In his way, Jim Rice had just as good a season at bat as Guidry had from the pitching mound.

The Red Sox had expected Rice to star since the day they had signed him in the high school players draft of June 1971. In his third full season, at Pawtucket of the International League, he had been named the Minor League Player of the Year by *The Sporting News* after he hit .337 with 25 homers and 93 RBIs, all league-leading figures, in just 117 games, before being brought up by the Red Sox for the final 24 games of the season.

As a rookie, Rice had an outstanding season before breaking his wrist in late September, hitting 22 homers, knocking in 102 runs, and batting .309, but he was overshadowed by teammate Fred Lynn, who became the first man to win both Rookie of the Year and Most Valuable Player awards. Lynn hit .331 with 21 homers and 105 RBIs, and he led the league with 47 doubles and 103 runs, while playing a virtually flawless center field.

In the next three years, though, Rice improved as a hitter, and it was Lynn who was overshadowed. In 1977, Rice had his best year to that point, leading the league with 39 homers while knocking in 114 runs and batting .320. But the best was yet to come. In 1978, Rice had one of the best all-round hitting seasons in the last 40 years.

He led the majors with 46 homers, 139 RBIs, 15 triples, 406 total bases, a .600 slugging percentage, 213 hits, and 214 runs produced (combining RBIs and runs, subtracting for homers). His total bases were a club record, and it was the first time a hitter had more than 400 total bases since Joe DiMaggio in 1937.

He was the first player ever to lead the league in triples, home runs, and

Jim Rice hit home runs of awesome length and also hit for a high average as he was named Most Valuable Player in 1978. *(Boston Red Sox)*

RBIs, and he also scored 121 runs and hit .315. With back-to-back 200-hit seasons, he became only the second player in Red Sox history to have more than one 200-hit season. (Johnny Pesky, with three, is the other, and Pesky was Rice's batting coach with the Red Sox.)

His hits came at critical moments, too; he led the club with 16 game-winning RBIs, and he hit .339 with men on base. He was named American League Player of the Month in both May and August, and was also twice named Player of the Week.

At the age of 25, Rice had 133 career homers, a Hall of Fame pace. Consider that, of the twelve hitters who had hit 500 or more home runs at the time, seven of them had more homers than Rice at that stage of the career, but five had fewer. The figures: Mel Ott, 210; Eddie Mathews, 190, Hank Aaron, 179; Mickey Mantle, 177; Jimmie Foxx, 176; Frank Robinson, 165; Willie Mays, 152; Harmon Killebrew, 130; Ted Williams, 127; Willie McCovey, 108; Babe Ruth, 103, Ernie Banks, 93. Rice was traveling in great company.

Rice's timing was exquisite, because his contract was up in 1978. The Red Sox weren't about to let him get away, and they signed him to a six-year contract which was estimated at $5.4 million.

Questions about the new contract tended to make Rice bristle, which was not unusual; a lot of questions make Rice bristle. Amiable enough with fans and teammates, he makes no secret of the fact that he would rather not answer questions from the media.

"Privacy is important to everyone," he told one reporter, Jim Laise of *The Charleston News and Courier.* "People say you owe the public this or that. You don't owe the public anything. . . . You're paid by your credentials. My statistics show I deserve what I'm getting."

This kind of ill-mannered talk, all too typical of athletes in these times, doesn't detract from Rice's playing ability, fortunately. He became a powerful draw around the league in '78, as people came out just to see him take batting practice. In every city, people pointed to spots where Rice had hit a ball, in batting practice or in a game, where balls had seldom been hit before.

Rice is not huge—6'2" and 205 pounds—but his power is awesome. He once snapped a bat in half just by checking`a swing. On the golf course, where he hits the ball mammoth distances, he is even harder on the equipment; he has snapped at least three clubs on the downswing.

So, how do you choose between Guidry and Rice after the seasons they had? Most voters, trying to make an impossible choice, split it down the middle, with each getting prestigious honors. Rice was named the American League's Most Valuable Player and named the league's Player of the Year by *The Sporting News,* while Guidry got the Cy Young Award and was named Major League Player of the Year and Man of the Year by *The Sporting News.*

Quite likely, Rice would have been the Man of the Year if the Red Sox had won the pennant, and for a time, it seemed that's exactly what would happen. The Red Sox got off to an incredible start, reminiscent of 1946, when they had run away with the pennant. After beating the White Sox at Chicago on July 6, five days before the All-Star game, the Red Sox stood at 55–24, a winning percentage of .696. Had they maintained that pace for a season, they would have won 112 or 113 games, which would have been an American League record. (The record of 111 wins, by the 1954 Cleveland Indians, was achieved in a 154-game season, of course.)

But the Red Sox could not continue at that pace. They had the best starting lineup in the league but no depth, and injuries to stars like Carlton Fisk, Carl Yastrzemski, Butch Hobson, and Rick Burleson began to weaken them. The 10-game lead they'd had as late as July 8 had slipped to 4½ by July 27. From their high mark on July 6 they won only 8 of the next 20.

For a time it seemed none of that would benefit the Yanks. If the Red Sox were to falter and lose, it seemed more likely that the Baltimore Orioles or the Milwaukee Brewers would win the pennant. The Yankees were too busy fighting among themselves to challenge another team.

The Yankees in some ways resembled the championship A's of the early '70s in their tendency to fight among themselves, and indeed, they had three of the old A's—Reggie Jackson, Catfish Hunter, and Ken Holtzman. They had an owner, George Steinbrenner, who was nearly as contentious in his way as the A's Charlie Finley. And they had the most argumentative manager in baseball, Billy Martin.

Inevitably, with these characters, the Yankees' considerable accomplishments were often overshadowed by what was being said and done away from the field.

Bob Lemon, then managing the White Sox, said he looked forward to reading the papers each day to see what new problem had erupted in the Yankee camp. "It's like 'Mary Hartman, Mary Hartman,' " he joked.

"When I was a little boy," said Yankee third baseman Graig Nettles, "I wanted to be a baseball player and join a circus. With the Yankees, I've accomplished both."

And when Sparky Lyle was traded away after the '78 season, he wrote a book entitled *The Bronx Zoo,* about his former team.

The "zoo" starts with the man on top, Steinbrenner, who turned the Yankee franchise around and created controversy as he did it.

When he bought the club in 1973, Steinbrenner promised that he wouldn't meddle in the day-to-day affairs of the club. Perhaps he even meant it at the time, but he was unable to keep his word. He has been more active—good and bad—in his club's affairs than any owner this side of Finley.

As he admits himself, Steinbrenner is a difficult man to work for. Some extremely competent men have left his employ, including Al Rosen, Gabe Paul, Lee MacPhail, Bob Fishel, and Tal Smith. A lot of people have given Paul much of the credit for rebuilding the Yankees, which irritated Steinbrenner.

When Paul left to become part-owner and president of the Cleveland Indians, Steinbrenner ungraciously commented: "He's been in baseball for 40 years, 25 as a general manager, and did he ever win a pennant before?"

Steinbrenner has created fear among his employees, which doesn't bother him. "I'm not trying to win any popularity contest," he says. "I know only one way, and that is to work my butt off and demand everybody else do the same.'

He has also irritated the players with petty demands about hair length and the type of uniform socks they wear. Some players have growled back at him—Graig Nettles, Sparky Lyle, and Catfish Hunter in particular.

But Steinbrenner is right out of the Yankee tradition in one respect: He knows how to win. The Yankees had always been able to adjust to changing circumstances. If they could buy players (like Babe Ruth) and win, they did that. If they could win with a top farm system and scouting, they did that. The free agent market opened up while Steinbrenner was in charge of the Yankees, and he has been more successful in signing top players than anybody. Hunter was the first, of course, and he has also signed such as Jackson, Don Gullett, Rich Gossage, Mike Torrez, Luis Tiant.

And the most controversial of all has been Jackson, the moody, articulate slugger who has—not by coincidence—played on so many championship teams, first with the A's and then the Yankees.

The Yankees had won the American League pennant in 1976 but were embarrassed by the Cincinnati Reds in four straight in the World Series. Steinbrenner was determined to improve the team, and he signed Jackson, who had played out his option after being traded from Oakland to Baltimore.

From the start, there were problems. Jackson was quoted in a *Sport* magazine article as saying he was the "straw that stirred the drink," which irritated catcher and team leader Thurman Munson—though Munson had urged Steinbrenner to sign Jackson.

More important, though, was the clash between Jackson and manager Billy Martin, hired by Steinbrenner mid-season, 1975. It was inevitable that Jackson and Martin wouldn't get along, because both crave the spotlight. Most managers, knowing that Jackson plays his best when the spotlight was hottest, would have willingly surrendered it to Jackson. Martin could not.

By the time Martin came to the Yankees, he had already been fired by three clubs—Minnesota, Detroit, and Texas. Everybody agreed he was a smart manager—he had won divisional titles with the first two clubs and gotten a young Texas team into second place—but he could not get along with either his players or his bosses.

Martin grew up as a street fighter in Berkeley, California, and he has never changed. As a player, he broke the jaw of an opposing pitcher, Jim Brewer. As a manager, he knocked out one of his own pitchers, Dave Boswell, at Minnesota.

He tried to tell everybody what to do. "He was even getting after the organist if he didn't like the tunes," said Texas owner Brad Corbett.

Because the Yankees had won the pennant by 10½ games in 1976, Martin felt the club didn't need Jackson. He also felt slighted because he had not been consulted; Reggie was Steinbrenner's man, not Martin's.

Martin seemed to go out of his way to show Reggie who was boss. When the '77 season was only a week old, he benched Jackson after Reggie had told some writers he had a sore elbow. "He didn't know I don't allow players to tell the press about injuries," said Martin. In May, he benched Reggie again without explanation.

Then, on June 18 in Fenway Park, Martin pulled Jackson out of right field because he felt Reggie had not hustled on a fielding play. The two argued and almost came to blows in the dugout—with the television camera recording it all.

That almost cost Martin his job. Ironically, Jackson helped save it by appealing to Steinbrenner not to fire Billy. Any gratitude that Martin had for that gesture was not apparent. Not until August 10 did he finally put Jackson in the cleanup spot, where Reggie clearly belonged. Jackson responded with outstanding hitting down the stretch—but then Martin benched him in the fifth game of the American League playoffs, because left-hander Paul Splittorff started for Kansas City. Jackson did pinch-hit, in the eighth inning, and got an RBI single in the 5–3 Yankee win.

Back in the cleanup spot for the World Series, Reggie hit .450 with five home runs as the Yankees beat the Dodgers. Incredibly, in the last game, he took only three swings and hit a home run with each swing. It was one of those moments that will last forever in people's minds.

"I must admit," said Dodger first baseman Steve Garvey, "when Reggie hit his third home run and I was sure nobody was looking, I applauded in my glove."

In all, Reggie set five Series records: five homers in a Series, three consecutive homers in a game, four homers in consecutive official at bats over two games, 25 total bases and ten runs. He tied records with three homers in a game, 12 total bases in a game, and four runs in a game.

That earned him the nickname, "Mr. October," but didn't help him any in the months of April, May, and June in the '78 season. Not in July, either.

The Yankees got off to a slow start and Steinbrenner, Martin, and Al Rosen, the club president, agreed something had to be done. The main thing they agreed on was to make Reggie a designated hitter, a role he hated, taking him out of right field on June 26. To make it worse for Jackson, Martin didn't even use him full-time as a designated hitter.

Jackson fretted, convinced the Yanks were trying to trade him. A meeting with Steinbrenner got him put back in the cleanup spot—but still as a designated hitter. On July 17, it all came to a head.

Jackson failed to get a hit in his first four appearances against Kansas City that night. His fifth time up, in the tenth inning, the score was tied, 5–5, and Munson was on first. Jackson was given the bunt sign. The first pitch was too high and inside to bunt, but the Kansas City infielders saw Jackson shortened up to bunt.

Martin then took off the bunt sign and third base coach Dick Howser came down the line to make sure that Jackson knew he was supposed to hit away. Nonetheless, Jackson tried to bunt three times, missing the first one and bunting foul on the next two, which counted as a strikeout.

Martin took Jackson out of the game (the Yankees lost, 9–7, in 11 innings). In the clubhouse after the game, he threw a radio and a beer bottle against the wall, and later announced that Jackson was suspended for at least a week. He soon changed that to five days, after a conference with Rosen.

When Jackson came back, Martin was still fuming, especially when Reggie did not apologize directly. Martin told Murray Chass of *The New York Times,* "I'm saying shut up, Reggie Jackson. We don't need none of your stuff. We're winning without you (the Yankees had won five straight). . . . I don't want to hear any more from him. It's like a guy getting out of jail and saying I'm innocent after he killed somebody. He and every one of the other players knew he defied me."

Billy Martin, later to become the Yankee manager, was an outstanding second baseman in the '50s. (George Brace)

At the time, the Yankees were waiting to board a flight to Kansas City. Chass asked Martin if he wanted that on the record, and the Yankee manager assured him that he did. Chass then phoned the story in to his paper.

When Chass returned, he was talking to Henry Hecht of *The New York Post* when Martin came by and asked if what he said was going to be in the paper. Chass told him it would be. Martin then added, "He's a born liar. The two of them (Jackson and Steinbrenner) deserve each other. One's a born liar, the other's convicted."

Steinbrenner, of course, had pleaded guilty to illegal campaign contributions to Richard Nixon, which cost him a $15,000 fine and a year's suspension from baseball. It was, obviously, a sore subject with him. When that appeared in print, Martin was through. He resigned the next day. He would have been fired if he hadn't.

There was much more to come in the Steinbrenner-Martin melodrama. At Old-Timers Day at Yankee Stadium on July 29, five days after Martin had resigned, Steinbrenner announced that Martin would be back as Yankee manager in 1980.

In fact, Martin was back by mid-season, 1979, but his return was a short one. After the 1979 season, Martin got into a fight in a bar and Steinbrenner fired him again. Presumably for good, this time.

But 1978 was to be Bob Lemon's year. Lemon had been the pitching coach for the Yanks in '76 before leaving to manage the Chicago White Sox in '77. He had been named Manager of the Year by UPI when his White Sox won 90 games and finished third, but when they were languishing in fifth place the next season, he was fired on June 30.

At one point under Martin, the Yankees had fallen 14 games behind the league-leading Red Sox, and they trailed Baltimore and Milwaukee as well. The trouble was by no means all because of Martin. The Yankees had had many injuries. Just before Martin's departure, they had finally gotten healthy, and they were making up some ground; on the day he left, they were in third place, 10 games back.

Nonetheless, it seems apparent that they could not have won if Martin had remained. The calm Lemon was exactly what the club needed. He smoothed over problems instead of exacerbating them, as Martin had so often done. And under his leadership, the Yankees won 48 of their last 68 games, a .706 pace.

By July 31st, they had climbed to within 7½ games of the fading Red Sox, though still in third place. By August 9, though still 7½ games behind, they had climbed to second, which was important; except for a four-day slip to third in late August, for the rest of the season, they would have only the Red Sox to beat.

But the real dramatics came in September, a month the Yankees entered still trailing by seven games. By September 7, they had closed the gap to four games and had a four-game series in Fenway Park, where the Red Sox are usually nearly unbeatable.

The Yankees not only beat them this time, they smothered them. The first game was a walloping 15–3, the second just as bad, 13–2. Guidry won his 21st the next day, 7–0. Finally, on the fourth day, the Yankees won, 7–4, the only reasonably close game of the series. They had won 6 straight, 16 of 18, had outscored the Red Sox, 42–9, in the series, and were tied for first place.

Three days later, after a 7–3 win in Detroit, they were in first place alone for the first time all season, and they never left it. The Red Sox came to town on the 15th for a three-game series, and the Yankees won the first, 4–0, Guidry's 22nd win, and the second, 3–2, before the Red Sox finally salvaged the final game of the series, 7–3. That seemed scant consolation for the Red Sox, who were 2½ games back and fading.

But to the Red Sox' credit, they battled back at a time when everybody thought they were folding. They won 12 of their last 14, including a 5–0 win over Toronto behind Luis Tiant's two-hitter on the final day of the season. When the Yankees fell to Cleveland, 9–2, the teams were tied after 162 games, and the second playoff game in league history would have to be played.

Just as in the first one, in 1948, the game was played at Fenway. And just as in the first one, the Red Sox lost, though much more dramatically than the first time, when Cleveland had beaten them.

Sometimes a game as important as this turns out to be a bad one because the players are too tense. Not this one. This game was a classic.

The Red Sox carried a 2–0 lead into the seventh, when light-hitting shortstop Bucky Dent came to bat with two men on base. Mike Torrez had pitched magnificently for the Red Sox to that point.

Dent fouled a ball off his instep and moved around in pain for several minutes. As it happened, though, that worked in the Yankees' favor, because it broke Torrez's concentration momentarily. When Dent stepped back into the box, waving a bat borrowed from teammate Mickey Rivers, he lashed a Torrez fastball up over the left field wall, the famed "Green Monster" that so many pitchers had cursed over the years.

Jackson added a homer in the eighth to make it 5–2, but the Red Sox came back with two runs in the bottom of the inning to close the margin to 5–4.

Guidry had started for the Yankees after just two days' rest, but he was not at his top form; he departed after seven with a 4–2 lead, a poor showing for him in that remarkable year. Rich "Goose" Gossage, one of the Yankees' free agent picks, came on to relieve him.

Gossage had pitched exceptionally well for the Yankees down the stretch. In his final 30 appearances, he had won 6 games and saved another 15, while losing only 3. He hadn't given up a home run in that time.

Gossage was even faster than Guidry; his fastball had been clocked at 98 mph. But like Guidry, he did not seem to be at his best this day, either, yielding the two eighth-inning runs.

With one out in the bottom of the ninth, Rick Burleson walked for the Red Sox. Jerry Remy singled, and Yankee right fielder Lou Piniella lost the ball momentarily in the sun. If it had gone through, Burleson would certainly have scored the tying run.

At the last moment, Piniella stabbed for the ball and stopped it, and Burleson stopped at second. All Gossage had to do now was to retire Jim Rice and Carl Yastrzemski. That's all.

But if Gossage had been struggling to that point, he now showed exactly why the Yankees had paid so much money to get him. He got Rice to hit a soft fly ball to Piniella and Yaz to pop out to third baseman Nettles. The Yankees were champions for the third straight year. The Red Sox had won 99 games, more than the champions in baseball's other three divisions, but they had no place to go but home.

For the third straight year, the Yankees played the Kansas City Royals in the American League championship series, and for the third straight year, they beat the Royals, this time in four games. Jackson hit a single, double and three-run homer in the first game, a 7–1 Yankee win, and drove in three runs with a homer, a single, and sacrifice fly in the third game, a 6–5 Yankee win. Guidry closed it out by beating the Royals, 2–1, in the fourth game.

But the fact that Guidry had to pitch that final game was bad news for the Yankees, because it meant he would not be able to pitch until the third game of the World Series. The Los Angeles Dodgers, the Yankees' opponent for the second straight year, took full advantage of that by beating the Yanks in the first two contests.

Then Guidry returned, and brought the Yankees' dominance back with him, beating the Dodgers, 5–1. He couldn't have done it, though, without some of the most remarkable third base efforts ever seen, as Graig Nettles

Rich Gossage became the Yankees' bull pen stopper in 1978, after playing out his option in Pittsburgh.
(New York Yankees)

made three great plays, off grounders by Reggie Smith in the third, Steve Garvey in the fifth, and Davey Lopes in the sixth. All three plays came on balls that should have been hits; all three came with two outs. There was one runner on when Smith hit his shot, and the bases were loaded on the other two chances. Had the balls gone through, at least five runs would have scored. Instead, Nettles turned them all into inning-ending outs.

That game turned everything around. The Yankees went on to win the next three, becoming the first team ever to lose the first two games of a World Series and then win the next four. Dent was the Series Most Valuable Player with 10 hits in 24 at bats and seven RBIs, four of them in the last two games.

The Yankees had won three straight pennants and two straight World Series. The baseball world seemed normal again.

28. Old Sluggers Never Die

It is usually sad to watch a great athlete at the end of his career, his reflexes gone and motivation reduced, limping through one final season, mocking his greatness. One thinks of Babe Ruth, exiled from the Yankees for his final season, of Jimmie Foxx dissipating his great talents, of Joe DiMaggio reduced to the status of an average player by a series of injuries.

But occasionally, as much by force of personality as ability, a great player will be able to call on a reserve deep within him for one last great effort. Nearing 42, Ty Cobb hit .323. Past 42, Ted Williams hit .316 and bowed out with a home run on his last at bat.

And so it was with Boston's Carl Yastrzemski in 1979. At 40, Yaz was ravaged by athletic old age; his damaged Achilles tendons were taped so tightly, he said, he had to look down to see if his feet were still there. But that sweet swing was still there, often enough for him to accomplish what no American Leaguer had ever done before: collect 400 home runs *and* 3,000 hits.

It was incredible. When you think of the American League, you think of great hitters—Ruth, Cobb, Williams, Foxx, DiMaggio, Lou Gehrig, Hank Greenberg, Joe Jackson, Al Simmons, George Sisler, Harry Heilmann. But none had done what Yastrzemski did.

There were extenuating circumstances with some of the others, of course. Ruth started his career as a pitcher, which reduced his at bats. Cobb and Jackson played in the dead ball era, which kept their home run totals low. Gehrig was cut down tragically by disease in his prime. Williams lost the equivalent of five seasons to military service.

But still, the fact remained that no American Leaguer had ever reached both goals. Indeed, there were great hitters—such as Greenberg and DiMaggio—who had not reached either goal. Only Al Kaline had come really close, stopping with 399 home runs after getting 3,007 hits. Yastrzemski's achievement was a remarkable one because he needed ability, durability, and consistency, and of the three, consistency was probably his biggest asset. His statistics were not padded by two or three extraordinary seasons; he never had more than 191 hits or 44 home runs in one season.

"He's a true superstar," said Reggie Jackson. "You really have to have other athletes comment on what he has achieved because you can't really appreciate what it means to perform as he has for as long as he has. It's an amazing human feat—the desire, the talent, the character, his makeup as a man. It takes a special human to perform at such a level for such a long time."

"It's a great accomplishment to blend power with consistency," said Frank Robinson, who hit 586 home runs but fell 57 hits short of 3,000.

Robinson and Kaline both played against Yastrzemski, Robinson for 10 years and Kaline for 14, and they appreciated what Yastrzemski had done.

"When I was playing in the league," said Robinson, "he was the only one I considered a true superstar, and he's still a dangerous hitter. He's been able to make adjustments in his stance to compensate for what he can't do because of his age. A lot of players can't do that. They hit a peak and go downhill immediately. But he's been able to avoid that."

Kaline remembered, wistfully, how close he had come to the double plateau. "I can remember a couple of home runs wiped out because of rain and a couple that were called foul that I thought were fair."

But he gave full credit to Yaz for his accomplishments. "I've always been

Frank Robinson, a great hitting star in both leagues, became the first black manager in the league with Cleveland in 1975.
(Cleveland Indians)

a Carl Yastrzemski fan," he said. "I've been absolutely amazed by what this guy can do. I'm not talking just about getting hits and home runs. Here's a guy who was signed out of college as a shortstop and moved to the outfield and became a great outfielder. Then one year he played third base for awhile and he did a good job. Then he moved to first base and did an outstanding job. To do what he's done, you have to be a superb athlete, and you have to endure it mentally."

It wasn't always like that for Yastrzemski. A good part of his early career was spent in frustration. Boston fans expected him to be the next Williams, and when he didn't hit .400 in his third season—as Williams had—he heard about it.

The Red Sox of that era, the early 1960s, were known as a "country club" team, pampered players who were overpaid and underproductive. Yastrzemski was linked to that group by the fans, which was unfair.

In truth, Yastrzemski had been a true professional, a man who kept playing even when he was hurt, which was often. Though he was lucky in avoiding the type of injury that would sideline him for a season, or even end his career, he had a series of injuries which curtailed his effectiveness. But he pleaded with managers and trainers not to let anyone know how serious these injuries were. It was part of his code not to make excuses.

One of the most telling instances occurred in 1978, when wrist and back injuries prevented him from keeping both hands on the bat at contact. He even considered taping his hand to the bat and tried it in batting practice; then he realized it wouldn't work. "What was I going to do if I got a hit and tried to run the bases with the bat still taped to my hand?"

Unaware of this, Boston fans often booed Yaz for not living up to their lofty expectations. He dealt with this in his own way—with earplugs.

The turning point for Yastrzemski—and the Red Sox—came in 1967, when he had a great season and the Red Sox won their first pennant in 21 years. "The whole attitude changed after that year," he said, "from a losing organization to a winning one. It even changed things all the way down to the minors."

Boston fans still booed Yastrzemski on occasion, just to keep in practice, but the occasions were further and further apart, as they realized they were watching a very special athlete.

His teammates realized it, too. George Scott recalled the time in 1968 when it seemed that the American League would not have a .300 hitter.

"He was hitting about .270," said Scott, "and he said to me, 'It would be embarrassing for the American league not to have one .300 hitter, wouldn't

Carl Yastrzemski became the first American Leaguer in history to collect 400 home runs and 3,000 hits in 1979. *(Boston Red Sox)*

it?' There was about a month to go, and he put on one of the greatest exhibitions I've ever seen, and he won the batting title with .301."

As he entered athletic old age, Yastrzemski conceded nothing. At 36, he drove in more than 100 runs and repeated the feat the next year, at 37. In 1977, he set an American League record by leading the league in, assists from the outfield (16) for the seventh time, and he won his seventh Gold Glove, with a 1.000 fielding percentage.

But 1979 was the sweetest year of all. Fans could enjoy what Yaz was still able to do while recalling nostalgically all that he had accomplished in the past, as he pursued his twin goals.

The home run mark came first, as he hit his 17th of the year and 400th of his career on July 24. That left only the 3,000-hit goal.

Fittingly, hit number 3,000 came in Boston, on September 13, against the

Yankees. After going ten official at bats without a hit since collecting number 2,999, Yaz finally grounded a single into right field in the eighth inning off Jim Beattie. The Red Sox won the game, 9–2, so the hit did not have any real effect on the outcome. "I'm glad for him," said Beattie. "It's a thrill to have been here to see it."

The next day, Yaz was honored by the city of Boston in a hastily called celebration, and two days later, he went to Washington, D.C. to meet President Carter. Typically, he took it all in stride.

"I haven't had the greatest ability in the world," he said, self-deprecatingly, "and I had to work hard for every accomplishment. But God gave me the body and something to go with it."

And with that "something," Carl Yastrzemski had made a unique contribution to the American League.

Historical Moments

1901　The American League becomes a major league; Nap Lajoie hits .422, still the league record.

1903　The Boston Pilgrims beat Pittsburgh in first World Series.

1904　Jack Chesbro wins 41 games, a modern record; Rube Waddell sets record with 343 strikeouts.

1907　Ty Cobb hits .350 to win first of 9 straight batting titles and 12 overall, both records.

1912　Walter Johnson and Joe Wood both win league record 16 straight.

1914　Hub Leonard as 1.01 ERA, still the league record.

1919　Babe Ruth sets major league home run record with 29.

1920　Ruth sets record with 54 homers.

1921　For third straight year, Ruth sets home run record, with 59.

1922　George Sisler hits in league record 41 straight games.

1924　Walter Johnson, pitching in his first World Series, wins in relief in seventh game.

1927　Ruth hits 60 homers, another record; Yankees set league record with 110 wins.

1931　Lefty Grove ties record with 16 straight wins in 31-4 season.

1932　Jimmie Foxx hits 58 homers.

1936-37　Johnny Allen wins league record 17 games straight over two seasons.

1938　Hank Greenberg hits 58 homers; Bob Feller strikes out major league record 18 batters in game.

1939　Yankees become first club to win four straight World Series.

1941　Joe DiMaggio hits in 56 straight games, major league record; Ted Williams hits .406.

1946　Feller is clocked at 98.6 mph and sets strikeout record with 348.

1948　Cleveland sets season attendance record and wins pennant in first American League playoff.

1953　Yankees become first club to win five straight World Series.

1954　Cleveland sets league record with 111 wins; St. Louis moves to Baltimore, first franchise shift in 52 years.

1955　Philadelphia moves to Kansas City.

1956　Don Larsen throws a perfect game in World Series.

1957   Ted Williams, at 39, hits .388 with 38 homers.

1960   Casey Stengel fired as Yankees manager despite unprecedented 10 pennants in 12 years.

1961   Roger Maris hits record 61 homers; expansion teams are put into Anaheim and Washington, D.C., and Senators are moved from Washington to Minneapolis-St. Paul.

1968   Denny McLain wins 31 games, first 30-game winner in 37 years; A's move from Kansas City to Oakland.

1969   Expansion franchises added in Kansas City and Seattle.

1970   Seattle team is moved to Milwaukee.

1973   Nolan Ryan sets strikeout mark with 383; American League adopts designated hitter rule.

1974   Ryan is clocked at 100.9 mph in a game and sets league record with 19 strikeouts in another game.

1975   Ryan throws fourth no-hitter, league record.

1977   Rod Carew hits .388 for sixth batting title; expansion franchises are added in Seattle and Toronto.

1978   Ron Guidry sets record for 20-game winner with .893 winning percentage (25–3).

1979   Carl Yastrzemski becomes the first American Leaguer to hit more than 400 home runs and collect 3,000 hits.

Nolan Ryan set strikeout records with a fastball timed at more than 100 miles an hour. *(California Angels)*

League Statistics

American League Team Standings: Year-By-Year

(* play-off to break tie)

1901

TEAM	W	L	PCT	MGR
CHI	83	53	.610	Griffith
BOS	79	57	.581	Collins
DET	74	61	.548	Stallings
PHI	74	62	.544	Mack
BAL	68	65	.511	McGraw
WAS	61	72	.459	Manning
CLE	54	82	.397	McAleer
MIL	48	89	.350	Duffy

1902

TEAM	W	L	PCT	MGR
PHI	83	53	.610	Mack
ST.L	78	58	.574	McAleer
BOS	77	60	.562	Collins
CHI	74	60	.552	Griffith
CLE	69	67	.507	Armour
WAS	61	75	.449	Loftus
DET	52	83	.385	Dwyer
BAL	50	88	.362	McGraw / Robinson

1903

TEAM	W	L	PCT	MGR
BOS	91	47	.659	Collins
PHI	75	60	.556	Mack
CLE	77	63	.550	Armour
N Y	72	62	.537	Griffith
DET	65	71	.478	Barrow
ST.L	65	74	.488	McAleer
CHI	60	77	.438	Callahan
WAS	43	94	.314	Loftus

1904

TEAM	W	L	PCT	MGR
BOS	95	59	.617	Collins
N Y	92	59	.609	Griffith
CHI	89	65	.578	Callahan / Jones
CLE	86	85	.570	Armour
PHI	81	70	.536	Mack
ST.L	65	87	.428	McAleer
DET	62	90	.408	Barrow / Lowe
WAS	38	113	.251	Kittredge / Donovan

1905

TEAM	W	L	PCT	MGR
PHI	92	56	.621	Mack
CHI	92	60	.605	Jones
DET	79	74	.516	Armour
BOS	78	74	.513	Collins
CLE	76	78	.494	Lajoie
N Y	71	78	.477	Griffith
WAS	64	87	.421	Stahl
ST.L	54	99	.354	McAleer

1906

TEAM	W	L	PCT	MGR
CHI	93	58	.615	Jones
N Y	90	61	.596	Griffith
CLE	89	64	.582	Lajoie
PHI	78	67	.536	Mack
ST.L	76	73	.510	McAleer
DET	71	78	.477	Armour
WAS	55	95	.367	Stahl. G.
BOS	49	105	.318	Collins / Stahl. C.

1907

TEAM	W	L	PCT	MGR
DET	92	58	.613	Jennings
PHI	88	57	.607	Mack
CHI	87	64	.576	Jones
CLE	85	57	.559	Lajoie
N Y	70	78	.473	Griffith
ST.L	69	83	.454	McAleer
BOS	59	90	.396	Young / Huff / Unglaub / McGuire
WAS	49	102	.325	Cantillon

1908

TEAM	W	L	PCT	MGR
DET	90	63	.588	Jennings
CLE	90	64	.584	Lajoie
CHI	88	64	.579	Jones
ST.L	83	69	.546	McAleer
BOS	75	79	.487	McGuire / Lake
PHI	68	85	.444	Mack
WAS	67	85	.441	Cantillon
N Y	51	103	.331	Griffith / Elberfeld

1909

TEAM	W	L	PCT	MGR
DET	98	54	.645	Jennings
PHI	95	58	.621	Mack
BOS	88	63	.583	Lake
CHI	78	74	.513	Sullivan
N Y	74	77	.490	Stallings
CLE	71	82	.464	Lajoie / McGuire
ST.L	61	89	.407	McAleer / O'Connor
WAS	42	110	.276	Cantillon

1910

TEAM	W	L	PCT	MGR
PHI	102	48	.680	Mack
N Y	88	63	.583	Stallings / Chase
DET	86	68	.558	Jennings
BOS	81	72	.529	Donovan
CLE	71	81	.467	McGuire
CHI	68	85	.444	Duffy
WAS	68	85	.437	McAleer
ST.L	47	107	.305	O'Connor

1911

TEAM	W	L	PCT	MGR
PHI	101	50	.669	Mack
DET	89	65	.578	Jennings
CLE	80	73	.523	McGuire / Stovall
CHI	77	74	.5099	Duffy,
BOS	78	75	.5098	Donovan
N Y	76	76	.500	Chase
WAS	64	90	.415	McAleer
ST.L	45	107	.296	Wallace

1912

TEAM	W	L	PCT	MGR
BOS	105	47	.691	Stahl
WAS	91	61	.599	Griffith
PHI	90	62	.592	Mack
CHI	78	76	.506	Callahan
CLE	75	78	.490	Davis / Birmingham
DET	69	84	.451	Jennings
ST.L	53	101	.344	Wallace / Stovall
N Y	50	102	.329	Wolverton

1913

PHI	96	57	.627	Mack
WAS	90	64	.584	Griffith
CLE	86	66	.566	Birmingham
BOS	79	71	.527	Stahl
				Carrigan
CHI	78	74	.513	Callahan
DET	66	87	.431	Jennings
N Y	57	94	.377	Chance
ST.L	57	96	.373	Stovall
				Austin
				Rickey

1914

PHI	99	53	.651	Mack
BOS	91	62	.595	Carrigan
WAS	81	73	.526	Griffith
DET	80	73	.523	Jennings
ST.L	71	82	.464	Rickey
CHI	70	84	.455	Callahan
N Y	70	84	.455	Chance
				Peckinpaugh
CLE	51	102	.333	Birmingham

1915

BOS	101	50	.669	Carrigan
DET	100	54	.649	Jennings
CHI	93	61	.604	Rowland
WAS	85	68	.556	Griffith
N Y	69	83	.454	Donovan
ST.L	63	91	.409	Rickey
CLE	57	95	.375	Birmingham
				Fohl
PHI	43	109	.283	Mack

1916

BOS	91	63	.591	Carrigan
CHI	89	65	.578	Rowland
DET	87	67	.565	Jennings
N Y	80	74	.519	Donovan
ST.L	79	75	.513	Jones
CLE	77	77	.500	Fohl
WAS	76	77	.497	Griffith
PHI	38	117	.235	Mack

1917

CHI	100	54	.649	Rowland
BOS	90	62	.592	Barry
CLE	88	68	.571	Fohl
DET	78	75	.510	Jennings
WAS	74	79	.484	Griffith
N Y	71	82	.464	Donovan
ST.L	57	97	.370	Jones
PHI	55	98	.359	Mack

1918

BOS	75	51	.595	Barrow
CLE	73	54	.575	Fohl
WAS	72	56	.563	Griffith
N Y	60	63	.488	Huggins
ST.L	58	64	.475	Jones
				Austin
				Burke
CHI	57	67	.460	Rowland
DET	55	71	.437	Jennings
PHI	52	76	.402	Mack

1919

CHI	88	52	.629	Gleason
CLE	84	55	.604	Fohl
				Speaker
N Y	80	59	.576	Huggins
DET	80	60	.571	Jennings
ST.L	67	72	.4820	Burke
BOS	66	71	.4817	Barrow
WAS	56	84	.400	Griffith
PHI	36	104	.257	Mack

1920

CLE	98	56	.636	Speaker
CHI	96	58	.623	Gleason
N Y	95	59	.617	Huggins
ST.L	76	77	.497	Burke
BOS	72	81	.471	Barrow
WAS	68	84	.447	Griffith
DET	61	93	.396	Jennings
PHI	48	106	.312	Mack

1921

N Y	98	55	.641	Huggins
CLE	94	60	.610	Speaker
ST.L	81	73	.526	Fohl
WAS	80	73	.523	McBride
BOS	75	79	.487	Duffy
DET	71	82	.464	Cobb
CHI	62	92	.403	Gleason
PHI	53	100	.346	Mack

1922

N Y	94	60	.610	Huggins
ST.L	93	61	.604	Fohl
DET	79	75	.513	Cobb
CLE	78	76	.507	Speaker
CHI	77	77	.500	Gleason
WAS	69	85	.448	Milan
PHI	65	89	.422	Mack
BOS	61	93	.396	Duffy

1923

N Y	98	54	.645	Huggins
DET	83	71	.539	Cobb
CLE	82	71	.536	Speaker
WAS	75	78	.490	Bush
ST.L	74	78	.487	Fohl
				Austin
PHI	69	83	.454	Mack
CHI	69	85	.448	Gleason
BOS	61	91	.401	Chance

1924

WAS	92	62	.597	Harris
N Y	89	63	.586	Huggins
DET	86	68	.558	Cobb
ST.L	74	78	.487	Sisler
PHI	71	81	.467	Mack
CLE	67	86	.438	Speaker
BOS	67	87	.435	Fohl
CHI	66	87	.431	Evers

1925

WAS	96	55	.636	Harris
PHI	88	64	.579	Mack
ST.L	82	71	.536	Sisler
DET	81	73	.526	Cobb
CHI	79	75	.513	Collins
CLE	70	84	.455	Speaker
N Y	69	85	.448	Huggins
BOS	47	105	.309	Fohl

1926

N Y	91	63	.591	Huggins
CLE	88	66	.571	Speaker
PHI	83	67	.553	Mack
WAS	81	69	.540	Harris
CHI	81	72	.529	Collins
DET	79	75	.513	Cobb
ST.L	62	92	.403	Sisler
BOS	48	107	.301	Fohl

1927

N Y	110	44	.714	Huggins
PHI	91	63	.591	Mack
WAS	85	69	.552	Harris
DET	82	71	.536	Moriarty
CHI	70	83	.458	Schalk
CLE	66	87	.431	McCallister
ST.L	59	94	.386	Howley
BOS	51	103	.331	Carrigan

1928

	W	L	PCT	Manager
N Y	101	53	.656	Huggins
PHI	98	55	.641	Mack
ST.L	82	72	.532	Howley
WAS	75	79	.487	Harris
CHI	72	82	.468	Schalk Blackburne
DET	68	86	.442	Moriarty
CLE	62	92	.403	Peckinpaugh
BOS	57	96	.373	Carrigan

1929

	W	L	PCT	Manager
PHI	104	46	.693	Mack
N Y	88	66	.571	Huggins Fletcher
CLE	81	71	.533	Peckinpaugh
ST.L	79	73	.520	Howley
WAS	71	81	.467	Johnson
DET	70	84	.455	Harris
CHI	59	93	.388	Blackburne
BOS	58	96	.377	Carrigan

1930

	W	L	PCT	Manager
PHI	102	52	.662	Mack
WAS	94	60	.610	Johnson
N Y	86	68	.558	Shawkey
CLE	81	73	.526	Peckinpaugh
DET	75	79	.487	Harris
ST.L	64	90	.416	Killefer
CHI	62	92	.403	Bush
BOS	52	102	.338	Wagner

1931

	W	L	PCT	Manager
PHI	107	45	.704	Mack
N Y	94	59	.614	McCarthy
WAS	92	62	.597	Johnson
CLE	78	76	.506	Peckinpaugh
ST.L	63	91	.409	Killefer
BOS	62	90	.406	Collins
DET	61	93	.396	Harris
CHI	56	97	.366	Bush

1932

	W	L	PCT	Manager
N Y	107	47	.695	McCarthy
PHI	94	80	.610	Mack
WAS	93	61	.604	Johnson
CLE	87	65	.572	Peckinpaugh
DET	76	75	.503	Harris
ST.L	63	91	.409	Killefer
CHI	49	102	.325	Fonseca
BOS	43	111	.279	Collins McManus

1933

	W	L	PCT	Manager
WAS	99	53	.651	Cronin
N Y	91	59	.607	McCarthy
PHI	79	72	.523	Mack
CLE	75	76	.497	Peckinpaugh Johnson
DET	75	79	.487	Harris Baker
CHI	67	83	.447	Fonseca
BOS	63	86	.423	McManus
ST.L	55	96	.364	Killefer Sothoron Hornsby

1934

	W	L	PCT	Manager
DET	101	53	.656	Cochrane
N Y	94	60	.610	McCarthy
CLE	85	69	.552	Johnson
BOS	76	76	.500	Harris
PHI	68	82	.453	Mack
ST.L	67	85	.441	Hornsby
WAS	66	86	.434	Cronin
CHI	53	99	.349	Fonseca Dykes

1935

	W	L	PCT	Manager
DET	93	58	.616	Cochrane
N Y	89	60	.597	McCarthy
CLE	82	71	.536	Johnson O'Neill
BOS	78	75	.510	Cronin
CHI	74	78	.487	Dykes
WAS	67	86	.438	Harris
ST.L	65	87	.428	Hornsby
PHI	58	91	.389	Mack

1936

	W	L	PCT	Manager
N Y	102	51	.667	McCarthy
DET	83	71	.539	Cochrane
CHI	81	70	.5386	Dykes
WAS	82	71	.5364	Harris
CLE	80	74	.519	O'Neill
BOS	74	80	.481	Cronin
ST.L	57	95	.375	Hornsby
PHI	53	100	.346	Mack

1937

	W	L	PCT	Manager
N Y	102	52	.662	McCarthy
DET	89	65	.576	Cochrane
CHI	86	68	.558	Dykes
CLE	83	71	.539	O'Neill
BOS	80	72	.526	Cronin
WAS	73	80	.477	Harris
PHI	54	97	.358	Mack
ST.L	46	108	.299	Hornsby Bottomley

1938

	W	L	PCT	Manager
N Y	99	53	.651	McCarthy
BOS	88	61	.591	Cronin
CLE	86	66	.566	Vitt
DET	84	70	.545	Cochrane Baker
WAS	75	76	.497	Harris
CHI	65	83	.439	Dykes
ST.L	55	97	.362	Street Melillo
PHI	53	99	.349	Mack

1939

	W	L	PCT	Manager
N Y	106	45	.702	McCarthy
BOS	89	62	.589	Cronin
CLE	87	67	.565	Vitt
CHI	85	69	.552	Dykes
DET	81	73	.526	Baker
WAS	65	87	.428	Harris
PHI	55	97	.362	Mack
ST.L	43	111	.279	Haney

1940

	W	L	PCT	Manager
DET	90	64	.584	Baker
CLE	89	65	.578	Vitt
N Y	88	66	.571	McCarthy
BOS	82	72	.532	Cronin
CHI	82	72	.532	Dykes
ST.L	67	87	.435	Haney
WAS	64	90	.416	Harris
PHI	54	100	.351	Mack

1941

	W	L	PCT	Manager
N Y	101	53	.656	McCarthy
BOS	84	70	.545	Cronin
CHI	77	77	.500	Dykes
CLE	75	79	.487	Peckinpaugh
DET	75	79	.487	Baker
ST.L	70	84	.455	Haney Sewell
WAS	70	84	.455	Harris
PHI	64	90	.416	Mack

1942

	W	L	PCT	Manager
N Y	103	51	.669	McCarthy
BOS	93	59	.612	Cronin
ST.L	82	69	.543	Sewell
CLE	75	79	.487	Boudreau
DET	73	81	.474	Baker
CHI	66	82	.446	Dykes
WAS	62	89	.411	Harris
PHI	55	99	.357	Mack

1943

	W	L	PCT	Manager
N Y	98	56	.636	McCarthy
WAS	84	69	.549	Bluege
CLE	82	71	.536	Boudreau
CHI	82	72	.532	Dykes
DET	78	76	.506	O'Neill
ST.L	72	80	.474	Sewell
BOS	68	84	.447	Cronin
PHI	49	105	.318	Mack

1944

	W	L	PCT	Manager
ST.L	89	65	.578	Sewell
DET	88	66	.571	O'Neill
N Y	83	71	.539	McCarthy
BOS	77	77	.500	Cronin
CLE	72	82	.468	Boudreau
PHI	72	82	.468	Mack
CHI	71	83	.461	Dykes
WAS	64	90	.416	Bluege

1945

	W	L	PCT	Manager
DET	88	65	.575	O'Neill
WAS	87	67	.565	Bluege
ST.L	81	70	.536	Sewell
N Y	81	71	.533	McCarthy
CLE	73	72	.503	Boudreau
CHI	71	78	.477	Dykes
BOS	71	83	.461	Cronin
PHI	52	98	.347	Mack

1946

	W	L	PCT	Manager
BOS	104	50	.675	Cronin
DET	92	62	.597	O'Neill
N Y	87	67	.565	McCarthy
				Dickey
				Neun
WAS	76	78	.494	Bluege
CHI	74	80	.481	Dykes
				Lyons
CLE	68	96	.442	Boudreau
ST.L	66	88	.429	Sewell
				Taylor
PHI	49	105	.318	Mack

1947

	W	L	PCT	Manager
N Y	97	57	.630	Harris
DET	85	69	.552	O'Neill
BOS	83	71	.539	Cronin
CLE	80	74	.519	Boudreau
PHI	78	76	.506	Mack
CHI	70	84	.455	Lyons
WAS	64	90	.416	Bluege
ST.L	59	95	.383	Ruel

1948

	W	L	PCT	Manager
CLE	97*	58	.626	Boudreau
BOS	95*	59	.619	McCarthy
N Y	94	60	.610	Harris
PHI	84	70	.545	Mack
DET	78	75	.506	O'Neill
ST.L	59	94	.386	Taylor
WAS	56	97	.366	Kuhel
CHI	51	101	.336	Lyons

1949

	W	L	PCT	Manager
N Y	97	57	.630	Stengel
BOS	98	58	.623	McCarthy
CLE	89	65	.578	Boudreau
DET	87	67	.565	Rolfe
PHI	81	73	.526	Mack
CHI	63	91	.409	Onslow
ST.L	53	101	.344	Taylor
WAS	50	104	.324	Kuhel

1950

	W	L	PCT	Manager
N Y	98	56	.636	Stengel
DET	95	59	.617	Rolfe
BOS	94	60	.610	McCarthy
				O'Neill
CLE	92	62	.597	Boudreau
WAS	67	87	.435	Harris
CHI	60	94	.390	Onslow
				Corriden
ST.L	58	96	.377	Taylor
PHI	52	102	.338	Mack

1951

	W	L	PCT	Manager
N Y	98	56	.636	Stengel
CLE	93	61	.604	Lopez
BOS	87	67	.585	O'Neill
CHI	81	73	.526	Richards
DET	73	81	.474	Rolfe
PHI	70	84	.455	Dykes
WAS	62	92	.403	Harris
ST.L	52	102	.338	Taylor

1952

	W	L	PCT	Manager
N Y	95	59	.617	Stengel
CLE	93	61	.604	Lopez
CHI	81	73	.526	Richards
PHI	79	75	.513	Dykes
WAS	78	76	.506	Harris
BOS	76	78	.494	Boudreau
ST.L	64	90	.416	Hornsby
				Marion
DET	50	104	.325	Rolfe
				Hutchinson

1953

	W	L	PCT	Manager
N Y	99	52	.656	Stengel
CLE	92	62	.597	Lopez
CHI	89	65	.578	Richards
BOS	84	69	.549	Boudreau
WAS	76	76	.500	Harris
DET	60	94	.390	Hutchinson
PHI	59	93	.383	Dykes
ST.L	54	100	.351	Marion

1954

	W	L	PCT	Manager
CLE	111	43	.721	Lopez
N Y	103	51	.669	Stengel
CHI	94	60	.610	Richards
				Marion
BOS	69	85	.448	Boudreau
DET	68	86	.442	Hutchinson
WAS	66	88	.429	Harris
BAL	54	100	.351	Dykes
PHI	51	103	.331	Joost

1955

	W	L	PCT	Manager
N Y	96	58	.623	Stengel
CLE	93	61	.604	Lopez
CHI	91	63	.591	Marion
BOS	84	70	.545	Higgins
DET	79	75	.518	Harris
K C	63	91	.409	Boudreau
BAL	57	97	.370	Richards
WAS	53	101	.344	Dressen

1956

	W	L	PCT	Manager
N Y	97	57	.630	Stengel
CLE	88	66	.571	Lopez
CHI	85	69	.552	Marion
BOS	84	70	.545	Higgins
DET	82	72	.532	Harris
BAL	69	85	.448	Richards
WAS	59	95	.383	Dressen
K C	52	102	.338	Boudreau

1957

	W	L	PCT	Manager
N Y	98	56	.636	Stengel
CHI	90	64	.584	Lopez
BOS	82	72	.532	Higgins
DET	78	76	.506	Tighe
BAL	76	76	.500	Richards
CLE	76	77	.497	Farrell
K C	59	94	.386	Boudreau
				Craft
WAS	55	99	.357	Dressen
				Lavagetto

1958

N Y	92	62	.597	Stengel
CHI	82	72	.532	Lopez
BOS	79	75	.513	Higgins
CLE	77	76	.503	Bragan
				Gordon
DET	77	77	.500	Tighe
				Norman
BAL	74	79	.484	Richards
K C	73	81	.474	Craft
WAS	61	93	.396	Lavagetto

1959

CHI	94	60	.610	Lopez
CLE	89	65	.578	Gordon
N Y	79	75	.513	Stengel
DET	76	78	.494	Norman
				Dykes
				Higgins
BOS	75	79	.487	York
				Jurges
BAL	74	80	.481	Richards
K C	66	88	.429	Craft
WAS	63	91	.409	Lavagetto

1960

N Y	97	57	.630	Stengel
BAL	89	65	.578	Richards
CHI	87	67	.563	Lopez
CLE	76	78	.494	Gordon
				White
				Dykes
WAS	78	81	.474	Lavagetto
DET	71	83	.461	Dykes
				Hitchcock
				Gordon
BOS	65	89	.422	Jurges
				Higgins
K C	58	96	.377	Elliott

1961

N Y	109	53	.673	Houk
DET	101	61	.623	Scheffing
BAL	95	67	.586	Richards
				Harris
CHI	86	76	.531	Hitchcock
CLE	78	83	.484	Dykes
				Harder
BOS	76	86	.469	Higgins
MIN	70	90	.438	Lavagetto
				Mele
L A	70	91	.435	Rigney
K C	61	100	.379	Gordon
				Bauer
WAS	61	100	.379	Vernon

1962

N Y	96	66	.593	Houk
MIN	91	71	.562	Mele
L A	86	76	.531	Rigney
DET	85	76	.528	Scheffing
CHI	85	77	.525	Lopez
CLE	80	82	.494	McGaha
BAL	77	85	.475	Hitchcock
BOS	76	84	.475	Higgins
K C	72	90	.444	Bauer
WAS	60	101	.373	Vernon

1963

N Y	104	57	.646	Houk
CHI	94	68	.580	Lopez
MIN	91	70	.565	Mele
BAL	86	76	.531	Hitchcock
CLE	79	83	.488	Tebbetts
DET	79	83	.488	Scheffing
				Dressen
BOS	76	85	.472	Pesky
K C	73	89	.451	Lopat
L A	70	91	.435	Rigney
WAS	56	106	.346	Vernon
				Hodges

1964

N Y	99	63	.611	Berra
CHI	98	64	.605	Lopez
BAL	97	65	.599	Bauer
DET	85	77	.525	Dressen
L A	82	80	.506	Rigney
CLE	79	83	.488	Tebbetts
MIN	79	83	.488	Mele
BOS	72	90	.444	Pesky
				Herman
WAS	62	100	.383	Hodges
K C	57	105	.352	Lopat
				McGaha

1965

MIN	102	60	.630	Mele
CHI	95	67	.586	Lopez
BAL	94	68	.580	Bauer
DET	89	73	.549	Dressen
CLE	87	75	.537	Tebbetts
N Y	77	85	.475	Keane
CAL	75	87	.463	Rigney
WAS	70	92	.432	Hodges
BOS	62	100	.383	Herman
K C	59	103	.364	McGaha
				Sullivan

1966

BAL	97	63	.606	Bauer
MIN	89	73	.549	Mele
DET	88	74	.543	Dressen
				Swift
				Skaff
CHI	83	79	.512	Stanky
CLE	81	81	.500	Tebbetts
				Strickland
CAL	80	82	.494	Rigney
K C	74	86	.463	Dark
WAS	71	88	.447	Hodges
BOS	72	90	.444	Herman
				Runnels
N Y	70	89	.440	Keane
				Houk

1967

BOS	92	70	.568	Williams
DET	91	71	.562	Smith
MIN	91	71	.562	Mele
				Ermer
CHI	89	73	.549	Stanky
CAL	84	77	.522	Rigney
BAL	76	85	.472	Bauer
WAS	76	85	.472	Hodges
CLE	75	87	.463	Adcock
N Y	72	90	.444	Houk
K C	62	99	.385	Dark
				Appling

1968

DET	103	59	.636	Smith
BAL	91	71	.562	Bauer
				Weaver
CLE	86	75	.534	Dark
BOS	86	76	.531	Williams
N Y	83	79	.512	Houk
OAK	82	80	.506	Kennedy
MIN	79	83	.488	Ermer
CAL	67	95	.414	Rigney
CHI	67	95	.414	Stanky
				Moss
				Lopez
WAS	65	96	.404	Lemon

1969—EASTERN DIVISION

BAL	109	53	.673	Weaver
DET	90	72	.556	Smith
BOS	87	75	.537	R. Williams
				Popowski
WAS	86	76	.531	T. Williams
N Y	80	81	.497	Houk
CLE	62	99	.385	Dark

1969—WESTERN DIVISION

MIN	97	65	.599	Martin
OAK	88	74	.543	Bauer
				McNamara
CAL	71	91	.438	Rigney
				Phillips
K C	69	93	.426	Gordon
CHI	68	94	.420	Lopez
				Gutteridge
SEA	64	98	.395	Schultz

1970—EASTERN DIVISION

BAL	108	54	.667	Weaver
N Y	93	69	.574	Houk
BOS	87	75	.537	Kasko
DET	79	83	.488	Smith
CLE	76	86	.469	Dark
WAS	70	92	.432	T. Williams

1970—WESTERN DIVISION

MIN	98	64	.605	Rigney
OAK	89	73	.549	McNamara
CAL	86	76	.531	Phillips
K C	65	97	.401	Metro
				Lemon
MIL	65	97	.401	Bristol
CHI	56	106	.346	Gutteridge
				Adair
				Tanner

1971—EASTERN DIVISION

BAL	101	57	.629	Weaver
DET	91	71	.562	Martin
BOS	85	77	.525	Kasko
N Y	82	80	.506	Houk
WAS	63	96	.396	T. Williams
CLE	60	102	.370	Dark
				Lipon

1971—WESTERN DIVISION

OAK	101	60	.627	R. Williams
K C	85	76	.528	Lemon
CHI	79	83	.488	Tanner
CAL	76	86	.469	Phillips
MIN	74	86	.463	Rigney
MIL	69	92	.429	Bristol

1972—EASTERN DIVISION

DET	86	70	.551	Martin
BOS	85	70	.548	Kasko
BAL	80	74	.519	Weaver
N Y	79	76	.510	Houk
CLE	72	84	.462	Aspromonte
MIL	65	91	.417	Bristol
				McMillan
				Crandall

1972—WESTERN DIVISION

OAK	93	62	.600	R. Williams
CHI	87	67	.565	Tanner
MIN	77	77	.500	Rigney
				Quilici
K C	76	78	.494	Lemon
CAL	75	80	.484	Rice
TEX	54	100	.351	T. Williams

1973—EASTERN DIVISION

BAL	97	65	.599	Weaver
BOS	89	73	.549	Kasko
				Popowski
DET	85	77	.525	Martin
				Schultz
N Y	80	82	.494	Houk
MIL	74	88	.457	Crandall
CLE	71	91	.438	Aspromonte

1973—WESTERN DIVISION

OAK	94	68	.580	Williams
K C	88	74	.543	McKeon
MIN	81	81	.500	Quilici
CAL	79	83	.488	Winkles
CHI	77	85	.475	Tanner
TEX	57	105	.352	Herzog
				Wilber
				Martin

1974—EASTERN DIVISION

BAL	91	71	.562	Weaver
N Y	89	73	.549	Virdon
BOS	84	78	.519	Johnson
CLE	77	85	.475	Aspromonte
MIL	76	86	.469	Crandall
DET	72	90	.444	Houk

1974—WESTERN DIVISION

OAK	90	72	.556	Dark
TEX	84	76	.525	Martin
MIN	82	80	.506	Quilici
CHI	80	80	.500	Tanner
K C	77	85	.475	McKeon
CAL	68	94	.420	Winkles
				Herzog
				Williams

1975—EASTERN DIVISION

BOS	95	65	.594	Johnson
BAL	90	69	.566	Weaver
N Y	83	77	.519	Virdon
				Martin
CLE	79	80	.497	Robinson
MIL	68	94	.420	Crandall
				Kuenn
DET	57	102	.358	Houk

1975—WESTERN DIVISION

OAK	98	64	.605	Dark
K C	91	71	.562	McKeon
				Herzog
TEX	79	83	.488	Martin
				Lucchesi
MIN	76	83	.478	Quilici
CHI	75	86	.466	Tanner
CAL	72	89	.447	Williams

1976—EASTERN DIVISION

N Y	97	62	.610	Martin
BAL	88	74	.543	Weaver
BOS	83	79	.512	Johnson
				Zimmer
CLE	81	78	.509	Robinson
DET	74	87	.460	Houk
MIL	66	95	.410	Grammas

1976—WESTERN DIVISION

K C	90	72	.556	Herzog
OAK	87	74	.540	Tanner
MIN	85	77	.525	Mauch
CAL	76	86	.469	Williams
				Sherry
TEX	76	86	.469	Lucchesi
CHI	64	97	.398	Richards

1977—EASTERN DIVISION

N Y	100	62	.617	Martin
BAL	97	64	.602	Weaver
BOS	97	64	.602	Zimmer
DET	74	88	.457	Houk
CLE	71	90	.441	Torborg
MIL	67	95	.414	Grammas
TOR	54	107	.335	Hartsfield

1977—WESTERN DIVISION

K C	102	60	.630	Herzog
TEX	94	68	.580	Lucchesi
				Stanky
				Ryan
				Hunter
CHI	90	72	.556	Lemon
MIN	84	77	.522	Mauch
CAL	74	88	.457	Sherry
				Garcia
SEA	64	98	.395	Johnson
OAK	63	98	.391	McKeon
				Winkles

1978—EASTERN DIVISION

N Y	99	64	.613	Martin
				Howser
				Lemon
BOS	99	64	.607	Zimmer
MIL	93	69	.574	Bamberger
BAL	90	71	.559	Weaver
DET	86	76	.531	Houk
CLE	69	90	.434	Torborg
TOR	59	102	.366	Hartsfield

1978—WESTERN DIVISION

K C	92	70	.568	Herzog
CAL	87	75	.537	Garcia
				Fregosi
TEX	87	75	.537	Hunter
				Corrales
MIN	73	89	.451	Mauch
CHI	71	90	.441	Lemon
				Deby
OAK	69	93	.426	Winkles
				McKeon
SEA	56	104	.350	Johnson

1979—EASTERN DIVISION

BAL	102	57	.642	Weaver
MIL	95	66	.590	Bamberger
BOS	91	69	.569	Zimmer
N Y	89	71	.556	Lemon
				Martin
DET	85	76	.528	Moss
				Anderson
CLE	81	80	.503	Torborg
				Garcia
TOR	53	109	.327	Hartsfield

1979—WESTERN DIVISION

CAL	88	74	.543	Fregosi
K C	85	77	.525	Herzog
TEX	83	79	.512	Corrales
MIN	82	80	.506	Mauch
CHI	73	87	.456	Kessinger
				LaRussa
SEA	67	95	.414	Johnson
OAK	54	108	.333	Marshall

CHAMPIONSHIP SERIES

1969
BAL (East) 3, MIN (West) 0
1970
BAL (East) 3, MIN (West) 0
1971
BAL (East) 3, OAK (West) 0
1972
OAK (West) 3, DET (East) 2
1973
OAK (West) 3, BAL (East) 2
1974
OAK (West) 3, BAL (East) 1
1975
BOS (East) 3, OAK (West) 0
1976
NY (East) 3, KC (West) 2
1977
NY (East) 3, KC (West) 2
1978
NY (East) 3, KC (West) 1
1979
BAL (East) 3, CAL (West) 1

World Series Results and Receipts

Year	National League	American League	Games W-L	Attendance	Receipts	Winning Player's Share	Losing Player's Share
1903	Pittsburgh	* Boston	3-5	100,429	55,500.00	1,316.25	1,182.00
1905	* New York	Philadelphia	4-1	91,723	68,437.00	1,142.00	833.75
1906	Chicago	* Chicago	2-4	99,845	106,550.00	1,874.63	439.50
1907	* Chicago	Detroit	4-0a	78,068	101,728.50	2,142.85	1,945.96
1908	* Chicago	Detroit	4-1	62,232	94,975.50	1,317.58	870.00
1909	* Pittsburgh	Detroit	4-3	145,295	188,302.50	1,825.22	1,274.76
1910	Chicago	* Philadelphia	1-4	124,222	173,980.00	2,062.79	1,375.16
1911	New York	* Philadelphia	2-4	179,851	342,164.50	3,654.58	2,436.39
1912	New York	* Boston	3-4a	252,037	490,449.00	4,024.68	2,566.47
1913	New York	* Philadelphia	1-4	151,000	325,980.00	3,246.36	2,164.22
1914	* Boston	Philadelphia	4-0	111,009	225,739.00	2,812.28	2,031.65
1915	Philadelphia	* Boston	1-4	143,351	320,361.50	3,780.25	2,520.17
1916	Brooklyn	* Boston	1-4	162,859	385,590.50	3,910.28	2,834.82
1917	New York	* Chicago	2-4	186,654	425,878.00	3,669.32	2,442.61
1918	Chicago	* Boston	2-4	128,483	179,619.00	1,102.51	671.09
1919	* Cincinnati	Chicago	5-3	236,928	722,414.00	5,207.01	3,254.36
1920	Brooklyn	* Cleveland	2-5	178,737	564,800.00	4,168.00	2,419.60
1921	* New York	New York	5-3	269,976	900,233.00	5,265.00	3,510.00
1922	* New York	New York	4-0a	185,947	605,475.00	4,470.00	3,225.00
1923	New York	* New York	2-4	301,430	1,063,815.00	6,143.49	4,112.89
1924	New York	* Washington	3-4	283,665	1,093,104.00	5,969.64	3,820.29
1925	* Pittsburgh	Washington	4-3	282,848	1,182,854.00	5,332.72	3,734.60
1926	* St. Louis	New York	4-3	328,051	1,207,864.00	5,584.51	3,417.75
1927	Pittsburgh	* New York	0-4	201,705	783,217.00	5,592.17	3,728.10
1928	St. Louis	* New York	0-4	199,072	777,290.00	5,531.91	4,197.37
1929	Chicago	* Philadelphia	1-4	190,490	859,494.00	5,620.57	3,782.01
1930	St. Louis	* Philadelphia	2-4	212,619	953,772.00	5,785.00	3,875.00
1931	* St. Louis	Philadelphia	4-3	231,567	1,030,723.00	4,467.59	3,032.09
1932	Chicago	* New York	0-4	191,998	713,377.00	5,231.77	4,244.60
1933	* New York	Washington	4-1	163,076	679,365.00	4,256.72	3,019.86
1934	* St. Louis	Detroit	4-3	281,510	1,031,341.00	5,389.57	3,354.57
1935	Chicago	* Detroit	2-4	286,672	1,073,794.00	6,544.76	4,198.53
1936	New York	* New York	2-4	302,924	1,204,399.00	6,430.55	4,655.58
1937	New York	* New York	1-4	238,142	985,994.00	6,471.10	4,489.05
1938	Chicago	* New York	0-4	200,833	851,166.00	5,782.76	4,674.87
1939	Cincinnati	* New York	0-4	183,849	745,329.00	5,614.26	4,282.58
1940	* Cincinnati	Detroit	4-3	281,927	1,222,328.21	5,803.62	3,531.81
1941	Brooklyn	* New York	1-4	235.773	1.007.762.00	5.943.31	4.829.40
1942	* St. Louis	New York	4-1	277.101	1.105.249.00	5.573.78	3.018.77
1943	St. Louis	* New York	1-4	277.312	1.105.784.00	6.139.46	4.321.96
1944	* St. Louis	St. Louis	4-2	206.708	906.122.00	4.626.01	2.743.79
1945	Chicago	* Detroit	3-4	333.457	1.492.454.00	6.443.34	3.930.22
1946	* St. Louis	Boston	4-3	250.071	1.052.900.00	3.742.34	2.140.89
1947	Brooklyn	* New York	3-4	389.763	1.781.348.92	5.830.03	4.081.19
1948	Boston	* Cleveland	2-4	358.362	1.633.685.56	6.772.05	4.651.51
1949	Brooklyn	* New York	1-4	236.710	1.129.627.88	5.665.54	4.272.73

World Series Results and Receipts (Continued)

Year	National League	American League	Games W-L	Attendance	Receipts	Winning Player's Share	Losing Player's Share
1950	Philadelphia	* New York	0-4	196.009	953.669.03	5.737.95	4.081.34
1951	New York	* New York	2-4	341.977	1.633.457.47	6.446.09	4.951.03
1952	Brooklyn	* New York	3-4	340.906	1.622.753.01	5.982.65	4.200.64
1953	Brooklyn	* New York	2-4	307.350	1.779.269.44	8.280.68	6.178.42
1954	* New York	Cleveland	4-0	251.507	1.566.203.38	11.147.90	6.712.50
1955	* Brooklyn	New York	4-3	362.310	2.337.515.34	9.768.00	5.598.00
1956	Brooklyn	* New York	3-4	345.903	2.183.254.59	8.714.76	6.934.34
1957	* Milwaukee	New York	4-3	394.712	2.475.978.94	8.924.36	5.606.06
1958	Milwaukee	* New York	3-4	393.909	2.397.223.03	8.759.10	5.896.09
1959	* Los Angeles	Chicago	4-2	420.784	2.628.809.44	11.231.18	7.257.17
1960	* Pittsburgh	New York	4-3	349.813	2.230.627.88	8.417.94	5.214.64
1961	Cincinnati	* New York	1-4	223.247	1.480.059.95	7.389.13	5.356.37
1962	San Francisco	* New York	3-4	376.864	2.878.891.11	9.882.74	7.291.49
1963	* Los Angeles	New York	4-0	247.279	1.995.189.09	12.794.00	7.874.32
1964	* St. Louis	New York	4-3	321.807	2.243.187.96	8.622.19	5.309.29
1965	* Los Angeles	Minnesota	4-3	364.326	2.975.041.60	10.297.43	6.634.36
1966	Los Angeles	* Baltimore	0-4	220.791	2.047.142.46	11.683.04	8.189.36
1967	* St. Louis	Boston	4-3	304.085	2.350.607.10	8.314.81	5.115.23
1968	St. Louis	* Detroit	3-4	379.670	3.018.113.40	10.936.66	7.078.71
1969	* New York	Baltimore	4-1	272.378	2.857.782.78	18.338.18	14.904.21
1970	Cincinnati	* Baltimore	1-4	253.183	2.599.170.26	18.215.78	13.687.59
1971	* Pittsburgh	Baltimore	4-3	351.091	3.049.803.46	18.164.58	13.906.46
1972	Cincinnati	* Oakland	3-4	363.149	3.954.542.99	20.705.01	15.080.25
1973	New York	* Oakland	3-4	358.289	3.923.968.37	24.617.57	14.950.17
1974	Los Angeles	* Oakland	1-4	260.004	3.007.194.00	22.219.09	15.703.97
1975	* Cincinnati	Boston	4-3	308.272	3.380.579.61	19.060.46	13.325.87
1976	* Cincinnati	New York	4-0	223.009	2.498.416.53	26.366.68	19.935.48
1977	Los Angeles	* New York	2-4	337.708	3.978.825.33	27.758.04	20.899.05
1978	Los Angeles	* New York	2-4	337.304	4.650.164.57	31.236.99	25.483.21
1979	* Pittsburgh	Baltimore	4-3	367.597	4.390.766.14	28.236.87	22.113.94

Note: Player's shares for 1969 to date include League Championship Series

* indicates winning team   a indicates one game tied

American League Annual Attendance

1901 —	1,683,584	1928 —	4,221,188	1954 —	7,922,364
1902 —	2,206,454	1929 —	4,662,470	1955 —	8,942,971
1903 —	2,344,888	1930 —	4,685,730	1956 —	7,893,683
1904 —	3,024,028	1931 —	3,883,292	1957 —	8,196,218
1905 —	3,120,752	1932 —	3,133,232	1958 —	7,296,034
1906 —	2,938,076	1933 —	2,926,210	1959 —	9,149,454
1907 —	3,398,764	1934 —	2,763,606	1960 —	9,226,526
1908 —	3,611,366	1935 —	3,688,007	1961 —	10,163,016
1909 —	3,739,570	1936 —	4,178,922	1962 —	10,015,056
1910 —	3,270,689	1937 —	4,735,835	1963 —	9,094,487
1911 —	3,339,514	1938 —	4,445,684	1964 —	9,235,151
1912 —	3,263,631	1939 —	4,270,602	1965 —	8,860,764
1913 —	3,526,805	1940 —	5,433,791	1966 —	10,166,738
1914 —	2,747,591	1941 —	4,911,956	1967 —	11,336,923
1915 —	2,434,684	1942 —	4,200,216	1968 —	11,317,387
1916 —	3,451,885	1943 —	3,696,569	1969 —	12,134,745
1917 —	2,858,858	1944 —	4,798,158	1970 —	12,085,135
1918 —	1,707,999	1945 —	5,580,420	1971 —	11,868,560
1919 —	3,654,236	1946 —	9,621,182	1972 —	11,438,538
1920 —	5,084,300	1947 —	9,486,069	1973 —	13,433,604
1921 —	4,620,328	1948 —	11,150,099	1974 —	13,047,294
1922 —	4,874,355	1949 —	10,730,647	1975 —	13,189,423
1923 —	4,602,589	1950 —	9,142,361	1976 —	14,657,802
1924 —	5,255,439	1951 —	8,882,674	1977 —	19,639,551
1925 —	5,186,851	1952 —	8,293,896	1978 —	20,529,965
1926 —	4,912,583	1953 —	6,964,076	1979 —	22,372,820
1927 —	4,612,951				

American League Record Single Game Attendance

Baltimore	51,798	(vs. Bos., Sept. 18, 1977)
Boston	41,766	(vs. N.Y., Aug. 12, 1934)
California	53,591	(vs. N.Y., July 13, 1962) *
Chicago	55,555	(vs. Minn., May 20, 1976)
Cleveland	84,587	(vs. N.Y., Sept. 12, 1954)
Detroit	58,888	(vs. Clev., Sept. 26, 1948)
Kansas City	40,903	(vs. N.Y., May 13, 1978) *
Milwaukee	55,120	(vs. Balt., Apr. 12, 1977)
Minnesota	46,463	(vs. Chi., June 16, 1977)
New York	81,841	(vs. Bos., May 30, 1938)
Oakland	48,758	(vs. Det., June 6, 1970)
Seattle	57,762	(vs. Cal., Apr. 6, 1977) *
Texas	40,854	(vs. Cal., May 21, 1976) *
Toronto	44,649	(vs. Chi., Apr. 7, 1977)

* Night Game

Stadium Dimensions

Active Stadiums

Team	Stadium	Home Run Distances (in ft.)			Seating
		LF	CF	RF	Capacity
Baltimore Orioles	Memorial Stadium	309	405	309	52,860
Boston Red Sox	Fenway Park	315	390	302	33,538
California Angels	Anaheim Stadium	333	404	333	43,250
Chicago White Sox	Comiskey Park	352	445	352	44,492
Cleveland Indians	Cleveland Stadium	320	400	320	76,713
Detroit Tigers	Tiger Stadium	340	440	325	53,676
Kansas City Royals	Royals Stadium	330	410	330	40,760
Milwaukee Brewers	County Stadium	320	402	315	53,192
Minnesota Twins	Metropolitan Stadium	343	406	330	45,919
New York Yankees	Yankee Stadium	312	417	310	57,545
Oakland Athletics	Oakland Coliseum	330	400	330	50,000
Seattle Mariners	The Kingdome	316	410	316	59,438
Texas Rangers	Arlington Stadium	330	400	330	41,907
Toronto Blue Jays	Exhibition Stadium	330	400	330	43,737

Former Stadiums

Team	Stadium	Home Run Distances (in ft.)			Seating
		LF	CF	RF	Capacity
Philadelphia Athletics	Connie Mack Stadium	334	440	331	33,233
St. Louis Browns	Sportsman's Park	351	422	310	30,000
Washington Senators	Griffith Stadium	408	426	328	29,731
Kansas City A's	Municipal Stadium	353	421	353	32,561
California Angels	Chavez Ravine Stadium	330	410	330	56,000
California Angels	Wrigley Field	340	412	339	20,543
Seattle Pilots	Sicks Stadium	305	405	320	28,500

American Leaguers in Baseball Hall of Fame

Luke Appling, Chicago.*

Earl Averill, Cleveland, Detroit.

Frank Baker, Philadelphia, New York.

Ed Barrow, Boston, Detroit, New York (Executive).*

Chief Bender, Philadelphia, Chicago.

Yogi Berra, New York.

Lou Boudreau, Cleveland, Boston, Kansas City (Manager).*

Roger Bresnahan, Baltimore.

Jesse Burkett, St. Louis, Boston.

Frank Chance, New York, Boston (Manager).

Jack Chesbro, New York, Boston.

Ty Cobb, Detroit, Philadelphia.*

Mickey Cochrane, Philadelphia, Detroit.*

Eddie Collins, Philadelphia, Chicago.*

Jimmy Collins, Boston, Philadelphia.

Earle Combs, New York.*

Charles Comiskey, Chicago (Manager, Owner).

Tommy Connolly (Umpire).*

Stan Coveleskie, Philadelphia, Cleveland, Washington, New York.*

Sam Crawford, Detroit.

Joe Cronin, Washington, Boston.

Dizzy Dean, St. Louis.

Ed Delahanty, Washington.

Bill Dickey, New York.*

Joe DiMaggio, New York.*

Hugh Duffy, Milwaukee.

Billy Evans (Umpire, Executive).*

Johnny Evers, Chicago.

Bob Feller, Cleveland.*

Red Faber, Chicago.*

Elmer Flick, Philadephia, Cleveland.

Whitey Ford, New York.*

Jimmy Foxx, Philadelphia, Boston.

Lou Gehrig, New York.*

Charlie Gehringer, Detroit.*

Lefty Gomez, New York, Washington.*

Goose Goslin, Washington, St. Louis, Detroit.*

Hank Greenberg, Detroit.

Clark Griffith, Chicago, New York, Washington (Manager, Owner).

Burleigh Grimes, New York.

Lefty Grove, Philadelphia, Boston.*

Will Harridge (League President).*

Bucky Harris, Washington, Detroit, Boston, New York (Manager).

Harry Heilmann, Detroit.

Harry Hooper, Boston, Chicago.*

Rogers Hornsby, St. Louis.

Waite Hoyt, New York, Boston, Detroit, Philadelphia.

Cal Hubbard (Umpire).*

Miller Huggins, New York (Manager).

Hugh Jennings, Detroit (Manager).

Ban Johnson (League President).*

Walter Johnson, Washington.*

Addie Joss, Cleveland.*

Al Kaline, Detroit.*

Willie Keeler, New York.

Joe Kelly, Baltimore.

Ralph Kiner, Cleveland.

Napoleon Lajoie, Philadelphia, Cleveland.

Bob Lemon, Cleveland.*

Al Lopez, Cleveland, Chicago (A.L. Manager).

Ted Lyons, Chicago.*

Connie Mack, Philadelphia (Manager, Owner).

Larry MacPhail, New York (Executive).

Mickey Mantle, New York.*

Heinie Manush, Detroit, St. Louis, Washington, Boston.

Eddie Mathews, Detroit.

Joe McCarthy, New York, Boston (Manager).

Joe McGinnity, Baltimore.

John McGraw, Baltimore
(Manager).

Bill McKechnie, New
York.

Satchel Paige, Cleveland,
St. Louis, Kansas City.

Herb Pennock,
Philadelphia, Boston,
New York.*

Eddie Plank, Philadelphia,
St. Louis.

Sam Rice, Washington,
Cleveland.*

Branch Rickey, St. Louis
(Manager, Executive).

Robin Roberts, Baltimore.

Wilbert Robinson,
Baltimore.

Edd Roush, Chicago.

Red Ruffing, Boston, New
York, Chicago.*

Babe Ruth, Boston, New
York.

Ray Schalk, Chicago.

Joe Sewell, Cleveland,
New York.*

Al Simmons, Philadelphia,
Chicago, Detroit,
Washington, Boston.

George Sisler, St. Louis,
Washington.

Tris Speaker, Boston,
Cleveland, Washington,
Philadelphia.*

Casey Stengel, New York
(Manager).

Dazzy Vance, New York.

Rube Waddell,
Philadelphia, St. Louis.

Bobby Wallace, St. Louis.

Ed Walsh, Chicago.

Paul Waner, New York.

George Weiss, New York
(Executive).

Zack Wheat, Philadelphia.

Ted Williams, Boston.*

Early Wynn, Washington,
Cleveland, Chicago.*

Cy Young, Boston,
Cleveland.

Includes all Hall of Famers who played or worked
in American League.

* Performed exclusively in the American League.

Individual Batting Records

GAMES
> *Season:* 164, Cesar Tovar, Minnesota, 1967
> *Career:* 3,033, Ty Cobb, Detroit/Philadelphia, 1905-28

AT BATS
> *Season:* 692, Bobby Richardson, New York, 1962
> *Career:* 11,429, Ty Cobb, Detroit/Philadelphia, 1905-28

HITS
> *Season:* 257, George Sisler, St. Louis, 1920
> *Career:* 4,191, Ty Cobb, Detroit/Philadelphia, 1905-28

BATTING AVERAGE
> *Season:* .422, Nap Lajoie, Cleveland, 1901
> *Career:* .367, Ty Cobb, Detroit/Philadelphia, 1905-28

SLUGGING PERCENTAGE
> *Season:* .847, Babe Ruth, New York, 1920
> *Career:* .692, Babe Ruth, Boston/New York, 1914-34

HOME RUNS
> *Season:* 61, Roger Maris, New York, 1961
> *Career:* 708, Babe Ruth, Boston/New York, 1914-34 *

TRIPLES
> *Season:* 26, Joe Jackson, Cleveland, 1920; Sam Crawford, Detroit, 1914
> *Career:* 297, Ty Cobb, Detroit/Philadelphia, 1905-28

DOUBLES
> *Season:* 67, Earl Webb, Boston, 1931
> *Career:* 793, Tris Speaker, Boston/Cleveland/Washington/Philadelphia, 1907-28

RBIs
> *Season:* 184, Lou Gehrig, New York, 1931
> *Career:* 1,990, Lou Gehrig, New York, 1923-39

RUNS
> *Season:* 177, Babe Ruth, New York, 1921
> *Career:* 2,244, Ty Cobb, Detroit/Philadelphia, 1905-28

STOLEN BASES
> *Season:* 96, Ty Cobb, Detroit, 1915
> *Career:* 892, Ty Cobb, Detroit/Philadelphia, 1905-28

Individual Pitching Records

GAMES
> *Season:* 88, Wilbur Wood, Chicago, 1968
> *Career:* 802, Walter Johnson, Washington, 1907–27

GAMES STARTED
> *Season:* 51, Jack Chesbro, New York, 1904
> *Career:* 666, Walter Johnson, Washington, 1907–27

COMPLETE GAMES
> *Season:* 48, Jack Chesbro, New York, 1904
> *Career:* 531, Walter Johnson, Washington, 1907–27

INNINGS PITCHED
> *Season:* 464, Ed Walsh, Chicago, 1908
> *Career:* 5,924, Walter Johnson, Washington, 1907–27

WINS
> *Season:* 41, Jack Chesbro, New York, 1904
> *Career:* 416, Walter Johnson, Washington, 1907–27

WINNING PERCENTAGE
> *Season:* .893 (25–3), Ron Guidry, New York, 1978
> *Career:* .690 (236–106), Whitey Ford, New York, 1950–67

EARNED RUN AVERAGE
> *Season:* 1.01, Hub Leonard, Boston, 1914
> *Career:* 2.37, Walter Johnson, Washington, 1913–27 (earned run averages
> not recorded before 1913)

SHUTOUTS
> *Season:* 13, Jack Coombs, Philadelphia, 1910
> *Career:* 113, Walter Johnson, Washington, 1907–27

STRIKEOUTS
> *Season:* 383, Nolan Ryan, Philadelphia, 1973
> *Career:* 3,508, Walter Johnson, Washington, 1907–27

Best Lifetime Marks

SEASONS MANAGED: Connie Mack, Philadelphia, 50.*

PENNANTS WON: Casey Stengel, New York, 10.

WORLD SERIES WON: Joe McCarthy, New York; Casey Stengel, New York, 7.

HITTERS WITH THREE THOUSAND HITS:
    Ty Cobb, 4,191
    Tris Speaker, 3,515
    Eddie Collins, 3,313
    Nap Lajoie, 3,251
    Carl Yastrzemski, 3,009
    Al Kaline, 3,007

PITCHERS WITH THREE HUNDRED WINS:
    Walter Johnson, 416
    Eddie Plank, 326
    Lefty Grove, 300
    Early Wynn, 300

HITTERS WITH 500 CAREER HOME RUNS:
    Babe Ruth, 708 *
    Harmon Killebrew, 573
    Mickey Mantle, 536
    Jimmie Foxx, 534
    Ted Williams, 521

HITTERS WITH .340 LIFETIME AVERAGE OR BETTER:
    Ty Cobb, .367
    Joe Jackson, .356
    Tris Speaker, .344
    Ted Williams, .344
    Babe Ruth, .342
    Harry Heilmann, .342
    George Sisler, .340
    Lou Gehrig, .340

* American League totals only

TRIPLE CROWN WINNERS (HOME RUNS, RBIs, BATTING AVERAGE):
    Ty Cobb, Detroit, 1909
    Jimmie Foxx, Philadelphia, 1933
    Lou Gehrig, New York, 1934
    Ted Williams, Boston, 1942
    Ted Williams, Boston, 1947
    Mickey Mantle, New York, 1956
    Frank Robinson, Baltimore, 1966
    Carl Yastrzemski, Boston, 1967

GRAND-SLAM HOME RUNS:
    Lou Gehrig, 23
    Jimmie Foxx, 17
    Ted Williams, 17
    Babe Ruth, 16
    Joe DiMaggio, 13
    Rudy York, 12
    Hank Greenberg, 11
    Harmon Killebrew, 11

* American League totals only

Most Valuable Players

American League

Chalmers
1911 Ty Cobb, Detroit (OF)
1912 Tris Speaker, Boston (OF)
1913 Walter Johnson, Washington (P)
1914 Eddie Collins, Philadelphia (2B)

League
1922 George Sisler, St. Louis (1B)
1923 Babe Ruth, New York (OF)
1924 Walter Johnson, Washington (P)
1925 Roger Peckinpaugh, Washington (SS)
1926 George Burns, Cleveland (1B)
1927 Lou Gehrig, New York (1B)
1928 Mickey Cochrane, Philadelphia (C)
1929 No Selection

Baseball Writers Association of America
1931 Lefty Grove, Philadelphia (P)
1932 Jimmie Foxx, Philadelphia (1B)
1933 Jimmie Foxx, Philadelphia (1B)
1934 Mickey Cochrane, Detroit (C)
1935 Hank Greenberg, Detroit (1B)
1936 Lou Gehrig, New York (1B)
1937 Charlie Gehringer, Detroit (2B)
1938 Jimmie Foxx, Boston (1B)
1939 Joe DiMaggio, New York (OF)
1940 Hank Greenberg, Detroit (1B)
1941 Joe DiMaggio, New York (OF)
1942 Joe Gordon, New York (2B)
1943 Spud Chandler, New York (P)
1944 Hal Newhouser, Detroit (P)
1945 Hal Newhouser, Detroit (P)
1946 Ted Williams, Boston (OF)
1947 Joe DiMaggio, New York (OF)
1948 Lou Boudreau, Cleveland (SS)
1949 Ted Williams, Boston (OF)
1950 Phil Rizzuto, New York (SS)
1951 Yogi Berra, New York (C)
1952 Bobby Shantz, Philadelphia (P)
1953 Al Rosen, Cleveland (3B)
1954 Yogi Berra, New York (C)
1955 Yogi Berra, New York (C)
1956 Mickey Mantle, New York (OF)
1957 Mickey Mantle, New York (OF)
1958 Jackie Jensen, Boston (OF)
1959 Nellie Fox, Chicago (2B)

1960 Roger Maris, New York (OF)
1961 Roger Maris, New York (OF)
1962 Mickey Mantle, New York (OF)
1963 Ellie Howard, New York (C)
1964 Brooks Robinson, Baltimore (3B)
1965 Zoilo Versalles, Minnesota (SS)
1966 Frank Robinson, Baltimore (OF)
1967 Carl Yastrzemski, Boston (OF)
1968 Denny McLain, Detroit (P)
1969 Harmon Killebrew, Minnesota (3B)
1970 Boog Powell, Baltimore (1B)
1971 Vida Blue, Oakland (P)
1972 Richie Allen, Chicago (1B)
1973 Reggie Jackson, Oakland (OF)
1974 Jeff Burroughs, Texas (OF)
1975 Fred Lynn, Boston (OF)
1976 Thurman Munson, New York (C)
1977 Rod Carew, Minnesota (1B)
1978 Jim Rice, Boston (OF)
1979 Don Baylor, California (OF)

AL Rookie of the Year
(one selection 1947–48)

1949 Roy Sievers, St. Louis (OF)
1950 Walt Dropo, Boston (1B)
1951 Gil McDougald, New York (3B)
1952 Harry Byrd, Philadelphia (P)
1953 Harvey Kuenn, Detroit (SS)
1954 Bob Grim, New York (P)
1955 Herb Score, Cleveland (P)
1956 Luis Aparicio, Chicago (SS)
1957 Tony Kubek, New York (SS)
1958 Albie Pearson, Washington (OF)
1959 Bob Allison, Washington (OF)
1960 Ron Hansen, Baltimore (SS)
1961 Don Schwall, Boston (P)
1962 Tom Tresh, New York (SS)
1963 Gary Peters, Chicago (P)
1964 Tony Oliva, Minnesota (OF)
1965 Curt Blefray, Baltimore (OF)
1966 Tommie Agee, Chicago (OF)
1967 Rod Carew, Minnesota (2B)
1968 Stan Bahnsen, New York (P)

1969	Lou Piniella, Kansas City (OF)		1975	Fred Lynn, Boston (OF)
1970	Thurman Munson, New York (C)		1976	Mark Fidryich, Detroit (P)
1971	Chris Chambliss, Cleveland (1B)		1977	Eddie Murray, Baltimore (1B)
1972	Carlton Fisk, Boston (C)		1978	Lou Whitaker, Detroit (2B)
1973	Al Bumbry, Baltimore (OF)		1979	John Castino, Minnesota (3B)
1974	Mike Hargrove, Texas (1B)		(tie)	Alfredo Griffin, Toronto (SS)

Cy Young Award Winners

(one selection 1956–66)

1958	Bob Turley, New York (RH)		1972	Gaylord Perry, Cleveland (RH)
1959	Early Wynn, Chicago (RH)		1973	Jim Palmer, Baltimore (RH)
1961	Whitey Ford, New York (LH)		1974	Jim (Catfish) Hunter, Oakland (RH)
1964	Dean Chance, Los Angeles (RH)		1975	Jim Palmer, Baltimore (RH)
1967	Jim Lonborg, Boston (RH)		1976	Jim Palmer, Baltimore (RH)
1968	Denny McLain, Detroit (RH)		1977	Sparky Lyle, New York (LH)
1969	Mike Cuellar, Baltimore (tie) (LH)		1978	Ron Guidry, New York (LH)
1969	Denny McLain, Detroit (tie) (RH)		1979	Mike Flanagan, Baltimore (LH)
1970	Jim Perry, Minnesota (RH)			
1971	Vida Blue, Oakland (LH)			

American League Batting Champions

1901	Lajoie, Philadelphia	.422		1925	Heilmann, Detroit	.393
1902	Delahanty, Washington	.376		1926	Manush, Detroit	.377
1903	Lajoie, Cleveland	.355		1927	Heilmann, Detroit	.398
1904	Lajoie, Cleveland	.381		1928	Goslin, Washington	.379
1905	Flick, Cleveland	.306		1929	Fonseca, Cleveland	.369
1906	Stone, St. Louis	.358		1930	Simmons, Philadelphia	.381
1907	Cobb, Detroit	.350		1931	Simmons, Philadelphia	.390
1908	Cobb, Detroit	.324		1932	Alexander, Det./Boston	.367
1909	Cobb, Detroit	.377		1933	Foxx, Philadelphia	.356
1910	Cobb, Detroit	.385		1934	Gehrig, New York	.363
1911	Cobb, Detroit	.420		1935	Myer, Washington	.349
1912	Cobb, Detroit	.410		1936	Appling, Chicago	.388
1913	Cobb, Detroit	.390		1937	Gehringer, Detroit	.371
1914	Cobb, Detroit	.368		1938	Foxx, Boston	.349
1915	Cobb, Detroit	.370		1939	DiMaggio, New York	.381
1916	Speaker, Cleveland	.386		1940	DiMaggio, New York	.352
1917	Cobb, Detroit	.383		1941	Williams, Boston	.406
1918	Cobb, Detroit	.382		1942	Williams, Boston	.356
1919	Cobb, Detroit	.384		1943	Appling, Chicago	.328
1920	Sisler, St. Louis	.407		1944	Boudreau, Cleveland	.327
1921	Heilmann, Detroit	.394		1945	Stirnweiss, New York	.309
1922	Sisler, St. Louis	.420		1946	Vernon, Washington	.353
1923	Heilmann, Detroit	.403		1947	Williams, Boston	.343
1924	Ruth, New York	.378		1948	Williams, Boston	.369

1949	Kell, Detroit	.3429	1965	Oliva, Minnesota	.321
1950	Goodman, Boston	.354	1966	Robinson, F., Baltimore	.316
1951	Fain, Philadelphia	.344	1967	Yastrzemski, Boston	.326
1952	Fain, Philadelphia	.327	1968	Yastrzemski, Boston	.301
1953	Vernon, Washington	.337	1969	Carew, Minnesota	.332
1954	Avila, Cleveland	.341	1970	Johnson, California	.3289
1955	Kaline, Detroit	.340	1971	Oliva, Minnesota	.337
1956	Mantle, New York	.353	1972	Carew, Minnesota	.318
1957	Williams, Boston	.388	1973	Carew, Minnesota	.350
1958	Williams, Boston	.328	1974	Carew, Minnesota	.364
1959	Kuenn, Detroit	.353	1975	Carew, Minnesota	.359
1960	Runnels, Boston	.320	1976	Brett, Geo., Kansas City	.333
1961	Cash, Detroit	.361	1977	Carew, Minnesota	.388
1962	Runnels, Boston	.326	1978	Carew, Minnesota	.333
1963	Yastrzemski, Boston	.321	1979	Lynn, Boston	.336
1964	Oliva, Minnesota	.323			

Designated Hitter

		AVG.	HRs	RBIs
1973	Orlando Cepeda (Bos)	.289	20	86
1974	Tommy Davis (Bal)	.289	11	83
1975	Willie Horton (Det)	.275	25	92
1976	Hal McRae (KC)	.329	7	62
1977	Jim Rice (Bos)	.316	31	87
1978	Rusty Staub (Det)	.273	24	121
1979	Willie Horton (Det)	.279	29	106

American League Home Run Champions

1901	Lajoie, Philadelphia	13	1918	Ruth, Boston	11
1902	Seybold, Philadelphia	16		C. Walker, Philadelphia	11
1903	Freeman, Boston	13	1919	Ruth, Boston	29
1904	Harry Davis, Philadelphia	10	1920	Ruth, New York	54
1905	H. Davis, Philadelphia	8	1921	Ruth, New York	59
1906	H. Davis, Philadelphia	12	1922	K. Williams, St. Louis	39
1907	H. Davis, Philadelphia	8	1923	Ruth, New York	43
1908	Crawford, Detroit	7	1924	Ruth, New York	46
1909	Cobb, Detroit	9	1925	Meusel, New York	33
1910	G. Stahl, Boston	10	1926	Ruth, New York	47
1911	Baker, Philadelphia	9	1927	Ruth, New York	60
1912	Baker, Philadelphia	10	1928	Ruth, New York	54
1913	Baker, Philadelphia	12	1929	Ruth, New York	46
1914	Baker, Philadelphia	8	1930	Ruth, New York	49
	Crawford, Detroit	8	1931	Ruth and Gehrig, New York	46
1915	Roth, Cleveland	7	1932	Foxx, Philadelphia	58
1916	Pipp, New York	12	1933	Foxx, Philadelphia	48
1917	Pipp, New York	9	1934	Gehrig, New York	49

Al Kaline became only the fifth American Leaguer to collect 3,000 hits when he stopped at 3,007 in 1974. *(Detroit Tigers)*

Year	Player	HR		Year	Player	HR
1935	Greenberg, Detroit	36		1959	Colavito, Cleveland	42
	Foxx, Philadelphia	36			Killebrew, Washington	42
1936	Gehrig, New York	49		1960	Mantle, New York	40
1937	DiMaggio, New York	46		1961	Maris, New York	61
1938	Greenberg, Detroit	58		1962	Killebrew, Minnesota	48
1939	Foxx, Boston	35		1963	Killebrew, Minnesota	45
1940	Greenberg, Detroit	41		1964	Killebrew, Minnesota	49
1941	Williams, Boston	37		1965	Conigliaro, Boston	32
1942	Williams, Boston	36		1966	Robinson, F., Baltimore	49
1943	York, Detroit	34		1967	Killebrew, Minnesota	44
1944	Etten, New York	22			Yastrzemski, Boston	44
1945	Stephens, St. Louis	24		1968	F. Howard, Washington	44
1946	Greenberg, Detroit	44		1969	Killebrew, Minnesota	49
1947	Williams, Boston	32		1970	F. Howard, Washington	44
1948	DiMaggio, New York	39		1971	Melton, Chicago	33
1949	Williams, Boston	43		1972	Allen, Chicago	37
1950	Rosen, Cleveland	37		1973	R. Jackson, Oakland	32
1951	Zernial, Philadelphia	33		1974	Allen, Chicago	32
1952	Doby, Cleveland	32		1975	Scott, Milwaukee	36
1953	Rosen, Cleveland	43			R. Jackson, Oakland	36
1954	Doby, Cleveland	32		1976	Nettles, New York	32
1955	Mantle, New York	37		1977	Rice, Boston	39
1956	Mantle, New York	52		1978	Rice, Boston	46
1957	Sievers, Washington	42		1979	Thomas, Milwaukee	44
1958	Mantle, New York	42				

Bobby Bonds combined power and speed as the only man in major league history to have five seasons in which he hit at least 30 home runs and stole at least 30 bases; the last three seasons came in the American League. *(Cleveland Indians)*

AL Runs Batted In Leaders

Year	Player	RBI		Year	Player	RBI
1907	Cobb, Detroit	116		1929	Simmons, Philadelphia	157
1908	Cobb, Detroit	101		1930	Gehrig, New York	174
1909	Cobb, Detroit	115		1931	Gehrig, New York	184
1910	Crawford, Detroit	115		1932	Foxx, Philadelphia	169
1911	Cobb, Detroit	144		1933	Foxx, Philadelphia	163
1912	Baker, Philadelphia	133		1934	Gehrig, New York	165
1913	Baker, Philadelphia	126		1935	Greenberg, Detroit	170
1914	Crawford, Detroit	112		1936	Trosky, Cleveland	162
1915	Crawford, Detroit	116		1937	Greenberg, Detroit	183
1916	Pipp, New York	99		1938	Foxx, Boston	175
1917	Veach, Detroit	115		1939	Williams, Boston	145
1918	Burns, Philadelphia	74		1940	Greenberg, Detroit	150
	Veach, Detroit	74		1941	DiMaggio, New York	125
1919	Ruth, Boston	112		1942	Williams, Boston	137
1920	Ruth, New York	137		1943	York, Detroit	118
1921	Ruth, New York	171		1944	Stephens, St. Louis	109
1922	Williams, St. Louis	155		1945	Etten, New York	111
1923	Ruth, New York	131		1946	Greenberg, Detroit	127
1924	Goslin, Washington	129		1947	Williams, Boston	114
1925	Meusel, New York	138		1948	DiMaggio, New York	155
1926	Ruth, New York	145		1949	Williams, Boston	159
1927	Gehrig, New York	175			Stephens, Boston	159
1928	Ruth, New York	142		1950	Dropo, Boston	144
	Gehrig, New York	142			Stephens, Boston	144

1951	Zernial, Chicago/Phila.	129		1965	Colavito, Cleveland	108
1952	Rosen, Cleveland	105		1966	F. Robinson, Baltimore	122
1953	Rosen, Cleveland	145		1967	Yastrzemski, Boston	121
1954	Doby, Cleveland	126		1968	Harrelson, Boston	109
1955	Boone, Detroit	116		1969	Killebrew, Minnesota	140
	Jensen, Boston	116		1970	Howard, Washington	126
1956	Mantle, New York	130		1971	Killebrew, Minnesota	119
1957	Sievers, Washington	114		1972	Allen, Chicago	113
1958	Jensen, Boston	122		1973	R. Jackson, Oakland	117
1959	Jensen, Boston	112		1974	Burroughs, Texas	118
1960	Maris, New York	112		1975	Scott, Milwaukee	109
1961	Maris, New York	142		1976	May, L., Baltimore	109
1962	Killebrew, Minnesota	126		1977	Hisle, Minnesota	119
1963	Stuart, Boston	118		1978	Rice, Boston	139
1964	B. Robinson, Baltimore	118		1979	Baylor, California	138

36 or More Home Runs—Season

61	Roger Maris, Yankees	1961		45	Harmon Killebrew, Twins	1963
60	Babe Ruth, Yankees	1927		44	Jimmie Foxx, Athletics	1934
59	Babe Ruth, Yankees	1921		44	Hank Greenberg, Tigers	1946
58	Jimmie Foxx, Athletics	1932		44	Harmon Killebrew, Twins	1967
58	Hank Greenberg, Tigers	1938		44	Carl Yastrzemski, Red Sox	1967
54	Babe Ruth, Yankees	1920		44	Frank Howard, Senators	1968
54	Babe Ruth, Yankees	1928		44	Frank Howard, Senators	1970
54	Mickey Mantle, Yankees	1961		44	Gordon Thomas, Brewers	1979
52	Mickey Mantle, Yankees	1956		43	Ted Williams, Red Sox	1949
50	Jimmie Foxx, Red Sox	1938		43	Al Rosen, Indians	1953
49	Babe Ruth, Yankees	1930		42	Hal Trosky, Indians	1936
49	Lou Gehrig, Yankees	1934		42	Gus Zernial, Athletics	1953
49	Lou Gehrig, Yankees	1936		42	Roy Sievers, Senators	1957
49	Harmon Killebrew, Twins	1964		42	Mickey Mantle, Yankees	1958
49	Frank Robinson, Orioles	1966		42	Rocky Colavito, Indians	1959
49	Harmon Killebrew, Twins	1969		42	Harmon Killebrew, Senators	1959
48	Jimmie Foxx, Athletics	1933		42	Dick Stuart, Red Sox	1963
48	Harmon Killebrew, Twins	1962		41	Babe Ruth, Yankees	1923
48	Frank Howard, Senators	1969		41	Lou Gehrig, Yankees	1930
47	Babe Ruth, Yankees	1926		41	Babe Ruth, Yankees	1932
47	Lou Gehrig, Yankees	1927		41	Jimmie Foxx, Red Sox	1936
47	Reggie Jackson, A's	1969		41	Hank Greenberg, Tigers	1940
46	Babe Ruth, Yankees	1924		41	Rocky Colavito, Indians	1958
46	Babe Ruth, Yankees	1929		41	Norm Cash, Tigers	1961
46	Babe Ruth, Yankees	1931		41	Harmon Killebrew, Twins	1970
46	Lou Gehrig, Yankees	1931		40	Hank Greenberg, Tigers	1937
46	Joe DiMaggio, Yankees	1937		40	Mickey Mantle, Yankees	1960
46	Jim Gentile, Orioles	1961		40	Rico Petrocelli, Red Sox	1969
46	Harmon Killebrew, Twins	1961		40	Carl Yastrzemski, Red Sox	1969
46	Jim Rice, Boston	1978		40	Carl Yastrzemski, Red Sox	1970
45	Rocky Colavito, Tigers	1961		39	Ken Williams, Browns	1922

Mike Caldwell was American League Comeback Player of the Year when he rebounded from five wins in 1977 to 22 in '78 with Milwaukee.
(Milwaukee Brewers)

39	Joe DiMaggio, Yankees	1948		37	Al Rosen, Indians	1950
39	Vern Stephens, Red Sox	1949		37	Mickey Mantle, Yankees	1955
39	Roy Sievers, Senators	1956		37	Rocky Colavito, Tigers	1962
39	Roger Maris, Yankees	1960		37	Leon Wagner, Angels	1962
39	Norm Cash, Tigers	1962		37	Boog Powell, Orioles	1969
39	Boog Powell, Orioles	1964		37	Dick Allen, Chicago	1972
39	Harmon Killebrew, Twins	1966		37	Bobby Bonds, Angels	1977
39	Jim Rice, Red Sox	1977		37	Graig Nettles, Yankees	1977
39	Jim Rice, Red Sox	1979		36	Al Simmons, Athletics	1930
39	Fred Lynn, Red Sox	1979		36	Jimmie Foxx, Athletics	1935
38	Ted Williams, Red Sox	1946		36	Hank Greenberg, Tigers	1935
38	Ted Williams, Red Sox	1957		36	Jimmie Foxx, Red Sox	1937
38	Bob Cerv, Athletics	1958		36	Jimmie Foxx, Red Sox	1940
38	Jim Lemon, Senators	1960		36	Ted Williams, Red Sox	1942
37	Tilly Walker, Athletics	1922		36	Frank Howard, Senators	1967
37	Jimmie Foxx, Athletics	1930		36	Willie Horton, Tigers	1968
37	Goose Goslin, Nats-Browns	1930		36	Tony Conigliaro, Red Sox	1970
37	Lou Gehrig, Yankees	1937		36	Reggie Jackson, Athletics	1975
37	Ted Williams, Red Sox	1941		36	George Scott, Brewers	1975

20 Game Winners

1901

Cy Young, Boston	32
Joe McGinnity, Baltimore	26
Clark Griffith, Chicago	24
Roscoe Miller, Detroit	23
Chick Fraser, Philadelphia	20

1902

Cy Young, Boston	32
Rube Waddell, Philadelphia	23
Frank Donahue, St. Louis	22
John Powell, St. Louis	22
Bill Dinneen, Boston	21
Ed Plank, Philadelphia	20
Roy Patterson, Chicago	20

1903

Cy Young, Boston	28
Ed Plank, Philadelphia	23
Rube Waddell, Philadelphia	22
Earl Moore, Cleveland	22
Jack Chesbro, New York	21
William Sudhoff, St. Louis	21
Tom Hughes, Boston	21
Bill Dinneen, Boston	21

1904

Jack Chesbro, New York	41
Bill Bernhard, Cleveland	29
Cy Young, Boston	26
Ed Plank, Philadelphia	26
Rube Waddell, Philadelphia	25
John Powell, New York	23
Bill Dinneen, Boston	23
Jesse Tannehill, Boston	21
Frank Owen, Chicago	21

1905

Rube Waddell, Philadelphia	27
Ed Plank, Philadelphia	24
Nick Altrock, Chicago	24
Ed Killian, Detroit	23
Jesse Tannehill, Boston	22
Frank Owen, Chicago	21
George Mullin, Detroit	21
Addie Joss, Cleveland	20

Boston's Fred Lynn became the first player to win both Rookie-of-the-Year and Most Valuable Player honors in 1975. *(Boston Red Sox)*

1906		1912	
Al Orth, New York	27	Joe Wood, Boston	34
Jack Chesbro, New York	24	Walter Johnson, Washington	32
Frank Owen, Chicago	22	Ed Walsh, Chicago	27
Bob Rhodes, Cleveland	22	Ed Plank, Philadelphia	26
George Mullin, Detroit	21	Bob Groom, Washington	24
Addie Joss, Cleveland	21	Jack Coombs, Philadelphia	21
Nick Altrock, Chicago	20	Vean Gregg, Cleveland	20
Otto Hess, Cleveland	20	Hugh Bedient, Boston	20
1907		1913	
Addie Joss, Cleveland	27	Walter Johnson, Washington	36
Guy White, Chicago	27	Fred Falkenberg, Cleveland	23
Bill Donovan, Detroit	25	Ewell Russell, Chicago	22
Ed Killian, Detroit	25	Vean Gregg, Cleveland	20
Ed Plank, Philadelphia	24	Jim Scott, Chicago	20
Ed Walsh, Chicago	24		
Cy Young, Boston	22	1914	
Frank Smith, Chicago	22	Walter Johnson, Washington	28
George Mullin, Detroit	20	Harry Coveleskie, Detroit	22
Jim Dygert, Philadelphia	20	Ray Collins, Boston	20
1908		1915	
Ed Walsh, Chicago	40	Walter Johnson, Washington	27
Addie Joss, Cleveland	24	Jim Scott, Chicago	24
Edgar Summers, Detroit	24	Urban Faber, Chicago	24
Cy Young, Boston	21	Harry Coveleskie, Detroit	23
		George Dauss, Detroit	23
1909		George Foster, Boston	20
George Mullin, Detroit	29		
Frank Smith, Chicago	25	1916	
Ed Willett, Detroit	22	Walter Johnson, Washington	25
		Bob Shawkey, New York	23
1910		Babe Ruth, Boston	23
Jack Coombs, Philadelphia	31	Harry Coveleskie, Detroit	23
Russ Ford, New York	26		
Walter Johnson, Washington	25	1917	
Chief Bender, Philadelphia	23	Ed Cicotte, Chicago	28
George Mullin, Detroit	21	Jim Bagby, Cleveland	25
		Babe Ruth, Boston	24
1911		Walter Johnson, Washington	23
Jack Coombs, Philadelphia	28	Carl Mays, Boston	22
Ed Walsh, Chicago	27	Stan Coveleskie, Cleveland	20
Walter Johnson, Washington	25		
Vean Gregg, Cleveland	23	1918	
Joe Wood, Boston	23	Walter Johnson, Washington	23
Ed Plank, Philadelphia	22	Stan Coveleskie, Cleveland	22
Russ Ford, New York	22	Carl Mays, Boston	21
		Scott Perry, Philadelphia	21

1919		
Ed Cicotte. Chicago	29	
Stan Coveleskie. Cleveland	24	
Claude Williams. Chicago	23	
George Dauss. Detroit	21	
Walter Johnson. Washington	20	
Bob Shawkey. New York	20	
Allan Sothoron. St. Louis	20	

1920		
Jim Bagby. Cleveland	31	
Carl Mays. New York	26	
Stan Coveleskie. Cleveland	24	
Urban Faber. Chicago	23	
Claude Williams. Chicago	22	
Dickie Kerr. Chicago	21	
Ed Cicotte. Chicago	21	
Bob Shawkey. New York	20	
Urban Shocker. St. Louis	20	
Ray Caldwell. Cleveland	20	

1921		
Carl Mays. New York	27	
Urban Shocker. St. Louis	27	
Urban Faber. Chicago	25	
Stan Coveleskie. Cleveland	23	
Sam Jones. Boston	23	

1922		
Ed Rommel. Philadelphia	27	
Joe Bush. New York	26	
Urban Shocker. St. Louis	24	
George Uhle. Cleveland	22	
Urban Faber. Chicago	21	
Bob Shawkey. New York	20	

1923		
George Uhle. Cleveland	26	
Sam Jones. New York	21	
George Dauss. Detroit	21	
Urban Shocker. St. Louis	20	
Howard Ehmke. Boston	20	

1924		
Walter Johnson. Washington	23	
Herb Pennock. New York	21	
Joe Shaute. Cleveland	20	
Hollis Thurston. Chicago	20	

1925		
Ted Lyons. Chicago	21	
Ed Rommel. Philadelphia	21	
Walter Johnson. Washington	20	
Stan Coveleskie. Washington	20	

Allie Reynolds starred both as a starting pitcher and reliever during the Casey Stengel years with the Yankees. *(George Brace)*

1926	
George Uhle, Cleveland	27
Herb Pennock, New York	23

1927	
Waite Hoyt, New York	22
Ted Lyons, Chicago	22
Bob Grove, Philadelphia	20

1928	
Bob Grove, Philadelphia	24
George Pipgras, New York	24
Waite Hoyt, New York	23
Al Crowder, St. Louis	21
Sam Gray, St. Louis	20

1929	
George Earnshaw, Philadelphia	24
Wes Ferrell, Cleveland	21
Bob Grove, Philadelphia	20

1930	
Bob Grove, Philadelphia	28
Wes Ferrell, Cleveland	25
George Earnshaw, Philadelphia	22
Ted Lyons, Chicago	22
Walter Stewart, St. Louis	20

1931	
Bob Grove, Philadelphia	31
Wes Ferrell, Cleveland	22
George Earnshaw, Philadelphia	21
Vernon Gomez, New York	21
Rube Walberg, Philadelphia	20

1932	
Al Crowder, Washington	26
Bob Grove, Philadelphia	25
Vernon Gomez, New York	24
Wes Ferrell, Cleveland	23
Monte Weaver, Washington	22

1933	
Al Crowder, Washington	24
Bob Grove, Philadelphia	24
Earl Whitehill, Washington	22

1934	
Vernon Gomez, New York	26
Lynwood Rowe, Detroit	24
Tom Bridges, Detroit	22
Mel Harder, Cleveland	20

1935	
Wes Ferrell, Boston	25
Mel Harder, Cleveland	22
Tom Bridges, Detroit	21
Bob Grove, Boston	20

1936	
Tom Bridges, Detroit	23
Vern Kennedy, Chicago	21
Charles Ruffing, New York	20
Johnny Allen, Cleveland	20
Wes Ferrell, Boston	20

1937	
Vernon Gomez, New York	21
Charles Ruffing, New York	20

1938	
Charles Ruffing, New York	21
Louis Newsom, St. Louis	20

1939	
Bob Feller, Cleveland	24
Charles Ruffing, New York	21
Emil Leonard, Washington	20
Louis Newsom, St. Louis/Detroit	20

1940	
Bob Feller, Cleveland	27
Louis Newsom, Detroit	21

1941	
Bob Feller, Cleveland	25
Thornton Lee, Chicago	22

1942	
Cecil Hughson, Boston	22
Ernie Bonham, New York	21

1943	
Spurgeon Chandler, New York	20
Paul Trout, Detroit	20

1944	
Hal Newhouser, Detroit	29
Paul Trout, Detroit	27

1945	
Hal Newhouser, Detroit	25
Dave Ferriss, Boston	21
Roger Wolff, Washington	20

1946	
Bob Feller, Cleveland	26
Hal Newhouser, Detroit	26
Dave Ferriss, Boston	25
Spurgeon Chandler, New York	20
Cecil Hughson, Boston	20

1947	
Bob Feller, Cleveland	20

1948	
Hal Newhouser, Detroit	21
Bob Lemon, Cleveland	20
Gene Bearden, Cleveland	20

1949	
Mel Parnell, Boston	25
Ellis Kinder, Boston	23
Bob Lemon, Cleveland	22
Vic Raschi, New York	21
Alex Keliner, Philadelphia	20

1950	
Bob Lemon, Cleveland	23
Vic Raschi, New York	21

1951	
Bob Feller, Cleveland	22
Ed Lopat, New York	21
Vic Raschi, New York	21
Mike Garcia, Cleveland	20
Early Wynn, Cleveland	20
Ned Garver, St. Louis	20

1952	
Bobby Shantz, Philadelphia	24
Early Wynn, Cleveland	23
Mike Garcia, Cleveland	22
Bob Lemon, Cleveland	22
Allie Reynolds, New York	20

1953	
Bob Porterfield, Washington	22
Mel Parnell, Boston	21
Bob Lemon, Cleveland	21
Virgil Trucks, Chicago	20

1954	
Early Wynn, Cleveland	23
Bob Lemon, Cleveland	23
Bob Grim, New York	20

1955	
(None)	

1956	
Frank Lary, Detroit	21
Billy Pierce, Chicago	20
Bill Hoeft, Detroit	20
Bob Lemon, Cleveland	20
Herb Score, Cleveland	20
Early Wynn, Cleveland	20

1957	
Jim Bunning, Detroit	20
Billy Pierce, Chicago	20

1958	
Bob Turley, New York	21

1959	
Early Wynn, Chicago	22

1960	
(None)	

1961	
Whitey Ford, New York	25
Frank Lary, Detroit	23

1962	
Ralph Terry, New York	23
Dick Donovan, Cleveland	20
Ray Herbert, Chicago	20
Camilo Pascual, Minnesota	20

1963	
Whitey Ford, New York	24
Jim Bouton, New York	21
Camilo Pascual, Minnesota	21
Steve Barber, Baltimore	20
Bill Monbouquette, Boston	20

1964	
Dean Chance, Los Angeles	20
Gary Peters, Chicago	20

1965	
Jim Grant, Minnesota	21
Mel Stottlemyre, New York	20

1966	
Jim Kaat, Minnesota	25
Dennis McLain, Detroit	20

1967	
Jim Lonborg, Boston	22
Earl Wilson, Detroit	22
Dean Chance, Minnesota	20

1968	
Dennis McLain, Detroit	31
Dave McNally, Baltimore	22
Mel Stottlemyre, New York	21
Luis Tiant, Cleveland	21

1969	
Dennis McLain, Detroit	24
Mike Cuellar, Baltimore	23
Dave Boswell, Minnesota	20
Dave McNally, Baltimore	20
Jim Perry, Minnesota	20
Mel Stottlemyre, New York	20

1970	
Mike Cuellar, Baltimore	24
Dave McNally, Baltimore	24
Jim Perry, Minnesota	24
Clyde Wright, California	22
Sam McDowell, Cleveland	20
Jim Palmer, Baltimore	20
Fritz Peterson, New York	20

1971	
Mickey Lolich, Detroit	25
Vida Blue, Oakland	24
Wilbur Wood, Chicago	22
Jim Hunter, Oakland	21
Dave McNally, Baltimore	21
Joe Coleman, Detroit	20
Mike Cuellar, Baltimore	20
Pat Dobson, Baltimore	20
Andy Messersmith, California	20
Jim Palmer, Baltimore	20

1972	
Gaylord Perry, Cleveland	24
Wilbur Wood, Chicago	24
Mickey Lolich, Detroit	22
Jim Hunter, Oakland	21
Jim Palmer, Baltimore	21
Stan Bahnsen, Chicago	21

1973	
Wilbur Wood, Chicago	24
Joe Coleman, Detroit	23

Jim Palmer, Baltimore	22
Jim Hunter, Oakland	21
Ken Holtzman, Oakland	21
Nolan Ryan, California	21
Vida Blue, Oakland	20
Bert Blyleven, Minnesota	20
Jim Colborn, Milwaukee	20
Bill Singer, California	20
Paul Splittorff, Kansas City	20
Luis Tiant, Boston	20

1974	
Jim Hunter, Oakland	25
Ferguson Jenkins, Texas	25
Mike Cuellar, Baltimore	22
Luis Tiant, Boston	22
Nolan Ryan, California	22
Steve Busby, Kansas City	22
Jim Kaat, Chicago	21
Gaylord Perry, Cleveland	21
Wilbur Wood, Chicago	20

1975	
Jim Palmer, Baltimore	23
Jim Hunter, New York	23
Vida Blue, Oakland	22
Mike Torrez, Baltimore	20
Jim Kaat, Chicago	20

1976	
Jim Palmer, Baltimore	22
Luis Tiant, Boston	21
Wayne Garland, Baltimore	20

1977	
Dave Goltz, Minnesota	20
Dennis Leonard, Kansas City	20
Jim Palmer, Baltimore	20

1978	
Ron Guidry, New York	25
Mike Caldwell, Milwaukee	22
Jim Palmer, Baltimore	21
Dennis Leonard, Kansas City	21
Dennis Eckersley, Boston	20
Ed Figueroa, New York	20

1979	
Mike Flanagan, Baltimore	23
Tommy John, New York	20
Jerry Koosman, Minnesota	20

Bibliography

Allen, Lee and Meany, Tom. *Kings of the Diamond.* New York: G. P. Putnam's Sons, 1965.

Allen, Lee. *The World Series.* New York: G. P. Putnam's Sons, 1969.

Allen, Maury. *Where Have You Gone, Joe DiMaggio?* New York: E. P. Dutton, 1975.

Allen, Mel, with Fitzgerald, Ed. *You Can't Beat the Hours.* New York: Harper & Row, 1964.

Anderson, Dave; Chass, Murray; Creamer, Robert; and Rosenthal, Harold. *The Yankees.* New York: Random House, 1979.

Angell, Roger. *Five Seasons: A Baseball Companion.* New York: Simon and Schuster, 1977.

Appel, Martin and Goldblatt, Burt. *Baseball's Best.* New York: McGraw-Hill, 1977.

Asinof, Eliot. *Eight Men Out.* New York: Holt, Rinehart, Winston, 1963.

Berry, Henry. *Boston Red Sox.* New York: Rutledge Books, 1975.

Book of Baseball Records. Edited and published by Seymour Siwoff, New York: 1979.

The Baseball Encyclopedia. New York: Macmillan Publishing Company, 1979.

Cobb, Ty with Stump, Al. *My Life in Baseball, The True Record.* New York: Doubleday & Co., Inc., 1961.

Creamer, Robert. *"Babe."* New York: Simon and Schuster, 1974.

Dickey, Glenn. *The Great No-Hitters.* Radnor, Pa.: Chilton Book Co., 1976.

Durso, Joseph. *Casey: The Life and Legend of Charles Dillon Stengel.* Englewood Cliffs, N.J.: Prentice-Hall, Inc., 1967.

Durso, Joseph; Ford, Whitey; and Mantle, Mickey. *Whitey and Mickey: An Autobiography of the Yankee Years.* New York: Viking Press, 1977.

Falls, Joe. *Detroit Tigers.* New York: Rutledge Books, 1975.

Feller, Bob. *Strikeout Story.* New York: A. S. Barnes & Co., 1947.

Holtzman, Jerome. *No Cheering in the Press Box.* New York: Holt, Rinehart and Winston, 1973.

Honig, Donald. *The October Heroes.* New York: Simon and Schuster, 1979.

———. *Baseball Between the Lines.* New York: Coward, McCann & Geoghegan, Inc., 1976.

———. *Baseball When the Grass Was Real.* New York: Coward, McCann and Geoghegan, Inc., 1975.

———. *The Man in the Dugout.* Chicago: Follett Publishing Co., 1971.

Kahn, Roger. *A Season in the Sun.* New York: Harper & Row, 1977.

Koppett, Leonard. *The Thinking Man's Guide to Baseball.* New York: E. P. Dutton & Co., 1967.

Meany, Tom. *Baseball's Greatest Teams.* Cranbury, N.J.: A. S. Barnes & Co., 1951.

———. *Baseball's Greatest Pitchers.* Cranbury, N.J.: A. S. Barnes & Co., 1952.

Michelson, Herb. *Charlie O.* Indianapolis/New York: Bobbs-Merrill, 1975.

Official Baseball Record Book. St. Louis: The Sporting News, 1975.

Paige, Satchel, as told to Lipman, David. *Maybe I'll Pitch Forever.* New York: Doubleday & Co., 1961.

Reichler, Joseph, editor. *The Game and the Glory.* Englewood Cliffs, N.J.: Prentice-Hall, Inc., 1976.

Ritter, Lawrence. *The Glory of Their Times.* New York: The Macmillan Company, 1966.

Salant, Nathan. *This Date in New York Yankees History.* New York: Stein and Day, 1979.

Sampson, Arthur. *Ted Williams.* New York: A. S. Barnes & Co., 1950.

Seymour, Harold. *Baseball: The Golden Age.* New York: Oxford University Press, 1971.

Smith, Robert. *Baseball.* New York: Simon and Schuster, 1970.

Treat, Roger L. *Walter Johnson, King of the Pitchers.* New York: Julian Messner, Inc., 1948.

Turkin, Hy, and Thompson, S. C. *The Official Encyclopedia of Baseball.* New York: A. S. Barnes & Co., 1979.

Walton, Ed. *This Date in Boston Red Sox History.* New York: Stein and Day, 1978.

Index